The Celestial Odyssey
Journey Through Portals

Angel Viera

Copyright © 2024

All Rights Reserved

All content, including text, graphics, images, logos, and software, published on this website/publication is protected by international copyright laws. Unauthorized use, reproduction, or distribution of the content wihtin is strictly prohibited without prior written permission.

Table of Contents

Index i

Synopsis v

Dear Readers viii

Review of "The Celestial Odyssey: Journey Through Portals" ix

   Key Gains for Readers

The Zoo of Wonders 1

Dear Readers 436

About The Author 438

Index

Here's a list of portals in "The Celestial Odyssey: Journey Through Portals" along with what each portal represents:

1. **Enchanted Forest Portal:**
   ~Represents: Exploration and selfdiscovery. It symbolizes venturing into the unknown parts of oneself and uncovering hidden strengths and wisdom.

2. **Celestial Observatory Portal:**
   ~Represents: Vision and enlightenment. It symbolizes the quest for higher knowledge, cosmic understanding, and the pursuit of dreams.

3. **Cosmic Nexus Portal:**
   ~Represents: Interconnectedness. It symbolizes the unity and interdependence of all life and the realization that all actions have farreaching consequences.

4. **Mystic Mountain Portal:**
   ~Represents: Challenges and personal growth. It symbolizes the journey of overcoming obstacles to attain wisdom, strength, and enlightenment.

5. **Crystal Cave Portal:**
   ~Represents: Inner clarity and reflection. It symbolizes the process of introspection, finding inner truth, and gaining mental clarity.

6. **Ethereal Ocean Portal:**
   ~Represents: Emotional depth and subconscious exploration. It symbolizes the journey through deep emotions, intuition, and subconscious realms.

7. **Timeless Desert Portal:**
   ~Represents: Resilience and endurance. It symbolizes the strength needed to survive life's trials and the timeless wisdom gained through perseverance.

8. **Sky Island Portal:**
   ~Represents: Freedom and perspective. It symbolizes rising above challenges, gaining a broader perspective, and experiencing the liberating feeling of freedom.

9. Dreamscape Portal:

~Represents: Creativity and imagination. It symbolizes the power of dreams, creativity, and the endless possibilities within the human mind.

10. Forest of Whispers Portal:

~Represents: Secrets and ancient knowledge. It symbolizes the discovery of hidden truths and the wisdom passed down through generations.

11. Mirror Realm Portal:

~Represents: Selfawareness and alternate possibilities. It symbolizes selfreflection, the exploration of alternate realities, and the understanding of different aspects of oneself.

12. Frozen Tundra Portal:

~Represents: Isolation and resilience. It symbolizes the strength to endure hardships and the clarity that comes from facing difficult conditions.

13. Luminous Lagoon Portal:

~Represents: Beauty and tranquility. It symbolizes finding peace, inner beauty, and the calming influence of serene environments.

14. **Astral Plane Portal:**
~Represents: Spiritual exploration. It symbolizes the journey through metaphysical and spiritual realms, seeking higher consciousness and enlightenment.

15. **Ruins of Time Portal:**
~Represents: History and timeless wisdom. It symbolizes learning from the past, understanding historical cycles, and gaining wisdom that transcends time.

Each portal in "The Celestial Odyssey: Journey Through Portals" serves as a gateway to new adventures and profound lessons, reflecting various aspects of personal growth, emotional exploration, and spiritual enlightenment.

Synopsis

Embark on an extraordinary adventure with Manny the Lion, Silvia the Hippo, Lili the Melodic Butterfly, and Frank the Adventurous Monkey as they traverse mystical portals across celestial realms. Each character brings unique strengths and perspectives to the quest, bound by a deep friendship and a shared pursuit of wisdom and enlightenment.

Manny, revered for his wisdom and courage, navigates challenges that test his resolve and deepen his understanding of universal truths. Silvia discovers resilience in the tranquil embrace of nature, finding solace and strength amidst verdant landscapes and serene waters. Lili's ethereal melodies resonate through the cosmos, unraveling mysteries and overcoming adversaries with her unique musical prowess. Frank's adventurous spirit leads him through daring escapades and transformative encounters, shaping his journey towards self-discovery and growth.

Throughout their odyssey, guided by celestial mentors and confronted by mystical foes, each character confronts their fears, embraces their strengths, and unlocks profound insights that reshape their destinies. Together, they unravel the fabric of reality, uncovering ancient prophecies and cosmic secrets that illuminate the interconnectedness of all beings.

"The Celestial Odyssey: Journey Through Portals" is a captivating tale of personal growth and spiritual exploration, resilience, and the transformative power of friendship. As they traverse celestial realms and encounter celestial mentors, Manny, Silvia, Lili, and Frank inspire readers to embark on their own journeys of self-discovery, inviting them to explore the depths of existence and awaken to the magic that lies within and beyond.

"The Celestial Odyssey: Journey Through Portals." This book aims to guide people out of darkness through abstract parables. The portals symbolize our negative thoughts, fears, and anxieties, offering metaphorical representations of the challenges we face. Each story serves as a helping hand, providing guidance and support.

Throughout "The Celestial Odyssey," you'll join characters like Frank, Silvia the Hippo, Lili the Melodic Singing Butterfly, and Manny as they navigate enchanted forests, celestial observatories, and cosmic nexuses. These journeys are not only entertaining but also filled with valuable advice and life lessons imparted by my characters.

The aliases used by Frank, Silvia, Lili, and Manny add intrigue and depth to their quest, reflecting their adaptability and resilience. The chapters may jump from one realm to another, keeping you curious and engaged.

Embrace this journey with an open heart and mind. Let yourself be swept away by the wonders of the cosmos, the wisdom of ancient sages, and the mysteries that unfold with each turn of the page. Each chapter is a glimpse into a different facet of existence, challenging you to contemplate the interconnectedness of all things and your own place within this vast universe.

May "The Celestial Odyssey" inspire you to seek knowledge, ignite your imagination, and embrace the beauty of diversity in all its forms. Remember, life itself is a journey— a series of chapters that unfold before us, each offering its own lessons and revelations.

Thank you for joining me on this celestial adventure. May your own journey be filled with endless curiosity, profound insights, and the joy of discovery.

With warmest regards,

Angel Viera,

Author CR 2009/2024

Dear Readers

As you delve into "The Book of Journeys," you may notice a deliberate weaving of mystique around the groups. Frank, Silvia, Lili, and Manny, our mystical characters, often cloak themselves in aliases. These aliases are not static; they change and adapt, providing a shield against the forces they confront on their epic odyssey. Throughout the book, you'll find these aliases seamlessly integrated with their true names, adding an air of intrigue and depth to their quest.

This is more than just a tale of adventure; it's a book for self-awareness and growth. Each chapter is designed to mirror the journey within, encouraging you to confront your own inner demons, embrace self-discovery, and find balance in your life.

Enjoy the journey of discovery and adventure as you uncover the mysteries hidden within the pages.

Happy reading!

Angel Viera,

CR 2009/2024

Review of "The Celestial Odyssey: Journey Through Portals"

"The Celestial Odyssey: Journey Through Portals" is a compelling and multifaceted narrative that offers readers a rich tapestry of adventure, wisdom, and introspection.

Key Gains for Readers

1. **Personal Growth:**

~The characters in the book embark on transformative journeys through various portals, encountering challenges that test their resilience, courage, and integrity. These experiences provide valuable lessons in self-discovery and personal development.

2. **Spiritual Insight:**

~The parables woven into the storyline offer profound spiritual insights. The book delves into themes of enlightenment, inner peace, and the interconnectedness of all beings, encouraging readers to explore their spiritual paths and find deeper meaning in their lives.

3. **Entertainment:**

~At its core, "The Celestial Odyssey" is a captivating adventure. The imaginative and richly described realms, the intriguing characters, and the unexpected twists keep readers engaged and entertained throughout the book.

Overall Impact:

Readers will emerge from "The Celestial Odyssey: Journey Through Portals" with a renewed sense of hope and inspiration. The blend of entertainment, personal growth, and spiritual enlightenment ensures that this book resonates on multiple levels, offering something meaningful for every reader.

The Zoo of Wonders

Let me introduce you to the enchanting world of the zoo, a place where magic and imagination intertwine. As the sun rises over the sprawling landscape of enclosures and pathways, we are introduced to our first protagonist, Manny .

Manny stands out amidst the vibrant tapestry of the zoo, his scarlet coat gleaming in the morning light. With a wisdom far beyond his years, Manny serves as a guardian of the zoo, offering guidance and wisdom to all who seek it. As visitors pass by his enclosure, they are drawn to his gentle gaze and the soft timbre of his voice, eager to hear the tales of the wonders that lie beyond.

Amidst the hustle and bustle of the zoo's opening hours, Manny finds solace in the quiet moments of reflection, gazing out over the expanse of his domain with a sense of wonder and reverence. He knows that within the walls of the zoo, there are endless adventures waiting to be discovered, and he eagerly awaits the arrival of those who will join him on his journey through this magical realm.

As the day unfolds and visitors come and go, Manny stands tall as a beacon of hope and inspiration, his presence a reminder of the boundless potential that lies within each of us. And as the sun sets on another day in the Zoo of Wonders, Manny knows that the greatest adventures are yet to come, waiting just beyond the horizon.

"**Lili's Song,**" we are introduced to another enchanting inhabitant of the Zoo of Wonders: Lili, the singing butterfly. As dawn breaks and the zoo comes to life once more, Lili flutters gracefully through the air, her delicate wings shimmering in the morning sunlight.

Unlike any other butterfly in the zoo, Lili possesses a special gift: the ability to sing. Her ethereal voice carries on the breeze, weaving melodies that captivate all who hear them. As visitors wander through the gardens and pathways, they are drawn to the sound of Lili's song, their hearts lifted by its beauty and grace.

Lili's presence brings a sense of magic and wonder to the zoo, her songs echoing through the trees and filling the air with a sense of joy and tranquility. She is beloved by all who know her, her gentle spirit and radiant smile lighting up even the darkest corners of the zoo.

But beneath Lili's joyful exterior lies a deeper longing, a desire to share her gift with the world beyond the confines of the zoo. As she gazes out over the horizon, her heart swells with the hope of one day spreading her wings and soaring into the unknown, her songs echoing across the vast expanse of the world beyond.

As the day unfolds and Lili continues to sing, her voice becomes a beacon of light and hope in a world filled with darkness and uncertainty. And as the sun sets on another day in the Zoo of Wonders, Lili knows that her song will continue to echo through the hearts of all who hear it, guiding them on their own journeys of discovery and adventure.

"**Frank's Antics,**" the spotlight turns to a new character within the Zoo of Wonders: Frank, the mischievous white monkey. With his gleaming coat and twinkling eyes, Frank is a whirlwind of energy and excitement, always on the lookout for his next adventure.

Unlike the other inhabitants of the zoo, Frank's antics often lead him into trouble, much to the amusement of visitors and fellow residents alike. From swinging through the trees to playing pranks on unsuspecting passersby, there is never a dull moment when Frank is around.

Despite his playful nature, Frank possesses a heart of gold, always willing to lend a helping hand to those in need. Whether it's rescuing a lost bird from a thorny bush or cheering up a lonely visitor with his antics, Frank's kindness and compassion shine through in everything he does.

But beneath his mischievous exterior lies a longing for something more, a desire to explore the world beyond the confines of the zoo and discover what lies beyond. As he watches the sun set over the horizon, Frank dreams of embarking on his own epic adventure, filled with excitement, danger, and the promise of new discoveries.

As the day draws to a close and the zoo begins to quiet down, Frank knows that his adventures are far from over. With a mischievous grin and a twinkle in his eye, he swings off into the sunset, ready to take on whatever challenges the world may throw his way.

"Silvia's Charm," we are introduced to Silvia, the epitome of grace and beauty within the Zoo of Wonders. Silvia is a majestic hippopotamus, her ivory tusks gleaming in the sunlight as she gracefully glides through the tranquil waters of her enclosure.

Silvia's presence is magnetic, drawing visitors from far and wide to admire her elegance and charm. With each graceful movement, she exudes a sense of confidence and poise that captivates all who behold her. Her radiant smile lights up the faces of those around her, filling the air with a sense of warmth and joy.

But Silvia's beauty is more than skin deep. Beneath her regal exterior lies a heart of gold, overflowing with kindness and compassion for all living creatures. She spends her days basking in the sun, surrounded by a menagerie of friends who flock to her side seeking comfort and friendship.

As the sun sets on another day in the Zoo of Wonders, Silvia's gentle presence serves as a reminder of the power of love and friendship. With her unwavering grace and boundless charm, she brings light and joy to all who cross her path, leaving a lasting impression on the hearts of all who know her.

"The Enchanted Gardens," our journey through the Zoo of Wonders continues as the groups delve deeper into its mysteries. As they traverse the winding pathways and lush greenery of the Enchanted Gardens, they stumble upon the zoo's hidden treasure: the Mysterious Menagerie.

This secluded corner of the zoo is a haven for creatures both magical and mundane, each one more wondrous than the last. From mythical beasts to rare species found nowhere else on Earth, the menagerie is a testament to the boundless creativity of the natural world.

As the groups explore the menagerie, they uncover secrets hidden within its depths. They encounter creatures that defy imagination, their forms shimmering with otherworldly beauty. From the majestic griffins that soar through the skies to the elusive unicorns that graze in the meadows, each creature holds a piece of the puzzle that is the Zoo of Wonders.

But amidst the wonders of the menagerie, the groups also discover darker truths lurking in the shadows. They encounter creatures of darkness and despair, their eyes filled with sorrow and longing. As they navigate through the maze of secrets and revelations, they come to understand that even within the most enchanted of gardens, there are shadows that must be faced.

As the day draws to a close and the sun dips below the horizon, the groups emerge from the menagerie with a newfound sense of wonder and awe. They carry with them the memories of the creatures they have encountered and the secrets they have uncovered, knowing that their journey through the Zoo of Wonders has only just begun.

"The Labyrinth of Wonders," the groups find themselves faced with a daunting challenge as they enter a labyrinth nestled deep within the Enchanted Gardens. The labyrinth is a maze of twisting pathways and hidden passages, each one filled with magical traps and challenges that test the courage and ingenuity of those who dare to enter.

As they navigate through the labyrinth, the groups encounter obstacles both physical and mystical. They must overcome riddles and puzzles that guard the secrets of the maze, deciphering ancient symbols and unlocking hidden doors that lead deeper into its depths.

But the labyrinth is more than just a test of wit and intelligence. It is a reflection of the inner journey that the groups must undertake, a journey of self-discovery and growth. As they navigate its twists and turns, they confront their fears and doubts, learning to trust in themselves and each other as they face the challenges that lie ahead.

Despite the dangers that lurk around every corner, the groups press on, fueled by their determination to uncover the mysteries of the labyrinth and emerge victorious. With each step forward, they draw closer to the heart of the maze, where the greatest challenges and revelations await.

As they journey deeper into the labyrinth, the groups come to understand that the true magic lies not in the destination, but in the journey itself. For it is in the face of adversity that they discover their own strength and resilience, and it is through their trials and triumphs that they become the heroes of their own story.

"The Fountain of Dreams," the groups embark on a journey to discover the legendary Fountain of Dreams hidden within the depths of the Zoo of Wonders. As they traverse the enchanted pathways of the Enchanted Gardens, they are guided by whispers and echoes that lead them ever closer to their destination.

The Fountain of Dreams is said to possess magical properties, granting those who drink from its waters the power to see visions of the past, present, and future. Legends abound of travelers who have journeyed to the fountain seeking enlightenment and guidance, their hearts filled with hope and wonder.

As the groups approach the fountain, they are greeted by a sight of breathtaking beauty. The fountain stands at the center of a tranquil oasis, its waters shimmering with iridescent light. Surrounding the fountain are lush gardens filled with exotic flowers and rare plants, their colors vibrant and alive with the magic of the fountain.

With hearts full of anticipation, the groups approach the edge of the fountain and dip their hands into its waters. As they drink, they feel a surge of energy coursing through their veins, filling them with a sense of clarity and purpose. Visions dance before their eyes, revealing glimpses of the past and future intertwined in a tapestry of destiny.

But the Fountain of Dreams holds more than just visions of times long gone and times yet to come. It also holds the power to grant wishes, allowing those who seek its waters to manifest their deepest desires into reality. With each wish spoken, the fountain ripples with energy, its magic weaving through the air like threads of light.

As our group make their wishes and watch them soar into the sky, they are filled with a sense of wonder and gratitude. For in this moment, they have tasted the magic of the fountain and experienced the power of dreams made real. And as they journey onwards, they carry with them the knowledge that within the depths of their own hearts, the fountain of dreams will always flow.

"Confronting the Darkness," the groups are faced with their greatest challenge yet as they come face to face with the shadows that lurk within the Zoo of Wonders. As they journey deeper into the Enchanted Gardens, they sense a growing darkness that threatens to engulf them.

The air grows thick with tension as they navigate through the twisting pathways, their senses heightened as they prepare to confront whatever lies ahead. Suddenly, they find themselves surrounded by a veil of darkness, obscuring their vision and filling their hearts with fear.

But the groups refuse to be cowed by the darkness. With courage and determination, they press onwards, their footsteps echoing through the silence as they search for the source of the shadows. As they move deeper into the darkness, they come face to face with the embodiment of their fears: a creature of pure darkness, its eyes glowing with malevolent intent.

With hearts pounding and adrenaline coursing through their veins, the groups stand their ground, ready to confront the darkness that threatens to consume them. They draw upon the strength of their bonds and the power of their convictions, refusing to let fear dictate their actions.

In a climactic battle that tests their resolve and challenges their beliefs, the groups emerge victorious, banishing the darkness and restoring light to the Enchanted Gardens once more. As the shadows dissipate and the sunlight filters through the trees, they are filled with a sense of triumph and accomplishment.

But they know that their journey is far from over. With the darkness vanquished, they emerge from the Enchanted Gardens stronger and more determined than ever to uncover the secrets of the Zoo of Wonders and embark on the adventure that awaits them beyond its borders. And as they take their first steps into the unknown, they carry with them the knowledge to conquer any foe that stands in their way.

"**The Call to Action,**" the group receives a mysterious message that sets the wheels of adventure in motion. As they go about their daily routine in the Zoo of Wonders, they stumble upon an ancient scroll tucked away in a forgotten corner of the Enchanted Gardens.

The scroll is old and weathered, its parchment yellowed with age and its edges frayed from centuries of use. As the group unfurls the scroll, they are greeted by a message written in elegant script, its words shimmering with magic and mystery.

The message is a call for aid, beckoning the group to embark on a journey to a distant land in search of a lost artifact of great power. It speaks of danger and peril, of challenges that will test the limits of their courage and determination. But it also promises adventure and discovery, the chance to uncover secrets long hidden and treasures beyond imagination.

Filled with a sense of purpose and excitement, the group heeds the call to action, knowing that they must answer the summons and embark on this epic quest. With the scroll in hand and their heart set aflame with the promise of adventure, they set out into the unknown, ready to face it

As they journey beyond the borders of the Zoo of Wonders, the group carries with them the knowledge that they are destined for greatness, their fate intertwined with the destiny of the world itself. And as they take their first steps into the adventure that awaits them, they know that their journey will continue on.

"**Seeking Allies,**" the group and their friends embark on a quest to gather allies from different corners of the Zoo of Wonders. With the call to action ringing in their ears, they know that they cannot face the challenges ahead alone and must seek out those who will stand by their side in the coming trials.

Their journey takes them through the winding pathways and hidden alcoves of the zoo, where they encounter creatures both familiar and strange. From the majestic lions of the Savannah to the wise old tortoises of the Enchanted Forest, they seek out allies who possess the strength, wisdom, and courage needed to aid them in their quest.

As they journey from one end of the zoo to the other, the group and their friends face obstacles and challenges that test their resolve and determination. They must navigate through treacherous terrain, overcome cunning adversaries, and prove themselves worthy of the trust and loyalty of those they seek to recruit.

But with each ally they gather, their bond grows stronger, their resolve bolstered by the knowledge that they are not alone in their quest. Together, they form a fellowship united by a common purpose: to confront the darkness that threatens to engulf the Zoo of Wonders and restore peace and harmony to its enchanted realms.

As they continue their journey, the group and their friends know that the path ahead will be fraught with danger and uncertainty. But with allies at their side and courage in their hearts, they are ready to face it and emerge victorious in the battle against the forces of darkness. "Building Alliances," the group and their friends engage in negotiations and form alliances with various magical creatures within the Zoo of Wonders. As they journey through the

enchanted realms, they encounter beings of all shapes and sizes, each possessing unique powers and abilities that could prove invaluable in their quest.

Their first stop is the Celestial Aviary, home to the majestic griffins and phoenixes that soar through the skies above the zoo. Here, they must negotiate with the wise and ancient guardians of the sky, earning their trust and persuading them to join their cause.

Next, they venture into the depths of the Enchanted Forest, where they encounter the mystical beings that dwell within its shadowed glades. From the mischievous faeries to the noble centaurs, they must navigate the delicate politics of the forest and forge alliances with those who call it home.

Their journey takes them to the depths of the Oceanic Abyss, where they must negotiate with the elusive merfolk and sea serpents that rule the underwater kingdom. Here, they must prove their worthiness to the guardians of the deep and convince them to lend their strength to the fight against darkness.

Finally, they journey to the heart of the Elemental Nexus, where they must negotiate with the powerful elemental beings that govern the forces of nature within the zoo. From the fiery salamanders to the icy frost giants, they must demonstrate their respect for the balance of the elements and forge alliances that will stand the test of time.

As they gather allies from all corners of the zoo, the group and their friends know that their fellowship is stronger than ever. With each alliance formed, they draw closer to their ultimate goal: to confront the darkness that threatens to engulf the Zoo of Wonders and restore peace and harmony to its enchanted realms.

"**Preparing for Battle**," the group and their allies focus their efforts on training and strategizing for the upcoming confrontation with the forces of darkness. With their alliances forged and their fellowship united, they know that they must be prepared for whatever challenges lie ahead.

Their training begins in earnest as they gather in the heart of the Zoo of Wonders, where they hone their skills and abilities under the guidance of their mentors and allies. From mastering the art of swordplay to harnessing the power of magic, they devote themselves to becoming the strongest and most skilled warriors they can be.

But preparation for battle is not just physical— it is also mental and emotional. the group and their friends spend long hours in discussion and debate, strategizing their approach and planning their tactics for the coming conflict. They analyze the strengths and weaknesses of their adversaries, devising cunning strategies to outmaneuver and overcome them.

As the days pass and the hour of reckoning draws near, the group and their allies find themselves tested in ways they never thought possible. They confront their fears and doubts, pushing themselves to their limits and emerging stronger and more determined than ever before.

But amidst the preparations and the training, there are moments of camaraderie and friendship, where bonds are forged and memories are made that will last a lifetime. As they stand together on the eve of battle, they all know that they are ready to face any challenges that may come their way, determined to protect the Zoo of Wonders and all who call it home.

"**Eerie Encounters**," the group and their friends venture into the dark and mysterious Haunted Hollows within the Zoo of Wonders. As they step into the shadowed realm, a chill wind whispers through the trees, sending shivers down their spines.

The Haunted Hollows is a place of legend and mystery, rumored to be haunted by restless spirits and malevolent creatures that lurk in the shadows. Despite the warnings and the tales of danger, the group and their friends press onwards, determined to uncover the truth behind the legends.

As they journey deeper into the hollows, they are assailed by eerie sights and sounds that unsettle their nerves. Ghostly apparitions flit through the darkness, their eyes glowing with

otherworldly light. Strange whispers echo through the trees, speaking of secrets long forgotten and curses that cannot be broken.

But the group and their friends refuse to be deterred by the darkness that surrounds them. With courage and determination, they press onwards, their senses sharp and their wits keen as they navigate the treacherous terrain.

As they delve deeper into the hollows, they come face to face with the source of the darkness that plagues the land. A powerful entity, ancient and malevolent, lurks in the heart of the hollows, its presence casting a shadow over the entire zoo.

With their allies at their side, the group confronts the creature, their blades drawn and their hearts filled with determination. In a fierce battle that tests their strength and resolve, they emerge victorious, banishing the darkness from the hollows and restoring peace to the land.

As they emerge from the hollows, the group and their friends are filled with a sense of accomplishment and pride. They have faced the darkness and emerged triumphant, proving themselves worthy of the challenges that lie ahead. And as they continue on their journey, they know that any danger they may face, it must be faced with gorup power, united in their quest to protect the Zoo of Wonders and all who call it home.

"**Uncovering Secrets**," the group and their friends delve deeper into the Haunted Hollows, their curiosity piqued by the mysteries that lie hidden within its depths. As they explore the shadowed corridors and crumbling ruins, they stumble upon ancient artifacts and hidden passages that hint at the secrets buried within.

Their journey takes them through forgotten chambers and hidden alcoves, where they uncover relics of a bygone era. From dusty tomes filled with cryptic symbols to ornate jewels that sparkle with hidden power, each artifact holds a piece of the puzzle that is the Haunted Hollows.

As they piece together the clues they find, the group and their friends unravel the secrets of the haunted area, uncovering tales of love and betrayal, triumph and tragedy. They learn of the ancient guardians who once protected the hollows, their spirits bound to the land for eternity.

But amidst the tales of the past, they also discover clues that point towards the present, hints of a darkness that threatens to engulf the hollows once more. Shadows lurk in every corner, whispering of malevolent forces that seek to reclaim the land and unleash chaos upon the world.

Undeterred by the dangers that surround them, the group and their friends press onwards, their determination unwavering as they seek to uncover the truth behind the mysteries of the hollows. With each artifact they unearth and each passage they explore, they draw closer to unlocking the secrets that lie hidden within, knowing that the fate of the zoo and all who inhabit it hangs in the balance.

"Confronting Fears," the groups find themselves facing not only the external threats of the Haunted Hollows but also their own inner demons. As they navigate the treacherous landscape, each character is forced to confront their own fears and doubts, testing their courage and resolve in the face of adversity.

For the group, the journey into the Haunted Hollows dredges up memories of past failures and regrets, filling them with self-doubt and uncertainty. They must confront their fear of inadequacy, learning to trust in their own abilities and believe in their capacity to overcome the challenges that lie ahead.

Lili, the singing butterfly, struggles with her fear of being silenced, her voice trembling as she confronts the darkness that threatens to engulf her. She must find the strength within herself to stand up to her fears and reclaim her power, using her voice to drive back the shadows and light the way forward.

Frank, the mischievous white monkey, grapples with his fear of failure, his usual bravado faltering as he faces the dangers of the hollows. He must learn to rely on his friends and trust in their support, knowing that together they are stronger than any obstacle they may encounter.

Silvia, the majestic hippopotamus, battles with her fear of rejection, her confidence shaken as she confronts the unknown. She must find the courage to embrace her vulnerability and open her heart to the possibility of new friendships and alliances, knowing that true strength lies in unity and solidarity.

As they journey deeper into the Haunted Hollows, the groups come to realize that their fears are not obstacles to be overcome but opportunities for growth and self-discovery. With each step forward, they emerge stronger and more resilient, their bonds forged in the fires of adversity and their spirits tempered by the trials they face.

And as they confront their fears head-on, the groups come to understand that true courage is not the absence of fear but the willingness to face it, to embrace it, and to emerge from the darkness stronger and more determined than ever before.

"A Glimmer of Hope," amidst the darkness and uncertainty of the Haunted Hollows, the groups discover a glimmer of hope that shines through the shadows. Despite the dangers that surround them, they stumble upon clues that could lead them closer to defeating the darkness that looms over the zoo.

As they explore the hollows, the groups uncover ancient runes etched into the walls, cryptic symbols that hint at a power long forgotten. They piece together fragments of lore and legend, piecing together a puzzle that promises to reveal the secrets of the haunted area.

Among the relics and artifacts they uncover, they find a map that marks the location of a hidden chamber deep within the hollows. Rumored to hold the key to unlocking the mysteries of the land, this chamber could provide the answers they seek and the means to confront the darkness that threatens to engulf the zoo.

But the path to the hidden chamber is fraught with peril, guarded by ancient guardians and traps laid by those who sought to protect its secrets. the groups must tread carefully, using their wits and their skills to navigate the treacherous terrain and overcome the obstacles that stand in their way.

Despite the dangers that lie ahead, the groups are filled with a sense of determination and purpose. They know that the fate of the zoo and all who inhabit it hangs in the balance, and they are willing to risk everything to bring an end to the darkness that plagues the land.

With the clues they have uncovered and the hope that burns within their hearts, the groups set out on their next journey, their spirits buoyed by the knowledge that they are closer than ever to achieving their goal. And as they venture deeper into the heart of the Haunted Hollows, they know that whatever challenges lie ahead, they will face them together, united in their quest to bring light to the darkness and restore peace to the zoo once more.

"Summoned to the Council," the protagonist and their allies receive a summons to a meeting with the wise and ancient guardians of the Zoo of Wonders. As they gather in the heart of the zoo, they are filled with a sense of anticipation and curiosity, eager to learn the purpose of the council and the role they are to play in the events to come.

As they enter the council chamber, they are greeted by a sight of breathtaking beauty. The chamber is adorned with ancient tapestries and intricate carvings, each one depicting scenes from the zoo's rich history. At the head of the chamber sits the council of guardians, their faces lined with age and wisdom, their eyes shining with otherworldly light.

The guardians welcome the group and their friends, speaking in voices that echo with the power of the ancients. They reveal that the zoo is facing a threat unlike any it has ever known, a darkness that threatens to engulf the land and plunge it into chaos.

The guardians explain that the group and their allies have been chosen by fate to embark on a quest to confront the darkness and restore balance to the zoo. They are to seek out the ancient artifacts hidden within its depths, artifacts that hold the key to unlocking the secrets of the land and defeating the forces of darkness once and for all.

Filled with a sense of duty and determination, the group and their friends pledge themselves to the council's cause, swearing to do whatever it takes to protect the zoo and all who inhabit it. With the wisdom of the guardians to guide them and the strength of their bonds to sustain them, they set out on their next journey, ready to face it.

"Ancient Wisdom," the wise guardians of the Zoo of Wonders impart their knowledge of the zoo's rich history and the origins of the darkness threatening it. Gathered around the council chamber, the group and their allies listen intently as the guardians weave a tale as old as time itself.

The guardians reveal that the zoo was once a place of harmony and balance, a sanctuary where creatures of all shapes and sizes lived in peace and harmony. But eons ago, a great darkness descended upon the land, shrouding it in shadows and threatening to consume everything in its path.

As the guardians speak, images dance before the group's eyes, visions of ancient battles and heroic deeds that echo through the ages. They learn of the legendary heroes who once rose to face the darkness, wielding ancient artifacts and harnessing the power of the elements to drive back the shadows and restore peace to the land.

But despite their valiant efforts, the darkness could not be fully vanquished. It retreated into the shadows, biding its time and waiting for the opportunity to strike once more. And now, after centuries of slumber, it has awakened once again, more powerful and more dangerous than ever before.

As the group and their friends absorb the wisdom of the guardians, they realize the magnitude of the task that lies before them. They must follow in the footsteps of the heroes who came before them, seeking out the ancient artifacts and harnessing their power to confront the darkness and restore balance to the zoo.

With the knowledge of the guardians to guide them and the strength of their bonds to sustain them, the group and their allies are ready to embark on their next journey, knowing that the fate of the zoo and all who inhabit it hangs in the balance. And as they leave the council chamber behind, they carry with them the weight of history and the hope of a brighter future.

"**Prophecies Unveiled,**" the group and their friends are presented with ancient prophecies that foretell the coming conflict and the role they must play in it. As the guardians continue to share their knowledge, they reveal that the fate of the Zoo of Wonders has long been intertwined with the threads of destiny, woven by the hands of fate itself.

The prophecies speak of a time of great upheaval, when darkness shall rise to challenge the light and the fate of the world shall hang in the balance. They speak of heroes who shall rise from the ashes of adversity, wielding ancient artifacts and harnessing the power of the elements to confront the darkness and restore balance to the land.

But amidst the chaos and uncertainty, there is hope. For the prophecies also foretell of a chosen few who shall rise to the challenge, guided by the wisdom of the ancients and fueled by the strength of their bonds. They are the ones who shall lead the charge against the forces of darkness, their courage and determination lighting the way forward.

As the group and their friends listen to the prophecies, they feel a sense of awe and wonder wash over them. They realize that they have been chosen by fate to play a pivotal role in the events to come, their actions shaping the course of history and determining the fate of the zoo and all who inhabit it.

Filled with a renewed sense of purpose and determination, the group and their allies pledge themselves to the fulfillment of the prophecies, knowing that the path ahead will be fraught with danger and uncertainty. But with the knowledge of the prophecies to guide them and the strength of their bonds to sustain them, they are ready to face it and emerge victorious in the battle against the darkness.

"**A Call to Act**," empowered by the council's guidance and fueled by the prophecies they have unveiled, the group and their friends prepare to embark on a quest to fulfill their destiny and save the Zoo of Wonders from the encroaching darkness.

With a renewed sense of purpose and determination, they gather their supplies and make final preparations for the journey ahead. Each member of the group feels the weight of responsibility upon their shoulders, but they also feel a sense of excitement and anticipation as they prepare to face the challenges that lie ahead.

As they stand on the threshold of adventure, the group addresses their friends, rallying them with words of courage and inspiration. They remind them of the importance of their quest, of the lives that hang in the balance, and of the duty they have been called to fulfill.

With their hearts united and their resolve unshakable, the group and their friends set out from the council chamber, their footsteps echoing through the halls of the zoo. They know that the journey ahead will be long and perilous, but they also know that they are not alone. Together, they will face whatever challenges come their way, united in their quest to save the zoo and all who inhabit it.

And as they step out into the world beyond the council chamber, they carry with them the hope of a brighter future, knowing that their actions will shape the course of history and determine the fate of the zoo for generations to come. With the council's guidance to light their way and the prophecies to guide their steps, they set forth on their epic quest, to emerge victorious in the battle against the darkness.

"Journeying Forth," the protagonist and their friends set out on their quest, braving the perils of the magical world beyond the Zoo of Wonders. With hearts full of determination and minds focused on their mission, they venture forth into the unknown, ready to face it.

Leaving the safety of the zoo behind, the group and their friends step out into a world filled with wonders and dangers alike. They journey through enchanted forests, where trees whisper secrets and magical creatures dart through the shadows. They traverse treacherous mountains, where icy winds howl and ancient spirits roam. And they navigate through vast plains, where the sky stretches out endlessly and the horizon beckons with the promise of adventure.

As they journey forth, the group and their friends encounter trials and tribulations that test their strength, courage, and resolve. They must overcome obstacles both natural and supernatural, from raging rivers to cunning adversaries, as they make their way towards their destination.

But amidst the challenges and dangers, there are moments of beauty and wonder that take their breath away. They witness majestic waterfalls cascading down sheer cliffs, shimmering auroras dancing across the night sky, and rare creatures of myth and legend that roam the land.

Through it all, the group and their friends rely on each other for support and encouragement, their bonds of friendship growing stronger with each step they take. Together, they face the unknown with courage and determination, knowing that their quest is just beginning and that the fate of the zoo and all who inhabit it hangs in the balance. And as they journey forth into the magical world beyond, they do so with hearts full of hope and minds set on the ultimate goal: to fulfill the prophecy and save the zoo from the darkness that threatens to consume it.

"Trials and Tribulations," the group and their friends encounter challenges and obstacles that test their strength, resolve, and friendship as they journey through the magical world beyond the Zoo of Wonders.

Their path is fraught with peril, and at every turn, they face new trials that push them to their limits. They must navigate treacherous terrain, from dense forests filled with hidden dangers to barren deserts where the sun beats down mercilessly. They encounter fierce creatures that seek to thwart their progress, from cunning wolves to ancient guardians that jealously guard their domains.

But the greatest challenges they face are not always external. As they journey onwards, the group and their friends must confront their own fears and doubts, grappling with inner demons that threaten to undermine their quest. They must learn to trust in themselves and each other, drawing strength from their bonds of friendship and the knowledge that they are not alone in their journey.

Despite the trials and tribulations they face, the group and their friends press onwards, their determination unwavering in the face of adversity. They draw upon their skills and resourcefulness to overcome each obstacle that stands in their way, growing stronger with every challenge they overcome.

And through it all, they learn valuable lessons about themselves and each other, forging bonds that will withstand the tests of time. As they journey onwards, they come to understand that true strength lies not in individual prowess, but in the unity and camaraderie of those who stand together in the face of adversity.

With each challenge they overcome, the group and their friends grow closer to their goal, their resolve strengthened by the knowledge that they are capable of facing whatever challenges lie ahead. And as they continue on their journey, they do so with hearts full of courage and minds set on the ultimate prize: to fulfill the prophecy and save the zoo from the darkness that threatens to engulf it.

"Unexpected Allies," the group and their friends form alliances with unexpected allies who join their quest, each bringing their own unique skills and abilities to the group. As they journey through the magical world beyond the Zoo of Wonders, they encounter individuals who are willing to lend their aid to their cause, united in their desire to confront the darkness that threatens the land.

Among their newfound allies are creatures of myth and legend, beings whose powers and abilities surpass those of ordinary mortals. From noble centaurs who roam the forests to wise dragons who dwell in hidden caves, each ally offers their assistance to the group and their friends, eager to join their quest and lend their strength to the fight against the darkness.

But not all of their allies are of the supernatural variety. Along the way, the group and their friends also encounter fellow travelers who share their goals and ideals, ordinary individuals who have been touched by the darkness and are determined to see it vanquished. Together, they form a diverse and eclectic group, united in their determination to confront the darkness and restore peace to the land.

As they journey onwards, the group and their friends come to rely on their allies for support and guidance, drawing strength from their shared purpose and the knowledge that they are not alone in their quest. Each ally brings their own unique skills and abilities to the group, enriching their journey with their wisdom and experience.

And as they continue on their journey, the group and their friends are filled with a renewed sense of hope and determination, knowing that with their allies at their side, they are stronger than ever before, and united in their quest to fulfill the prophecy and save the zoo from the darkness that threatens it.

"The Path Ahead," the group and their friends find themselves contemplating the journey that lies before them as they venture deeper into the unknown. As they travel through the magical world beyond the Zoo of Wonders, they cannot help but reflect on the path they have chosen and the dangers that lie in wait.

The road ahead is fraught with uncertainty, and each step they take brings them closer to the heart of the darkness that threatens the land. They know that the challenges they will face will test them in ways they cannot yet imagine, and they are filled with a sense of apprehension and foreboding as they contemplate the perils that lie ahead.

But amidst the uncertainty, there is also hope. the group and their friends draw strength from the bonds of friendship that unite them, knowing that together they can overcome any obstacle that stands in their way. They take comfort in the knowledge that they are not alone in their journey, and that they have allies who will stand by their side no matter what dangers they may face.

As they journey onwards, the group and their friends steel themselves for the trials that lie ahead, their determination unwavering in the face of adversity. They know that the road ahead will not be easy, but they are ready to face whatever challenges come their way, united in their quest to fulfill the prophecy and save the zoo from the darkness that threatens to consume it.

And as they continue on their journey, they do so with hearts full of courage and minds set on the ultimate goal: to confront the darkness and restore balance to the land, no matter the cost. With their eyes fixed firmly on the horizon, they press onwards to face the battle against the forces of darkness.

"Lost History," the group stumbles upon ancient ruins hidden deep within the heart of the magical world beyond the Zoo of Wonders. As they explore the crumbling remnants of a once-great civilization, they uncover clues to the origins of the darkness that threatens to engulf the zoo.

The ruins are shrouded in mystery, their walls adorned with faded murals and inscriptions that speak of a time long forgotten. the group and their friends pore over the ancient carvings, searching for answers to the questions that plague their minds.

As they delve deeper into the ruins, they discover artifacts and relics that hint at the ancient civilization's connection to the darkness. They find ancient tomes filled with cryptic symbols, their pages yellowed with age but still filled with wisdom and knowledge. They uncover hidden chambers and secret passageways, each one revealing a piece of the puzzle that is the zoo's lost history.

But the more they uncover, the more questions arise. Who were the people who built these ruins? What role did they play in the events that led to the darkness that now threatens the land? And most importantly, what secrets do these ancient ruins hold that could help the group and their friends in their quest to save the zoo?

As they ponder these questions, the group and their friends realize that they have stumbled upon something far greater than they could have ever imagined. The ruins hold the key to unlocking the secrets of the past, and with that knowledge, they may be able to uncover the truth behind the darkness that plagues the land.

With newfound determination, the group and their friends set out to explore every corner of the ancient ruins, knowing that the answers they seek may be closer than they realize. And as they delve deeper into the mysteries of the past, they do so with hearts full of hope and minds open to the possibility of uncovering the truth that will set the zoo free from the darkness that threatens to consume it.

"Deciphering the Past," the group and their friends set to work deciphering the ancient inscriptions and symbols found within the ruins. With determination and perseverance, they begin piecing together the history of the magical world and its connection to the present crisis.

Armed with knowledge and curiosity, the group and their friends pore over the ancient texts, unraveling the secrets of a time long forgotten. They painstakingly translate the inscriptions, their minds racing as they piece together the puzzle that is the history of the magical world.

As they delve deeper into their research, they uncover startling revelations about the origins of the darkness that threatens the land. They learn of ancient wars and conflicts that tore the world apart, of powerful sorcerers who wielded dark magic in their quest for domination, and of heroes who rose to challenge the forces of darkness and restore peace to the land.

But amidst the tales of strife and conflict, they also discover stories of hope and redemption. They learn of ancient prophecies that foretold the coming of a chosen few who would rise to confront the darkness and restore balance to the world. They uncover legends of powerful artifacts and magical relics that hold the key to unlocking the secrets of the past and vanquishing the forces of evil once and for all.

As they piece together the fragments of the past, the group and their friends come to understand the magnitude of the task that lies before them. They realize that they are not just fighting to save the zoo, but to preserve the very fabric of the magical world itself. And with this knowledge burning in their hearts, they redouble their efforts, knowing that the fate of all who inhabit the land hangs in the balance.

"Guardians of the Ruins," the group and their friends encounter guardians or spirits protecting the ancient ruins. As they delve deeper into the labyrinthine passages of the crumbling structures, they come face to face with spectral beings who test their worthiness and determination.

The guardians of the ruins are ancient spirits bound to protect the secrets held within the crumbling walls. They manifest as ethereal figures, their forms shifting and shimmering in the dim light of the ruins. With eyes that seem to pierce the soul, they challenge the group and their friends to prove their worthiness to uncover the truths hidden within the ancient structures.

To pass the test of the guardians, the group and their friends must demonstrate courage, wisdom, and strength of character. They are faced with riddles and puzzles that test their intellect, trials of skill and agility that test their prowess, and moral dilemmas that test their integrity and resolve.

But as they face the trials set before them, the group and their friends draw upon their inner strength and the bonds of friendship that unite them. They support each other through moments of doubt and uncertainty, offering encouragement and guidance as they navigate the challenges that lie ahead.

With determination and perseverance, they overcome each trial that the guardians set before them, proving themselves to be worthy of uncovering the secrets of the ruins. And as they emerge victorious from the trials, they are granted passage deeper into the heart of the ruins, one step closer to uncovering the truth behind the darkness that threatens the land.

As they press onwards, the group and their friends are filled with a renewed sense of purpose and determination, knowing that they are on the right path to unraveling the mysteries of the past and saving the zoo from the darkness that looms on the horizon. And with the guardians' blessings to guide them, they venture forth into the unknown, ready to face it

"**Unleashing Power,**" the group and their friends uncover ancient artifacts or knowledge that could aid them in their quest to save the zoo from the encroaching darkness.

As they continue to explore the depths of the ancient ruins, the group and their friends stumble upon a chamber filled with treasures of untold value. Among the artifacts scattered about the room are ancient scrolls, glowing gemstones, and intricately crafted weapons imbued with powerful magic.

With a sense of awe and wonder, the group and their friends examine the artifacts, realizing that they hold the key to unlocking the secrets of the past and harnessing the power needed to confront the darkness that threatens the land.

Among the treasures they uncover is a scroll containing ancient spells and incantations, passed down through generations and imbued with the magic of the ancients. With careful study and practice, the group and their friends learn to wield the power of the spells, tapping into the elemental forces of the world to aid them in their quest.

They also discover a collection of enchanted weapons, each one crafted by master artisans and infused with the essence of the magical world. With these weapons in hand, the group and their friends feel a surge of power coursing through their veins, ready to be unleashed against the forces of darkness.

But perhaps the greatest treasure they uncover is a tome containing the lost history of the zoo and its connection to the darkness that threatens it. Within its pages are clues and revelations that shed light on the origins of the darkness, as well as the role the group and their friends must play in confronting it.

Armed with this newfound knowledge and the power of the artifacts they have uncovered, the group and their friends are ready to continue their journey, knowing that they have the tools and the strength they need to face whatever challenges lie ahead. With hearts full of courage and minds set on the ultimate goal, they venture forth into the unknown, ready to confront the darkness and save the zoo from its grip once and for all.

"Entrance to the Forest," the group ventures into the mysterious Forest of Whispers, where the trees seem to whisper secrets of ancient times as they sway in the gentle breeze. As the group and their friends step beneath the canopy of ancient trees, they feel a sense of wonder and trepidation wash over them.

The forest is alive with the sounds of nature, from the chirping of birds to the rustling of leaves in the wind. But there is also an eerie sense of silence that hangs in the air, broken only by the soft murmurs of the trees as they speak in hushed tones.

As they journey deeper into the heart of the forest, the group and their friends feel a sense of disorientation wash over them. The twisting paths and dense foliage seem to shift and change before their eyes, leading them deeper into the heart of the unknown.

But amidst the uncertainty, there is also a sense of awe and wonder that fills their hearts. The forest is teeming with life, from colorful flowers that bloom along the forest floor to majestic creatures that dart through the underbrush.

With each step they take, the group and their friends are filled with a sense of anticipation, knowing that they are on the brink of uncovering secrets that have long been hidden within the depths of the forest. And as they press onwards, they do so with hearts full of courage and minds open to the wonders that await them in the Forest of Whispers.

"Lost in the Shadows," the group and their friends find themselves ensnared in the dense foliage of the Forest of Whispers, facing illusions and mirages that challenge their perceptions and resolve.

As they venture deeper into the heart of the forest, the dense foliage begins to close in around them, obscuring their path and leading them astray. Shadows dance among the trees, playing tricks on their eyes and leading them down winding paths that seem to twist and turn endlessly.

Confusion sets in as the group and their friends struggle to navigate the labyrinthine maze of the forest. Each turn they take seems to lead them further from their intended path, and the whispers of the trees only serve to deepen their sense of disorientation.

But amidst the chaos, there is also a sense of determination that fills their hearts. They refuse to give in to despair, knowing that they must press onwards if they are to uncover the secrets hidden within the forest's depths.

With each passing moment, the group and their friends face new challenges that test their resolve. They must confront their own fears and doubts, overcoming illusions that seek to cloud their judgment and lead them astray.

But through it all, they rely on each other for support and guidance, drawing strength from the bonds of friendship that unite them. Together, they navigate the treacherous maze of the forest, determined to find their way back to the path that will lead them to their ultimate goal.

And as they press onwards, their resolve only grows stronger, fueled by the knowledge that they are on the right path and that their journey is far from over. With hearts full of courage and minds set on the task at hand, they continue their quest, ready to face it in the depths of the Forest of Whispers.

"Encounter with the Guardians," the group and their friends encounter the guardians of the Forest of Whispers, enigmatic beings who test their determination and purity of heart as they seek to navigate the treacherous depths of the forest.

The guardians of the forest are ancient spirits, their forms ethereal and ever-shifting as they move through the dense foliage. With eyes that seem to see into the very depths of their souls, they confront the group and their friends, challenging them to prove their worthiness to pass through the forest's sacred domain.

To pass the test of the guardians, the group and their friends must demonstrate their determination and purity of heart. They are faced with trials that test their resolve and courage, trials that push them to their limits and force them to confront their own inner demons.

But as they face the guardians' challenges, the group and their friends draw strength from the bonds of friendship that unite them. They support each other through moments of doubt and uncertainty, offering encouragement and guidance as they navigate the trials that lie before them.

With each trial they overcome, the group and their friends come one step closer to proving their worthiness to pass through the forest's sacred domain. And as they face the guardians with courage and determination, they do so with hearts full of hope and minds set on the ultimate goal: to uncover the secrets hidden within the depths of the Forest of Whispers and emerge victorious in their quest to save the zoo from the darkness that threatens to engulf it.

"**Finding the Way,**" the group and their friends summon their courage and determination as they navigate through the dense foliage of the Forest of Whispers. Despite the challenges they face, they persevere, determined to uncover clues that will lead them closer to their goal of saving the zoo from the encroaching darkness.

With each step they take, the group and their friends draw upon their inner strength and the bonds of friendship that unite them. They support each other through moments of doubt and uncertainty, offering encouragement and guidance as they navigate the labyrinthine paths of the forest.

As they press onwards, they keep their eyes and ears open for any signs or clues that may help them in their quest. They search for hidden symbols or markings, listen for whispers in the wind, and follow the guidance of their instincts as they seek to unravel the mysteries of the forest.

And finally, their perseverance pays off as they uncover a series of clues that lead them closer to their goal. They stumble upon ancient runes carved into the bark of the trees, pointing them in the direction they must go. They find hidden passages and secret clearings that reveal glimpses of the world beyond the forest, offering hope that they are on the right path.

With renewed determination, the group and their friends press onwards, knowing that they are one step closer to uncovering the secrets hidden within the depths of the Forest of Whispers. And as they continue their journey, they do so with hearts full of courage and minds set on the ultimate goal: to confront the darkness and save the zoo from its grip once and for all.

"Descending into Darkness," the group ventures into the depths of the Cave of Echoes, a foreboding cavern where the darkness seems to swallow all sound and light. As the group and their friends step cautiously into the mouth of the cave, they are greeted by an oppressive silence that hangs heavy in the air.

The walls of the cave are slick with moisture, and the only sound that echoes through the darkness is the steady drip of water from stalactites above. Shadows dance along the cavern walls, casting eerie shapes that seem to come alive in the flickering torchlight.

With each step they take, the group and their friends feel a sense of trepidation wash over them. The air is thick with an otherworldly chill, and a sense of foreboding hangs over the cavern like a shroud.

But despite the darkness that surrounds them, the group and their friends press onwards, determined to uncover the secrets that lie hidden within the depths of the Cave of Echoes. They steel themselves against the unknown, their hearts filled with courage and their minds focused on the task at hand.

As they venture deeper into the heart of the cave, they know that they are treading on dangerous ground. But they refuse to give in to fear, knowing that they must press onwards if they are to confront the darkness that threatens the land.

With each step they take, they draw closer to their goal, their determination unwavering in the face of adversity. And as they continue their journey into the depths of the Cave of Echoes, they do so with hearts full of courage and minds set on the ultimate goal: to uncover the truth behind the darkness that plagues the land and emerge victorious in their quest to save the zoo from its grip.

"Whispers of the Past," the group and their friends hear echoes of ancient voices and cryptic messages as they journey deeper into the depths of the Cave of Echoes. The cavern seems to come alive with the faint whispers of long-forgotten spirits, their words carrying hints of the cave's hidden secrets and dangers.

As they navigate the twisting passages of the cave, the group and their friends strain to catch the elusive whispers that seem to echo all around them. The voices speak in hushed tones, their words obscured by the shifting shadows and the steady drip of water from the cavern walls.

But amidst the echoes, the group and their friends discern fragments of ancient knowledge and cryptic messages that hint at the true nature of the cave. They hear tales of ancient civilizations that once inhabited the depths of the cave, of powerful sorcerers who wielded dark magic in their quest for dominion, and of heroes who rose to challenge the forces of darkness and restore balance to the land.

With each whispered word, the group and their friends piece together the puzzle of the cave's history, drawing closer to uncovering the truth behind the darkness that plagues the land. But they also sense the dangers that lie ahead, knowing that they must tread carefully if they are to emerge unscathed from the depths of the Cave of Echoes.

With hearts full of determination and minds open to the wisdom of the ancients, the group press onwards, ready to challenge the cave and emerge victorious in their quest to save the zoo from its grip.

"Trial of Reflection," the cave presents them with a trial that forces them to confront their innermost fears and doubts, testing their resolve. As they venture deeper into the cavernous depths, they come face to face with a series of challenges that push them to their limits.

The trial of reflection manifests as a series of illusions and mirages that play upon their deepest fears and insecurities. Shadows dance along the walls, morphing into sinister shapes

that seem to mock them with their every step. The air grows thick with tension as they struggle to discern reality from illusion, their senses heightened by the oppressive darkness that surrounds them.

But despite the overwhelming odds, they refuse to back down, drawing upon their inner strength and the support of their friends to face the trial head-on. With each challenge they overcome, they grow stronger, their resolve unwavering in the face of adversity.

As they confront their innermost demons, they come to realize that the true test lies not in overcoming the physical obstacles before them, but in overcoming the doubts and insecurities that linger within their own hearts. With each step they take, they learn to trust in themselves and in each other, knowing that together, they can overcome any obstacle that stands in their way.

With hearts full of courage and minds set on the task at hand, they press onwards, determined to emerge victorious in their quest to save the zoo from the darkness that threatens to engulf it. And as they face the trial of reflection with unwavering resolve, they do so with the knowledge that they are stronger than before.

"Illuminate the Shadows," they, through courage and unity, overcome the darkness of the cave and find a glimmer of hope that guides them forward. As they continue their journey through the depths of the Cave of Echoes, they draw upon the strength of their bonds and the light of their resolve to push back against the encroaching darkness.

With each step they take, they feel the weight of the shadows lifting, replaced by a sense of clarity and purpose that fills their hearts with hope. The oppressive darkness that once surrounded them begins to recede, replaced by the warm glow of their collective determination to see their quest through to the end.

Together, they stand as beacons of light in the midst of the darkness, illuminating the path ahead with their unwavering resolve and unwavering determination. With each obstacle they overcome, they grow stronger, their spirits lifted by the knowledge that they are not alone in their journey.

As they press onwards, guided by the glimmer of hope that shines bright within their hearts, they know that they are on the right path. With each passing moment, they draw closer to their goal of saving the zoo from the darkness that threatens to consume it, fueled by the knowledge that they are stronger together than they could ever be apart.

And as they emerge from the depths of the Cave of Echoes, they do so with renewed determination and a sense of purpose that burns bright within their souls. With hearts full of courage and minds set on the ultimate goal, they continue their journey, ready to face it.

"**A World of Wonder**," they discover the breathtaking beauty of the Crystal Caverns, where shimmering crystals light up the darkness. As they step into the cavernous expanse of the Crystal Caverns, they are greeted by a sight unlike any they have ever seen before.

The cavern walls are adorned with countless crystals of every shape and size, their surfaces sparkling and reflecting the light in a mesmerizing display of color and brilliance. The air is cool and crisp, filled with the faint hum of energy that emanates from the crystals themselves.

As they explore further into the depths of the caverns, they are surrounded on all sides by the radiant glow of the crystals, which seem to pulse with an otherworldly energy. Each step they take reveals new wonders to behold, from towering stalactites that stretch towards the cavern ceiling to delicate formations that glisten like jewels in the soft light.

With each passing moment, they are filled with a sense of awe and wonder at the beauty of the Crystal Caverns, their hearts lifted by the sheer magnificence of the sight before them. Despite the dangers that lurk in the shadows, they cannot help but feel a sense of peace and tranquility wash over them as they bask in the glow of the crystals.

As they continue their journey through the caverns, they are filled with a renewed sense of purpose and determination, knowing that they are one step closer to uncovering the secrets that lie hidden within the depths of the Crystal Caverns. And as they press onwards, guided by the light of the crystals and the hope that burns bright within their hearts, they do so with the knowledge that they are on the right path to saving the zoo from the darkness that threatens it.

"Trapped by Illusions," they become ensnared by illusions created by the crystals, facing visions of their deepest desires and greatest fears. As they journey deeper into the Crystal Caverns, they are surrounded by the shimmering light of the crystals, which seem to pulse with an otherworldly energy.

But amidst the beauty of their surroundings, danger lurks in the form of illusions that play tricks on their minds and distort their perceptions of reality. Visions of their deepest desires and greatest fears dance before their eyes, tempting them to lose themselves in the illusions and abandon their quest altogether.

With each step they take, the illusions grow stronger, threatening to overwhelm them with their hypnotic allure. They struggle to distinguish truth from fiction, their minds clouded by the shimmering light of the crystals and the powerful magic that surrounds them.

But despite the challenges they face, they refuse to give in to the illusions, drawing upon their inner strength and the support of their friends to break free from their grasp. With each passing moment, they fight against the temptations that surround them, their resolve unwavering in the face of adversity.

As they press onwards, they are filled with a sense of determination and purpose, knowing that they must overcome the illusions if they are to uncover the secrets that lie hidden within the depths of the Crystal Caverns. And as they face the illusions with courage and resolve, they do so with the knowledge that they are stronger together.

"Breaking the Spell," they, through self-awareness and determination, break free from the illusions and find clarity amidst the chaos. As they struggle against the illusions created by the crystals, they begin to realize that the key to breaking free lies within themselves.

With each passing moment, they delve deeper into their own minds, confronting their deepest fears and desires with unwavering resolve. They draw upon their inner strength and the support of their friends, refusing to succumb to the temptations that surround them.

Through self-awareness and introspection, they begin to see through the illusions, recognizing them for what they truly are: tricks of the mind designed to deceive and distract. With each revelation, they grow stronger, their determination unwavering in the face of adversity.

And finally, with a burst of clarity and insight, they break free from the illusions that have ensnared them, emerging from the chaos with a renewed sense of purpose and determination. With hearts full of courage and minds clear of doubt, they press onwards, ready to face it

As they continue their journey through the Crystal Caverns, they do so with a newfound sense of clarity and determination, knowing that they are stronger together than they could ever be apart. And as they face the trials that lie ahead with courage and resolve, they do so with the knowledge that they have overcome the illusions that once threatened to consume them, emerging victorious in their quest to save the zoo from the darkness.

"Unveiling Truths," they uncover hidden truths within the caverns that shed light on their quest and the nature of the darkness threatening the zoo. As they delve deeper into the Crystal Caverns, they stumble upon ancient writings and artifacts that reveal long-forgotten secrets hidden within the depths of the caverns.

With each discovery, they piece together the puzzle of the Crystal Caverns' history, uncovering clues that shed light on the true nature of the darkness that threatens the zoo.

They learn of ancient civilizations that once inhabited the caverns, of powerful sorcerers who harnessed the energy of the crystals for their own nefarious purposes, and of heroes who rose to challenge the forces of darkness and restore balance to the land.

But amidst the revelations, they also uncover darker truths that shake them to their core. They learn of the sacrifices made by those who came before them, of the trials and tribulations they faced in their quest to protect the zoo from the encroaching darkness, and of the dangers that still lie ahead.

With each new revelation, they are filled with a sense of awe and wonder at the magnitude of the task that lies before them. But they also feel a renewed sense of purpose and determination, knowing that they are on the right path to uncovering the secrets that lie hidden within the Crystal Caverns and saving the zoo from the darkness that threatens to consume it.

And as they press onwards, guided by the light of the crystals and the hope that burns bright within their hearts, they know that they should stay together. And with each step they take, they draw closer to their ultimate goal of saving the zoo from its impending doom.

"Flowing Mysteries," they embark on a journey down the River of Whispers, where the waters seem to carry secrets of the past and future. As they navigate the gentle currents of the river, they are surrounded by an atmosphere of mystery and intrigue.

The waters of the River of Whispers are clear and pristine, reflecting the soft light of the sun as it filters through the dense foliage overhead. Yet beneath the tranquil surface lies a sense of ancient wisdom, as if the river itself holds the key to unlocking the secrets of the world.

As they journey downstream, they are drawn deeper into the heart of the mystery that surrounds them. They listen intently to the whispers of the river, hoping to glean some insight into the challenges that lie ahead.

With each passing moment, they feel a sense of wonder and curiosity wash over them, as if they are being guided by unseen forces towards a greater understanding of the world around them. They sense that the answers they seek may lie hidden within the depths of the river, waiting to be discovered by those who dare to venture forth.

As they continue their journey down the River of Whispers, they do so with hearts full of anticipation and minds open to the mysteries that lie ahead. And as they listen to the gentle whispers of the river, they know that they are on the right path to uncovering the truths that will ultimately save the zoo.

"**Echoes of Destiny**," they hear whispers and echoes along the riverbanks, foretelling of trials and tribulations yet to come. As they journey down the River of Whispers, the air is filled with a sense of anticipation and unease, as if the very fabric of destiny is woven into the currents of the river itself.

The whispers and echoes that drift along the riverbanks speak of trials and tribulations yet to come, hinting at the challenges that lie ahead in their quest to save the zoo from the darkness that threatens to consume it. They listen intently to the cryptic messages, trying to decipher their meaning and glean some insight into the path that lies before them.

With each whispered word, they feel a sense of foreboding wash over them, as if they are being warned of the dangers that await them on their journey. Yet amidst the uncertainty, they also sense a glimmer of hope, as if the whispers are guiding them towards a greater understanding of their destiny.

As they continue their journey down the River of Whispers, they do so with hearts full of determination and minds open to the mysteries that lie ahead. And as they listen to the echoes of destiny that drift along the riverbanks, they know that they are on the right path to fulfilling their destiny and saving the zoo from its impending doom.

"**Navigating Rapids,**" they encounter treacherous rapids and obstacles along the river, testing their teamwork and resilience. As they navigate the swirling currents and jagged rocks, they are faced with a series of challenges that push them to their limits.

The rapids churn and roar as they rush downstream, threatening to capsize their vessel and send them tumbling into the icy waters below. They paddle furiously against the current, their muscles straining with exertion as they fight to maintain control of their craft.

But amidst the chaos, they also find strength in their unity, working together to navigate the treacherous waters and overcome each obstacle that stands in their way. With each passing moment, they grow stronger, their bonds forged in the heat of battle as they face the rapids head-on.

As they continue to battle against the raging waters, they draw upon their collective resilience and determination, refusing to give in to the despair that threatens to overwhelm them. With each obstacle they overcome, they grow closer to their goal, their spirits buoyed by the knowledge that they are stronger together than they could ever be apart.

And as they emerge victorious from the rapids, they do so with a renewed sense of purpose and determination, knowing that they have proven themselves capable of overcoming any challenge that stands in their way. With hearts full of courage and minds set on the ultimate goal, they press onwards, ready to face whatever trials and tribulations lie ahead.

"Towards the Horizon," despite the challenges, they press on towards the horizon, guided by hope and determination. As they leave the treacherous rapids behind, they set their sights on the distant horizon, their hearts filled with a renewed sense of purpose and resolve.

Despite the trials and tribulations they have faced along the River of Whispers, they refuse to be deterred from their quest to save the zoo from the darkness that threatens to consume it. With each stroke of the paddle and each passing mile, they draw closer to their goal, their spirits lifted by the promise of a brighter tomorrow.

As they journey onwards, they are buoyed by the bonds of friendship and the strength of their collective resolve. They know that the path ahead will not be easy, but they also know that they have faced adversity before and emerged victorious.

With each passing moment, they draw closer to the horizon, their determination unwavering in the face of uncertainty. And as they press onwards, guided by hope and fueled by determination, they know that they are on the right path to saving the zoo from its impending doom.

And so, with hearts full of courage and minds set on the ultimate goal, they continue their journey towards the horizon.

"Mirror Lake," the group arrives at the Isle of Reflection, where a tranquil lake mirrors the sky and surrounding landscape. As they step onto the shores of Mirror Lake, they are greeted by a sight of breathtaking beauty.

The surface of the lake is calm and still, reflecting the colors of the sky above and the lush greenery that surrounds it. It is as if the lake itself is a mirror, capturing the essence of the world around it in perfect clarity.

As they gaze upon the tranquil waters, they feel a sense of peace wash over them, as if the very air is infused with a sense of serenity and calm. The beauty of Mirror Lake is unlike anything they have ever seen before, filling them with a sense of wonder and awe.

They take a moment to pause and reflect on the journey that has brought them to this place, marveling at the twists and turns of fate that have led them to the Isle of Reflection. They know that their quest is far from over, but for now, they allow themselves to bask in the tranquility of this beautiful place.

As they explore the shores of Mirror Lake, they are filled with a sense of gratitude for the beauty of the natural world and the wonders that it holds. And as they continue their journey, they carry with them the memory of Mirror Lake, a reminder of the peace and serenity that can be found even in the midst of chaos and uncertainty.

"**Facing Truths**," they confront reflections of their true selves in the mirror lake, forced to confront their past actions and future aspirations. As they gaze into the tranquil waters of Mirror Lake, they see not only the beauty of their surroundings, but also the reflection of their own souls.

The mirror-like surface of the lake holds a mirror to their innermost thoughts and feelings, reflecting back to them the truth of who they are and who they aspire to be. They are forced to confront their past actions and decisions, as well as the consequences that those actions may have had on themselves and others.

For some, the reflection is a source of comfort and reassurance, a reminder of their strengths and virtues. For others, it is a harsh mirror that reveals flaws and weaknesses that they may have been reluctant to acknowledge.

But amidst the revelations, they also find hope and inspiration, as they are reminded of the potential for growth and change that lies within each of them. They see glimpses of the person they aspire to be, and are filled with a renewed sense of determination to strive towards that ideal.

As they confront their reflections in the mirror lake, they do so with courage and resolve, knowing that true growth and transformation can only come from facing the truth of who they are and who they wish to become. And as they emerge from this introspective journey, they do so with a deeper understanding of themselves and their place in the world.

"**Inner Battles**," each character wrestles with their inner demons and insecurities, seeking to find peace and clarity amidst the turmoil. As they gaze into the reflective surface of Mirror

Lake, they are confronted not only with their external reflections but also with the shadows of their innermost struggles.

For Manny , it is the fear of inadequacy and the burden of responsibility that weighs heavily on his heart. He grapples with doubts about his own worthiness and his ability to lead his friends on their quest.

Lili, the singing butterfly, is haunted by memories of past failures and the fear of not living up to her own potential. She struggles with self-doubt and uncertainty, questioning whether she has what it takes to make a difference in the world.

Frank, the mischievous white monkey, battles with his own reckless impulses and the desire to prove himself worthy of the trust placed in him by his friends. He struggles to find balance between his playful nature and the seriousness of their quest.

And Silvia, the beautiful hipo, faces her own inner demons of vanity and self-absorption, wrestling with the realization that true beauty lies not in outward appearances but in the strength of character and compassion.

As they confront their inner battles, they are forced to confront the parts of themselves that they would rather keep hidden, to acknowledge their weaknesses and flaws with humility and grace. But amidst the turmoil, they also find moments of clarity and insight, as they begin to understand that true strength comes not from denying their weaknesses but from embracing them and striving to overcome them.

As they emerge from their inner struggles, they do so with a newfound sense of purpose and determination, ready to face it with courage and resilience. And as they continue their journey, they do so with the knowledge that true growth and transformation can only come from facing their inner demons head-on and emerging stronger on the other side.

"Embracing Growth," through introspection and self-discovery, they emerge from the Isle of Reflection with newfound wisdom and inner strength. As they reflect on their experiences at Mirror Lake, they realize that the journey they have undertaken is not just about saving the zoo from darkness, but also about confronting the darkness within themselves.

Each character has faced their own inner demons and insecurities, and though the journey has been difficult, it has also been transformative. They have confronted their fears and doubts with courage and resilience, and in doing so, have discovered hidden reserves of strength and resilience within themselves.

For Manny , the journey has been one of self-acceptance and growth. He has come to realize that true leadership is not about being infallible, but about acknowledging one's own limitations and learning from them.

Lili, the singing butterfly, has learned to embrace her own uniqueness and the power of her voice. She has discovered that true strength lies not in perfection, but in authenticity and vulnerability.

Frank, the mischievous white monkey, has found a balance between his playful nature and the seriousness of their quest. He has learned that true courage is not about bravado, but about facing one's fears with humility and grace.

And Silvia, the beautiful hipo, has come to understand that true beauty is not skin-deep, but comes from within. She has learned to value herself for who she is, rather than for how others perceive her.As they emerge from the

Isle of Reflection, they do so with a sense of peace and clarity that they did not have before. They know that the journey ahead will not be easy, but they also know that they are stronger and more resilient than they ever thought possible.

And so, with hearts full of courage and minds open to the possibilities that lie ahead, they continue their journey, ready to face whatever challenges come their way with strength, resilience, and inner peace.

"**Ascending Heights**," the group ascends towards the Summit of Destiny, where the air is thin and the path treacherous. As they climb higher and higher, the landscape around them transforms, giving way to rugged terrain and towering cliffs.

The air grows thin and crisp, making each breath a struggle as they push onwards towards their goal. The path ahead is steep and unforgiving, with every step bringing them closer to the summit and the challenges that await them there.

Despite the difficulty of the journey, they press onwards with determination and resolve, fueled by the knowledge that their quest is nearing its climax. With each step they take, they draw closer to the summit and the ultimate confrontation with the darkness that threatens to consume the zoo.

As they ascend towards the heights of destiny, they do so with hearts full of courage and minds focused on the task at hand. And though the path ahead may be fraught with danger, they know that they are stronger together, and that together, they will overcome whatever obstacles lie in their way.

"Tests of Endurance," they face grueling challenges and tests of endurance as they climb higher, pushing themselves to their limits. The path to the Summit of Destiny is fraught with obstacles, each one more daunting than the last.

They must navigate treacherous rock faces, clinging to narrow ledges and footholds as they ascend ever higher. The air grows thinner with each passing moment, making it difficult to draw breath and causing their muscles to ache with exertion.

Despite the physical strain, they press onwards, driven by their determination to reach the summit and confront the darkness that threatens the zoo. With each obstacle they overcome, they grow stronger and more resilient, their bonds of friendship and camaraderie serving as a source of strength in the face of adversity.

As they climb higher and higher, they draw upon their inner reserves of courage and determination, refusing to give in to fatigue or despair. They know that the challenges they face are nothing compared to the importance of their mission, and that failure is not an option.

And so, with hearts full of determination and minds focused on the task at hand, they press on towards their journey to the Summit of Destiny.

"**Confronting Trials,**" at the summit, they encounter trials that test their courage, resilience, and loyalty to each other. As they reach the pinnacle of their journey, they are greeted by a series of challenges that push them to their limits.

These trials are not physical in nature, but rather tests of their character and resolve. They must confront their deepest fears and insecurities, facing them head-on with courage and determination.

For Manny, the trial may be one of leadership, forcing him to make difficult decisions for the good of the group, even in the face of uncertainty.

Lili, the singing butterfly, may be tested on her ability to trust in her own voice and instincts, even when others doubt her.

Frank, the mischievous white monkey, may face a trial of loyalty, being forced to choose between his own desires and the needs of his friends.

And Silvia, the beautiful hipo, may confront a trial of vanity, learning to see beyond outward appearances and value the strength of character within.

As they face these trials together, they draw strength from each other, their bonds of friendship and camaraderie serving as a source of support and encouragement. And though the challenges they face may be daunting, they know that together, they are capable of overcoming anything that stands in their way.

As they confront these trials with courage and determination, they emerge stronger than ever before, ready to face their journey to save the zoo.

"The Dawn of Fate," as they reach the pinnacle of their journey, they stand at the precipice of destiny, ready to face whatever lies ahead. The air is charged with anticipation as they gaze out over the vast expanse before them, knowing that the fate of the zoo hangs in the balance.

The summit of destiny stretches out before them, a stark reminder of the challenges they have overcome and the trials that still await them. But amidst the uncertainty, there is also a sense of hope and determination, as they know that they have come too far to turn back now.

With hearts full of courage and minds focused on the task at hand, they prepare to confront the darkness that threatens to consume the zoo. They draw upon the strength of their bonds and the lessons they have learned along the way, knowing that together, they are capable of facing whatever challenges lie ahead.

As they stand on the brink of destiny, they do so with a sense of purpose and resolve, ready to fight for the future of the zoo and all who call it home. And as they take their first steps into the unknown, they do so with the knowledge that their journey is far from over, but that they are ready to face any trials and tribulations come their way, united in their quest to bring light back to the darkness .

"Guidance Sought," the group seeks guidance from the Oracle, a wise and enigmatic seer who resides in a secluded sanctuary. As they approach the sanctuary, they are filled with a sense of awe and reverence, knowing that the Oracle possesses knowledge and insight beyond that of mortal beings.

The path to the sanctuary is treacherous, winding through dense forests and rugged terrain. But despite the challenges, they press onwards, driven by their desire for guidance and clarity in the face of uncertainty.

When they finally reach the sanctuary, they are greeted by an aura of tranquility and wisdom that permeates the air. The Oracle awaits them in the heart of the sanctuary, surrounded by ancient tomes and mystical artifacts that speak to the depth of their knowledge.

With hearts open and minds eager to receive guidance, they approach the Oracle and present their questions, seeking answers to the mysteries that have plagued them on their journey. And as they listen to the Oracle's words of wisdom, they are filled with a sense of hope and clarity, knowing that they are on the right path and that their quest is far from over.

As they leave the sanctuary, they carry with them the wisdom of the Oracle, renewed in their determination to face whatever challenges lie ahead. And though the journey ahead may be fraught with peril, they know that with the guidance of the Oracle, they will find the strength and courage to overcome any obstacle.

"Visions Revealed," the Oracle imparts cryptic visions and prophecies that offer insights into their quest and the challenges ahead. As they listen to the Oracle's words, they are filled with a sense of awe and wonder, knowing that they are being granted a glimpse into the future.

The visions are cryptic and mysterious, filled with symbols and imagery that are difficult to decipher. But amidst the confusion, they sense a thread of truth running through the Oracle's words, guiding them towards their destiny.

Each member of the group sees visions that are uniquely tailored to their own journey and experiences.

For Manny, the visions may offer clues to his true purpose and the role he is destined to play in the quest to save the zoo.

Lili's visions may reveal hidden talents and powers that she never knew she possessed, unlocking new possibilities for her to explore.

Frank's visions may challenge his perceptions of loyalty and friendship, forcing him to confront his own doubts and insecurities.

And Silvia's visions may offer insights into the nature of true beauty and the importance of inner strength and resilience.

As they listen to the Oracle's words and interpret the visions that unfold before them, they are filled with a sense of clarity and purpose, knowing that they are on the right path and that their journey is far from over. And though the challenges ahead may be daunting, they face them with courage and determination, ready to embrace whatever fate has in store.

"**Answers and Riddles,**" they grapple with the Oracle's cryptic messages, deciphering riddles and unraveling the threads of fate. The Oracle's words are like a puzzle, with each piece offering a glimpse into the larger picture of their quest.

They pore over the Oracle's words, searching for hidden meanings and clues that will guide them on their journey. Each riddle presents a new challenge, testing their intellect and intuition as they seek to unravel the mysteries that lie before them.

For Manny , the riddles may offer insights into his own past and the choices that have led him to this moment.

Lili, the singing butterfly, may find solace in the Oracle's words, uncovering hidden truths about her own identity and purpose.

Frank, the mischievous white monkey, may delight in the challenge of the riddles, using his cunning and wit to unravel their secrets.

And Silvia, the beautiful hipo, may find herself drawn to the deeper meanings behind the Oracle's words, searching for answers to questions that have long haunted her.

As they grapple with the Oracle's cryptic messages, they are filled with a sense of determination and resolve, knowing that each riddle solved brings them one step closer to their goal. And though the path ahead may be uncertain, they face it with courage and conviction.

"Leaving with Purpose,"

For Manny , the knowledge gained from the Oracle fills him with a sense of purpose, driving him forward towards his destiny.

Lili, the singing butterfly, feels the weight of her newfound knowledge settle upon her shoulders, but she embraces it with open wings, ready to soar to new heights.

Frank, the mischievous white monkey, grins with excitement as he anticipates the adventures that lie ahead, eager to test his skills against whatever challenges come his way.

And Silvia, the beautiful hipo, walks with grace and poise, her determination shining like a beacon in the darkness, guiding them towards their ultimate goal.

As they leave the sanctuary behind them, they do so with heads held high and hearts full of hope. They know that the road ahead will not be easy, but they face it with courage ready to live each moment to the fullest as they journey towards their destiny.

"Into Darkness," the group descends into the Valley of Shadows, a place shrouded in darkness and mystery. As they venture deeper into the valley, the air grows thick with a sense of foreboding, and the light of the sun dims, swallowed by the shadows that cling to the land.

Their footsteps echo softly in the gloom as they navigate the winding paths and treacherous terrain of the valley. Each step forward brings them deeper into the heart of darkness, closer to the secrets that lie hidden within its depths.

For Manny, the darkness of the valley serves as a reminder of the struggles he has faced in the past, and the challenges that still lie ahead.

Lili, the singing butterfly, feels a chill run down her spine as she senses the presence of unseen eyes watching her every move, their intentions unknown.

Frank, the mischievous white monkey, moves with caution, his senses alert for any signs of danger lurking in the shadows.

And Silvia, the beautiful hipo, draws upon her inner strength and courage, refusing to be cowed by the darkness that surrounds them.

As they journey deeper into the valley, they do so with hearts full of determination and minds focused on the task at hand. Though the darkness may be daunting, they press onwards, to face whatever challenges await them in the shadows.

"Haunted Whispers," they hear haunting whispers and echoes that seem to emanate from the very shadows themselves, filling them with unease. The air is heavy with the weight of the unseen, and each whisper sends shivers down their spines, raising the hairs on the backs of their necks. The whispers are indistinct, barely audible above the sound of their own footsteps, but they carry with them an undeniable sense of malevolence. It's as if the shadows themselves are alive, whispering secrets and half-truths to those who dare to venture into their domain.

For Manny , the whispers dredge up memories of past traumas and fears, threatening to overwhelm him with their insidious presence.

Lili, the singing butterfly, feels a chill run down her spine as the whispers seem to echo the fears and doubts that have plagued her since the beginning of their journey.

Frank, the mischievous white monkey, bares his teeth in a silent snarl, his instincts telling him that whatever is whispering in the shadows is not to be trusted.

And Silvia, the beautiful hipo, draws upon her inner strength and resolve, refusing to let the whispers shake her confidence or deter her from their mission.

As they press onwards, the whispers grow louder, their words becoming clearer and more sinister with each passing moment. But though the darkness may be scary, they do not falter, their determination unwavering as they continue their journey into the heart of the shadows.

"Confronting Nightmares," they confront their darkest fears and nightmares as they navigate through the valley, struggling to maintain their sanity. The darkness seems to seep into their very souls, twisting their perceptions and distorting reality with its malevolent presence.

For Manny , the valley dredges up memories of past traumas and nightmares that have haunted him for years, threatening to consume him with their relentless grip.

Lili, the singing butterfly, feels the weight of her fears pressing down on her, each step forward a struggle against the overwhelming sense of dread that threatens to overwhelm her.

Frank, the mischievous white monkey, fights to keep his wits about him, his mind assailed by visions of his worst nightmares come to life in the darkness.

And Silvia, the beautiful hipo, draws upon every ounce of strength and courage she possesses, refusing to let the darkness break her spirit or extinguish the light within her.

As they navigate through the valley, each step forward is a battle against the darkness that threatens to consume them. But though their fears may be great, they refuse to let them dictate their actions or control their destiny. And though the journey ahead may be fraught with peril, they coninue, their determination unwavering as they confront the nightmares that lurk in the shadows.

"Embracing Light," with courage and perseverance, they find a way to overcome the darkness and emerge into the light once more. As they press onwards through the valley, they draw upon the strength of their bonds and the light that burns within them, refusing to be consumed by the shadows that seek to envelop them.

For Manny, the light represents a beacon of hope in the darkness, guiding him forward and reminding him that there is always a way out, even in the bleakest of circumstances.

Lili, the singing butterfly, spreads her wings and lets her voice soar, filling the darkness with the sweet sound of her song and driving back the shadows with its purity and light.

Frank, the mischievous white monkey, swings from branch to branch, his laughter ringing out like a bell and banishing the darkness with its infectious joy.

And Silvia, the beautiful hipo, stands tall and proud, her radiant beauty casting a warm glow that dispels the shadows and illuminates the path ahead.

As they journey onwards, they do so with hearts full of hope and minds filled with determination. Though the darkness may have threatened to consume them, they have emerged into the light once more, stronger and more resolute than ever before. And as they continue their journey, they do so with the knowledge that no matter how dark the night may seem, the light of their friendship and courage will always guide them home.

"**Guardian's Challenge,**" the group faces a formidable guardian who stands between them and their ultimate goal, testing their strength and resolve. The guardian looms before them, a towering figure of power and might, its eyes gleaming with an otherworldly light.

For them, the guardian represents the final obstacle in their journey, the last trial they must overcome to reach their destination. Though the challenge ahead may be daunting, they stand firm in their determination to succeed, drawing upon the courage and strength that lies within them.

As they face the guardian, each member of the group must confront their own fears and doubts, pushing themselves to their limits as they strive to prove themselves worthy of passing the test. And though the road ahead may be fraught with danger, they press onwards, ready to face whatever challenges lie in store.

As they stand before the guardian, they do so with hearts full of determination and minds focused on the task at hand. Though the road ahead may be long and difficult, they know that with courage and perseverance, they can overcome any obstacle that stands in their way. And as they prepare to face the guardian's challenge, they do it with the knowledge that victory is within their grasp, if only they have the strength to seize it.

"**Battle of Wills,**" they engage in a battle of wills with the guardian, matching wits and courage against overwhelming odds. The air crackles with tension as they stand face to face with their adversary, each side unwilling to back down.

For them, the battle represents more than just a test of strength; it is a test of their resolve, their determination, and their belief in themselves. Though the guardian may seem

unbeatable, they refuse to give in to despair, drawing upon their inner strength and resilience to face the challenge head-on.

As they confront the guardian, they must rely not only on their physical prowess, but also on their intelligence and cunning. Each move they make is calculated, each decision weighed carefully as they seek to outmaneuver their opponent and emerge victorious.

Though the battle may be fierce and the odds may be stacked against them, they refuse to give up hope. With every fiber of their being, they fight on, knowing that the fate of their quest hangs in the balance. And as they clash with the guardian, they do so with the knowledge that they are not alone, that together they can overcome any obstacle that stands in their way.

"**Lessons Learned,**" through the trial, they learn valuable lessons about sacrifice, loyalty, and the true nature of heroism. As they face the challenges posed by the guardian, they are forced to confront their own limitations and weaknesses, and in doing so, they discover the strength that lies within them.

For them, the trial is not just a test of their physical abilities, but also a test of their character and resolve. Each obstacle they overcome teaches them something new about themselves and their friends, forging bonds of trust and loyalty that will carry them through the darkest of times.

As they reflect on their experiences, they come to understand that true heroism is not about glory or fame, but about selflessness and compassion. It is about standing up for what is right, even when the odds are stacked against you, and fighting for those who cannot fight for themselves.

Through the trial, they learn that sacrifice is sometimes necessary in order to achieve greatness, and that true loyalty means standing by your friends no matter what. And as they emerge from the trial, they do so with a newfound sense of purpose and determination, ready to face it with courage and resilience.

"Victory and Loss," with determination and sacrifice, they emerge victorious from the guardian's trial, though not without paying a heavy price. As they stand before the fallen guardian, their breaths coming in ragged gasps, they feel a sense of both triumph and sorrow. For them, victory is bittersweet, tinged with the knowledge of what they have lost along the way. Though they have overcome the guardian's challenge, they have done so at great cost, and the memory of their sacrifice weighs heavily upon them.

As they mourn their losses, they also celebrate their triumphs, knowing that their journey is far from over. Though they may have emerged from the trial battered and bruised, they are stronger and more determined than ever before, ready to face it with courage and resilience.

And as they stand together, united in their victory and their grief, they know that no matter what the future may hold, they will face it together, as friends and friends bound by a bond that can never be broken.

"Ancient Relics," the group discovers a forgotten temple hidden deep within the jungle, filled with ancient relics and artifacts. As they step into the dimly lit interior of the temple, they are struck by the sense of awe and wonder that surrounds them.

For them, the temple represents a link to the past, a glimpse into a time long forgotten. Each artifact they encounter tells a story, shedding light on the history of the jungle and the creatures that once called it home.

As they explore the temple, they uncover treasures beyond their wildest dreams, each relic more magnificent than the last. From ornate statues to intricately carved tablets, the temple is a treasure trove of ancient wonders waiting to be discovered.

But as they marvel at the beauty and craftsmanship of the relics, they also sense a deeper significance to their discovery. For them, the relics represent more than just material wealth; they are a connection to their past, a reminder of the journey they have undertaken and the challenges they have overcome.

And as they stand in the heart of the temple, surrounded by the echoes of ancient whispers and the soft glow of long-forgotten treasures, they know that their adventure is far from over. For beyond the walls of the temple lies a world waiting to be explored, filled with mysteries and wonders beyond imagination.

"Echoes of the Past," they uncover echoes of the temple's history, learning of its significance in the ancient world. As they delve deeper into the temple's chambers, they discover inscriptions and carvings that tell the story of its creation and purpose.

For them, the echoes of the past resonate through the temple's halls, revealing glimpses of a civilization long gone. They learn of the rituals and ceremonies that once took place within its walls, and of the people who worshipped at its altars.

As they piece together the fragments of the temple's history, they come to understand its importance in the ancient world. It was not just a place of worship, but a center of knowledge and learning, where scholars and sages gathered to study the mysteries of the universe.

But as they delve deeper into the temple's secrets, they also uncover darker truths hidden beneath its surface. They learn of ancient conflicts and betrayals, of wars fought and lives lost in the name of power and greed.

And as they listen to the echoes of the past, they come to realize that the temple holds secrets that could change the course of their journey forever. For buried within its depths lie clues to the mysteries they seek to unravel, and to the challenges that lie ahead.

"Traps and Tribulations," they face traps and trials left behind by the temple's builders, testing their agility and cunning. As they navigate through the ancient corridors and chambers, they encounter obstacles designed to thwart intruders and protect the temple's secrets.

For them, the traps are a reminder of the dangers that lurk within the temple's walls, and of the need to proceed with caution. Each step they take could trigger a hidden mechanism or trigger a deadly trap, and they must rely on their wits and instincts to survive.

As they encounter each new challenge, they must work together to overcome it, using their unique skills and abilities to outsmart the ancient traps. From dart traps to hidden pitfalls, the temple is a labyrinth of danger and intrigue, and they must tread carefully if they hope to emerge unscathed.

But as they face each trial head-on, they also come to understand the true meaning of teamwork and trust. For in the face of adversity, they rely on each other for support and guidance, knowing that together they are stronger than any trap or tribulation they may encounter.

And as they press onwards through the temple's depths, they do so with determination and resolve, knowing that the secrets they seek lie just beyond the next hidden door or ancient puzzle. For though the path ahead may be fraught with danger, they are ready to face it, united in their quest for knowledge and adventure.

"Unveiling Truths," through perseverance and determination, they unravel the mysteries of the temple and unlock its secrets. As they delve deeper into the heart of the temple, they uncover hidden chambers and ancient artifacts that hold the key to its secrets.

For them, the journey through the temple has been filled with challenges and obstacles, but with each trial they have grown stronger and more determined. Now, as they stand on the brink of discovery, they know that they must push forward with all their might if they are to uncover the truth hidden within the temple's walls.

As they piece together the clues they have gathered along the way, they begin to see a pattern emerging, a story of ancient civilizations and forgotten legends. They learn of the temple's true purpose and of the role it played in shaping the world around it.

But as they delve deeper into the temple's secrets, they also uncover darker truths that threaten to shake the foundations of everything they thought they knew. They learn of ancient conflicts and betrayals, of power struggles and wars fought in the name of greed and ambition.

And as they stand on the precipice of revelation, they know that the knowledge they have gained will change them forever. For they have glimpsed the true nature of the world they inhabit, and in doing so, they have unlocked the secrets of the temple and uncovered truths that have lain hidden for centuries.

"The air shimmered with waves of heat as our intrepid travelers ventured forth into the unforgiving expanse of the desert. Each step seemed to sink deeper into the shifting sands, as if the very earth conspired to impede their progress.

As the sun beat down relentlessly upon them, their resolve was tested to its limits. Water rations dwindled with each passing day, and the mirage of salvation danced tantalizingly on the horizon, forever out of reach.

Yet, amidst the vastness of the desert, a sense of unity emerged among the group. Each member lent their strength to the collective, offering words of encouragement and support in moments of despair.

With grit and determination, they pressed onward, guided by a flicker of hope that burned bright within their hearts. For beyond the dunes lay the promise of discovery, of secrets long buried beneath the sands of time. And though the journey ahead was fraught with peril, they embraced it eagerly, knowing that their destiny awaited just beyond the horizon.

Our travelers stumble upon an oasis amidst the vast expanse of the desert, a sanctuary of life in the midst of desolation. As they approach, weary and parched from their journey, the sight of lush greenery and shimmering waters fills them with a renewed sense of hope.

With each step towards the oasis, the oppressive heat of the desert begins to fade, replaced by a cool breeze that carries the scent of blooming flowers. Manny , takes the lead, his scarlet coat gleaming in the morning light as he guides his friends towards the oasis.

Lili, the singing butterfly, flutters gracefully alongside Manny, her delicate wings shimmering in the sunlight. Her ethereal voice fills the air with a sense of wonder and tranquility, lifting the spirits of all who hear her.

Frank, the mischievous white monkey, swings from branch to branch overhead, his twinkling eyes gleaming with excitement at the sight of the oasis. With boundless energy and enthusiasm, he leads the group onwards, eager to explore this newfound paradise.

Silvia, the majestic hippopotamus, follows behind, her ivory tusks gleaming as she gracefully navigates the terrain. Her presence brings a sense of calm and serenity to the group, her boundless compassion shining through in every step she takes.

Together, they approach the oasis, their hearts filled with anticipation and wonder at the beauty that lies before them. For in this moment, amidst the harsh realities of the desert, they have found a glimmer of hope, a sanctuary where they can rest and rejuvenate before continuing on their journey through the unknown.

Our intrepid travelers continue their journey through the unforgiving desert, facing adversity at every turn. The scorching sun beats down upon them relentlessly, testing their resolve to its limits.

Despite the harsh conditions, they press on, fueled by a deep sense of determination and resilience. With each step, they draw upon their inner strength, refusing to succumb to the challenges that threaten to overwhelm them.

As they navigate the treacherous terrain, their bonds grow stronger, forged in the crucible of adversity. Manny, Lili, Frank, and Silvia stand together as a beacon of hope in the face of uncertainty, their spirits undiminished by the trials they face.

Through sheer perseverance, they find renewal amidst the desolation of the desert. Each obstacle they overcome serves to strengthen their resolve, fueling their determination to continue onwards, no matter the cost.

And as they emerge from the crucible of adversity, they do so with a newfound sense of purpose and determination. For in the midst of the harshest trials, they have discovered the true source of their strength: the unwavering bond of friendship that binds them together as one.

The group of adventurers sets out on a daring journey to ascend towering peaks and reach the skyward realms above. With determination burning in their hearts and a sense of adventure driving them forward, they begin their ascent into the unknown.

The path ahead is rugged and steep, with sheer cliffs and treacherous terrain posing formidable obstacles. Yet, undeterred by the challenges that lie ahead, they press on, their spirits buoyed by the promise of discovery that awaits them at the summit.

As they climb higher and higher, the air grows thinner, and the landscape shifts around them, transforming into a realm of breathtaking beauty and majesty. Snow-capped peaks pierce the sky above, their towering summits obscured by wisps of cloud and mist.

With each step, they draw closer to the heavens, their hearts filled with awe and wonder at the spectacle unfolding before them. Despite the physical exertion and exhaustion that threaten to weigh them down, they are driven by a sense of purpose that propels them ever onwards.

Together, they navigate the perilous slopes and rocky outcrops, supporting each other every step of the way. For in the crucible of adversity, their bonds grow stronger, forging a unity that transcends the limits of mortal endurance.

And as they near the summit, their spirits soar with anticipation, for they know that beyond the towering peaks lies the promise of enlightenment and revelation. With each breath, they draw closer to the skyward realms above, their journey a testament to the indomitable spirit of the human heart.

Our adventurers find themselves facing aerial challenges and obstacles as they continue their ascent towards the towering peaks. The air around them grows turbulent, filled with swirling winds and ominous clouds that threaten to obscure their path.

Navigating through the treacherous skies, they must contend with sudden gusts and turbulent updrafts that buffet them from all sides. Each step forward is a battle against the elements, as they struggle to maintain their course amidst the chaos of the storm.

But despite the dangers that surround them, they press on with unwavering determination, their spirits unbroken by the challenges they face. With each obstacle overcome, they grow stronger, their bond as a group forged in the crucible of adversity.

Together, they weather the storm, their resolve shining bright amidst the darkness that threatens to engulf them. For in the face of adversity, they find strength in each other, drawing upon the collective courage that binds them together as one.

As they navigate through the tempestuous skies, their eyes remain fixed on the summit, their hearts filled with the promise of triumph that awaits them at the peak. For beyond the storm lies the skyward realms above, where the secrets of the cosmos await discovery by those brave enough to seek them.

Our intrepid travelers, fueled by determination and courage, reach the summit of their ascent. With every step, they draw closer to their goal, their spirits undaunted by the challenges that have tested their resolve along the way.

As they climb higher and higher, the air grows thinner, and the landscape shifts around them, transforming into a realm of breathtaking beauty and majesty. Snow-capped peaks tower above them, reaching towards the heavens like fingers stretching towards the stars.

With each breath, they feel a sense of exhilaration and anticipation building within them, driving them ever onwards towards the summit. Despite the physical exertion and exhaustion that threaten to weigh them down, they press on, their eyes fixed on the prize that awaits them at the peak.

And then, finally, they reach the summit, standing atop the highest peak with the world spread out before them. With outstretched arms, they reach for the stars themselves, their hearts filled with a sense of accomplishment and triumph that transcends words.

For in this moment, amidst the towering peaks and boundless skies, they have achieved the impossible. They have touched the stars and proven that with determination and courage, anything is possible. And as they stand together, bathed in the light of the heavens, they know that their journey is far from over.

Now the adventurers embark on a daring descent into the depths below, plunging into the mysteries of the underwater world. With each passing moment, the light fades, and darkness envelops them, casting a veil of uncertainty over their journey.

As they descend deeper and deeper into the abyss, they are surrounded by an otherworldly silence, broken only by the rhythmic pulse of their own breath. The water grows colder, and the pressure mounts, pressing in on them from all sides with an unrelenting force.

Yet, undeterred by the darkness that surrounds them, they press on, their senses heightened as they navigate through the underwater labyrinth. Strange and wondrous creatures dart in and out of the shadows, their forms illuminated by the faint glow of bioluminescent organisms that dot the ocean floor.

With each passing moment, they are drawn deeper into the mysteries of the underwater world, their hearts filled with a sense of awe and wonder at the beauty that lies hidden beneath the waves. For in this realm of darkness and silence, they have found a new frontier to explore, a world filled with secrets waiting to be uncovered.

And as they continue their descent into the depths below, they know that their journey is not finished. For beyond the darkness that surrounds them lies the promise of discovery and revelation, beckoning them ever onwards into the unknown.

They make a remarkable discovery as they explore the depths below: sunken treasures and ancient ruins hidden beneath the waves, remnants of a lost civilization that lies forgotten beneath the sea.

As they navigate through the murky waters, their eyes are drawn to the glimmer of gold and silver that lies scattered across the ocean floor. Jeweled artifacts and precious relics lay untouched for centuries, their secrets waiting to be uncovered by those brave enough to seek them.

Amidst the ruins of a once-great city, they marvel at the craftsmanship of ancient civilizations, their minds racing with questions about the people who once called this place home. Crumbling temples and towering statues stand as silent sentinels, bearing witness to the passage of time and the mysteries that lie hidden beneath the waves.

With each discovery, they piece together the story of a lost civilization, piecing together fragments of history that have long been forgotten by the world above. They marvel at the ingenuity of those who came before them, their hearts filled with a sense of reverence for the wonders that lie hidden beneath the sea.

But amidst the treasures they uncover, they also find danger lurking in the shadows. For the depths below hold secrets of their own, and not all who venture into the darkness emerge unscathed. Yet, undeterred by the risks that lie ahead, they press on, their thirst for knowledge driving them ever onwards into the unknown.

As the adventurers delve deeper into the ocean depths, they encounter guardians of the deep, formidable creatures that test their strength and resolve. Manny, Lili, Frank, and Silvia move cautiously through the underwater world, their senses alert for signs of danger. Suddenly, looming shadows materialize from the darkness, revealing the presence of ancient guardians that have long watched over the sunken treasures and ruins below. Manny, with his wisdom beyond his years, recognizes the importance of treading carefully in the presence of these majestic but potentially dangerous creatures.

Lili's ethereal songs resonate through the water, soothing the guardians and preventing an immediate confrontation. Frank's quick wit and agility prove invaluable as he navigates the treacherous waters, avoiding the guardians' watchful gaze.

Yet, despite their caution, a confrontation is inevitable. Silvia, with her imposing presence and unwavering courage, steps forward to face the guardians head-on, her determination unwavering in the face of danger.

With a combination of diplomacy, quick thinking, and sheer determination, our adventurers navigate past the guardians of the deep, earning their respect and forging a temporary truce. As they continue their exploration, they carry with them the knowledge that even in the darkest depths, bravery and unity can overcome any obstacle.

They embark on their final leg of the journey: rising back to the surface. With perseverance and teamwork, they navigate through the depths, their journey leaving them forever changed.

As they ascend, they reflect on the trials and triumphs of their underwater odyssey. Manny, Lili, Frank, and Silvia draw strength from each other, their bonds forged in the crucible of adversity.

Together, they rise towards the light, their spirits buoyed by the knowledge that they have faced the unknown and emerged victorious. The surface beckons, promising a return to the world above and the adventures that await them there.

And as they break through the surface, gasping for breath and bathed in the warm glow of the sun, they know that they are forever changed by their journey through the depths. With hearts full of gratitude and minds filled with memories, they stand united, ready to face any challenges the future holds.

For in the depths below, they have discovered the true power of perseverance and teamwork, lessons that will guide them on their adventures for years to come. And as they take their first steps back onto solid ground, they carry with them the knowledge that no matter how dark the journey may seem, there is always light waiting to guide them home.

The venture into the Whispering Woods, a forest alive with mysterious murmurs and rustling leaves. They tread cautiously into the heart of the woodland, their senses alert for any signs of danger or wonder.

As they step beneath the towering canopy of ancient trees, they are enveloped by a sense of tranquility and awe. The air is thick with the scent of earth and foliage, and shafts of golden sunlight filter through the dense foliage above, casting dappled patterns on the forest floor.

But amidst the natural beauty of the woods, there is an undercurrent of mystery and intrigue. Strange whispers seem to echo through the trees, their voices soft and ethereal, carrying secrets that have long been lost to time.

With each step, the group delves deeper into the heart of the forest, their curiosity piqued by the tantalizing whispers that surround them. They know that within the depths of the Whispering Woods lie untold mysteries waiting to be uncovered, and they are eager to unravel the secrets that lie hidden within.

As they journey deeper into the heart of the forest, their senses sharpen, and their hearts beat with anticipation. For in the heart of the Whispering Woods, they know that adventure awaits, and they are ready to embrace it.

Our adventurers continue their exploration of the Whispering Woods, discovering hidden glades and clearings within the forest, each with its own magical aura and inhabitants.

They venture deeper into the heart of the woods, guided by the whispers of the forest itself. As they wander through the dappled sunlight, they stumble upon hidden glades adorned with carpets of vibrant wildflowers and bathed in the soft glow of sunlight filtering through the trees.

Each glade they discover seems to possess its own unique enchantment, with inhabitants ranging from playful sprites and mischievous fairies to wise old tree spirits and elusive woodland creatures. The air is alive with the sound of laughter and song, as the denizens of the glades go about their mysterious rituals and celebrations.

Despite their initial caution, our adventurers are drawn into the magical allure of the glades, their spirits lifted by the joy and wonder that surrounds them. They interact with the inhabitants, sharing stories and laughter, and marveling at the beauty of their surroundings.

But amidst the enchantment of the glades, they remain ever vigilant, knowing that danger may lurk beneath the surface of this seemingly idyllic realm. With each new discovery, they tread carefully, their senses attuned to any signs of trouble or treachery.

Yet, for now, they allow themselves to be swept away by the magic of the Whispering Woods, embracing the wonder and enchantment that surrounds them. For in this hidden realm of beauty and mystery, they have found a moment of respite from the trials of their journey, and they savor every precious moment of it.

They find themselves entangled in the labyrinthine paths of the forest, struggling to navigate through twisting trails and deceptive illusions. Amidst the dense foliage and towering trees, they lose their sense of direction, unsure of which path leads to safety and which leads to further peril.

As they wander deeper into the heart of the woods, the trees seem to shift and rearrange themselves, creating an ever-changing maze of tangled branches and shadowy clearings. Each turn leads them further into the depths of the forest, their footsteps echoing through the silent groves.

Despite their best efforts to find their way, the forest seems determined to confound them at every turn. Strange illusions dance at the corners of their vision, leading them astray and blurring the boundaries between reality and fantasy.

With each passing moment, their sense of urgency grows, fueled by the knowledge that time is slipping away and danger lurks in the shadows. They must find a way out of the labyrinth before it's too late, before they become lost forever in the twisting paths of the Whispering Woods.

They find themselves enveloped in the ethereal glow of moonlight, which guides their way through the dense forest. Bathed in the soft silver light, they navigate through the twisting paths of the Whispering Woods with a renewed sense of purpose and clarity.

The moon casts long shadows that dance among the trees, illuminating hidden pathways and revealing the secrets of the forest's depths. With each step, they draw closer to escaping the labyrinthine maze that has ensnared them, their spirits buoyed by the gentle radiance that surrounds them.

Under the watchful gaze of the moon, they move with purpose and determination, their senses sharpened by the clarity of the night. The whispering of the trees seems to guide them, leading them towards the edge of the forest and the promise of freedom beyond.

As they journey through the enchanted woods, they find solace in the tranquility of the night, finding beauty in the stillness and serenity that surrounds them. And as they emerge from the depths of the forest, they carry with them the memory of the moonlight that guided their way, a beacon of hope in the darkness of the Whispering Woods.

They step into the Hall of Echoes, a place where the past seems to reverberate through the very air. The atmosphere is thick with a sense of history and nostalgia, as if every step they take echoes with the footsteps of those who came before them.

As they move deeper into the hall, they are surrounded by the remnants of a bygone era. Ancient tapestries line the walls, their faded colors telling stories of forgotten heroes and lost civilizations. Statues stand sentinel in the corners, their stoic expressions bearing witness to the passage of time.

With each breath, they feel the weight of centuries pressing down upon them, as if the very walls of the hall are alive with the memories of the past. They listen intently, hoping to catch a whisper of the secrets that lie hidden within the echoes of time.

But amidst the echoes of the past, there is also a sense of possibility and discovery. For within the Hall of Echoes, the past and present intertwine, creating a tapestry of stories waiting to be unraveled by those brave enough to seek them out.

As they journey deeper into the heart of the hall, they know that they are on the brink of uncovering secrets that have long been lost to the sands of time. With each step forward, they draw closer to unlocking the mysteries of the Hall of Echoes and revealing the truth that lies hidden within its hallowed halls.

The travelers, Manny and Silvia, step into the Hall of Echoes, where the air is thick with the echoes of ancient voices and whispers that speak of forgotten tales and legends.

As they move deeper into the hall, Manny's keen ears pick up on the faint murmurs that seem to reverberate through the very stones. Silvia, with her sharp senses, listens intently alongside him, her curiosity piqued by the mysterious voices that echo around them.

The voices speak of long-lost kingdoms and epic battles, of heroes and villains whose names have faded into obscurity. They tell of love and loss, triumph and tragedy, weaving a tapestry of stories that stretch back through the annals of time.

Together, Manny and Silvia follow the trail of whispers, their footsteps echoing in the vast chamber as they listen to the tales of the ancients. With each story they hear, they feel a deeper connection to the history of the hall, and to the souls who once walked its hallowed halls.

As they delve deeper into the mysteries of the Hall of Echoes, Manny and Silvia know that they are on the brink of uncovering secrets that have long been lost to the sands of time. With each whisper that fills the air, they draw closer to unlocking the truth that lies hidden within the ancient voices of the hall.

Silvia ventures deeper into the Hall of Echoes alone. As she moves through the ancient chamber, she is confronted by reflections of her own past actions and choices, forced to reckon with the consequences of her deeds.

The echoes of her footsteps seem to mock her as she walks, each sound a reminder of the paths she has chosen and the roads left untraveled. Images flicker in the shadows, showing moments from her past, both triumphs and failures, illuminated by the dim light that filters through the hall.

Silvia stands amidst the reflections, her heart heavy with the weight of her decisions. She sees the faces of those she has loved and lost, the friends she has made and the enemies she has faced. Each reflection is a mirror, reflecting back to her the truth of who she is and the choices she has made.

With each passing moment, Silvia is forced to confront the consequences of her actions, to reckon with the deeds that have shaped her destiny. She knows that she cannot change the past, but she can learn from it, using it to forge a path towards a future where hope and redemption await.

As she stands amidst the reflections of her own past, Silvia finds strength in the knowledge that she is not defined by her mistakes, but by her willingness to learn from them. With determination in her heart, she presses forward, ready to face whatever challenges the Hall of Echoes holds.

Silvia continues her solitary journey through the Hall of Echoes. As she traverses the ancient chamber, she is enveloped by a sense of introspection and acceptance, confronting the echoes of her past with a heart open to redemption.

With each step, Silvia delves deeper into the recesses of her soul, confronting the mistakes and regrets that linger in the shadows of her memories. Yet, instead of succumbing to despair, she embraces the opportunity for growth and transformation that the echoes of the hall offer.

Amidst the whispers of the past, Silvia finds solace in the knowledge that forgiveness begins with oneself. She acknowledges her faults and shortcomings, but refuses to be defined by

them. Instead, she chooses to focus on the lessons learned and the strength gained through adversity.

In the quiet depths of the hall, Silvia finds redemption not through absolution, but through acceptance. She accepts herself for who she is, flaws and all, and in doing so, finds the courage to forgive herself and others for past transgressions.

As she emerges from the Hall of Echoes, Silvia carries with her a newfound sense of peace and understanding. She knows that the journey towards redemption is ongoing, but she faces the future with renewed hope and a heart free from the burdens of the past.

They brave the frozen wastes, where the bitter cold seems to seep into their very bones. Together, they trek across the icy expanse, their breath forming misty clouds in the frigid air. The landscape stretches out before them, a desolate and unforgiving terrain of snow and ice as far as the eye can see.

With each step, the crunch of snow beneath their boots echoes in the stillness of the frozen wasteland. The biting wind lashes against their faces, stinging their skin and numbing their extremities. Yet, they press on, their determination unwavering in the face of adversity.

As they journey deeper into the icy expanse, they rely on each other for warmth and support, drawing strength from their unity in the face of nature's fury. Though the cold threatens to chill them to the core, they refuse to be defeated, their spirits burning bright against the backdrop of the frozen landscape.

Through sheer grit and determination, they forge ahead, their eyes fixed on the horizon and the promise of warmer days ahead. For in the heart of the frozen wastes, they know that the greatest trials often yield the greatest rewards, and they are ready to face it

Manny, known as the Sage of the Sands, Lili, the Melodic Butterfly, Frank, the Agile Trickster, and Silvia, the Majestic Hippo, venture deeper into the frozen wastes. Here, they uncover ancient glaciers and ice formations that hold secrets of ages long past.

Their journey leads them to towering glaciers, whose icy surfaces shimmer in the pale light of the frozen landscape. Each crevice and cavern holds the echoes of a forgotten time, whispering tales of ancient civilizations and lost knowledge.

As they explore the glacial mysteries, the group is captivated by the beauty and grandeur of the ice formations. They marvel at the intricate patterns carved into the ice by centuries of wind and weather, each line and curve telling a story of the world's ever-changing history.

Yet amidst the beauty of the glaciers, there is also a sense of foreboding. For within the frozen depths lie secrets that have been buried for eons, waiting to be uncovered by those brave enough to seek them out.

With each discovery, Manny, Lili, Frank, and Silvia feel a sense of wonder and awe, their curiosity driving them deeper into the heart of the glacial mysteries. Together, they stand on the precipice of discovery, ready to unlock the secrets that lie hidden within the icy depths of the frozen wastes.

Lili, the Melodic Butterfly, and her friends venture further into the frozen wastes, where they encounter formidable frost giants and creatures of ice that guard the secrets of this frigid realm.

As they press on through the icy expanse, the ground beneath their feet trembles with each step, and the air grows thick with anticipation. Suddenly, towering figures loom in the distance, their forms hulking and menacing against the backdrop of the frozen landscape.

The frost giants, guardians of the frozen wastes, stand sentinel before them, their eyes gleaming with a cold, unyielding resolve. With each breath, they exhale clouds of icy mist, their very presence sending shivers down the spines of our adventurers.

Yet, despite the daunting challenge that lies before them, Lili and her friends stand firm, their courage unwavering in the face of danger. With a melodic hum, Lili weaves a spell of enchantment, her ethereal voice carrying on the wind and captivating the frost giants with its beauty.

As the giants falter, momentarily entranced by Lili's song, the group seizes the opportunity to press onward, navigating past the towering guardians with skill and determination. Though the path ahead is fraught with peril, they know that together, they can overcome any obstacles.

Manny, and the group face a daunting challenge as they strive to thaw the ice and uncover the truths hidden beneath its frozen surface.

With bravery and determination, Manny leads the group in their efforts to melt the icy barriers that stand in their way. He calls upon his knowledge of ancient lore and elemental forces, seeking a solution to the frozen puzzle that surrounds them.

As they work tirelessly, their efforts are met with resistance from the unforgiving ice, which seems determined to guard its secrets at any cost. Yet, undeterred by the cold and the challenges they face, Manny and his friends press on, their spirits unbroken by the adversity they encounter.

Through sheer perseverance, they begin to make progress, slowly but surely chipping away at the frozen barriers that stand between them and the truths hidden beneath the ice. With each blow, they draw closer to their goal, their determination fueled by the knowledge that they are on the brink of discovery.

And then, finally, their efforts bear fruit as the ice begins to thaw, revealing the secrets that lie hidden beneath its frozen surface. With a sense of triumph and accomplishment, Manny and his friends uncover the truths that have been buried for centuries, their bravery and determination paving the way for a new chapter in their journey through the frozen wastes.

Our intrepid adventurers journey into the heart of a volcanic inferno, where the earth rumbles and spews forth molten lava.

With each step, the ground trembles beneath their feet, and the air is thick with the acrid scent of sulfur. They navigate through the rugged terrain, their eyes wide with awe and trepidation as they draw closer to the fiery heart of the volcano.

The roar of the inferno echoes in their ears, a constant reminder of the raw power that lies dormant within the earth. Molten rivers of lava flow like rivers of fire, carving paths through the rocky landscape and lighting up the night with an incandescent glow.

Yet, amidst the chaos and destruction of the volcanic inferno, there is also a sense of awe and wonder. The heat of the lava warms their skin, and the vibrant colors of the molten rock paint a mesmerizing picture against the darkened sky.

With each passing moment, they draw closer to the heart of the volcano, their resolve unyielding in the face of nature's fury. For in the heart of the volcanic inferno, they know that they will find the answers they seek, and perhaps uncover secrets that have long been hidden beneath the surface of the earth.

Frank, known as the Agile Trickster, and his friends face the searing heat and fiery trials of the volcano, testing their resilience and endurance.

As they journey deeper into the heart of the inferno, Frank and his friends feel the intense heat bearing down upon them, threatening to sap their strength and willpower. The air shimmers with waves of heat, and the ground beneath their feet grows hot to the touch.

Despite the overwhelming heat and the challenges they face, Frank remains steadfast, his determination unwavering in the face of adversity. He leads the group with courage and conviction, guiding them through the fiery trials with skill and agility.

Together, they navigate through rivers of molten lava and treacherous terrain, their spirits undaunted by the dangers that surround them. With each obstacle they overcome, they grow stronger and more resilient, their bonds forged in the crucible of the volcano's fiery embrace.

As they press onward, Frank and his friends draw upon their inner strength and determination, refusing to be consumed by the flames that rage around them. For in the heart of the inferno, they know that their resilience will be their greatest weapon, and that together, they can overcome any challenge that stands in their way.

Frank, and the group encounter elemental guardians of fire, beings of pure flame that challenge their courage and strength.

As they journey deeper into the heart of the volcano, they are confronted by the elemental guardians, towering figures of flame that dance and flicker in the intense heat. The guardians' fiery gaze bears down upon them, testing their resolve and daring them to prove their worth.

Frank stands at the forefront, his heart filled with determination as he faces the guardians head-on. With a quick wit and agile movements, he dodges their fiery attacks and rallies his friends to stand firm against the elemental onslaught.

Despite the overwhelming power of the guardians, Frank and his friends refuse to back down, drawing upon their courage and strength to face the fiery challenge before them. With each blow they exchange, they inch closer to victory, their spirits burning bright against the inferno that surrounds them.

As the battle rages on, Frank and his friends fight with all their might, their determination unwavering in the face of the elemental guardians' fury. And in the end, it is their courage and resilience that emerge victorious, proving that even in the heart of the flames, the spirit of adventure burns fiercer still.

Manny, the Sage of the Sands, and his friends harness the power of the volcano through unity and determination, using its fiery energy to fuel their quest.

With Manny's guidance, they work together to channel the raw power of the volcano, tapping into its fiery energy and using it to propel them forward on their journey. They draw upon their collective strength and determination, forging a bond that burns brighter than the flames that surround them.

As they harness the inferno's power, they feel its fiery energy coursing through their veins, fueling their spirits and igniting their resolve. With each step they take, they draw closer to their goal, their hearts ablaze with the passion of adventure and discovery.

Together, Manny and his friends navigate through the fiery depths of the volcano, their unity serving as a beacon of hope amidst the chaos and destruction that surrounds them. With each obstacle they overcome, they grow stronger and more determined, their bond forged in the crucible of the volcano's fiery embrace.

And as they emerge from the heart of the inferno, triumphant and unscathed, Manny and his friends carry with them the knowledge that with unity and determination, they can overcome any challenge that stands in their way. For in the fire of adversity, they have found the strength to fuel their quest and illuminate the path ahead.

Manny, the Sage of the Sands, Lili, the Melodic Butterfly, Frank, the Agile Trickster, and Silvia, the Majestic Hippo, ascend to a celestial observatory atop a towering mountain, where the heavens stretch out before them.

Together, they embark on the arduous journey to reach the observatory, their footsteps echoing against the rocky slopes as they climb higher and higher. With each step, they draw closer to the celestial realm above, their hearts filled with anticipation and wonder.

As they reach the summit, they are greeted by the sight of the celestial observatory, its gleaming spires reaching towards the heavens like outstretched arms. The air is crisp and clear, and the stars shine brightly overhead, casting their ethereal light upon the world below.

With awe and reverence, they enter the observatory, their eyes wide with wonder as they gaze upon the celestial wonders that await them. They stand in awe of the vastness of the cosmos, humbled by the beauty and majesty of the universe.

As they peer through the telescopes and observe the stars and planets that twinkle in the night sky, they feel a sense of connection to something greater than themselves. In the celestial observatory, they find solace and inspiration, their spirits lifted by the infinite possibilities that stretch out before them.

Together, they stand atop the mountain, bathed in the light of the stars, united in their quest to unlock the mysteries of the cosmos. For in the celestial observatory, they know that the journey to enlightenment has only just begun, and that the stars themselves hold the key to unlocking the secrets of the universe.

Lili, and her friends marvel at the wonders of the night sky within the celestial observatory. They observe constellations and celestial phenomena that ignite their imagination, filling their hearts with awe and wonder.

As they peer through the telescopes and gaze up at the vast expanse of the night sky, Lili is captivated by the beauty and majesty of the celestial wonders before them. They trace the patterns of the stars, connecting the dots to form intricate constellations that tell stories of heroes and mythical creatures.

The air is alive with excitement as Lili and her friends discuss the mysteries of the cosmos, sharing stories and legends passed down through the ages. They marvel at the dance of the planets and the shimmering light of distant galaxies, each celestial phenomenon a testament to the wonders of the universe.

In the celestial observatory, Lili finds solace and inspiration, their hearts filled with a sense of wonder and possibility. They are reminded of the interconnectedness of all things and the eternal dance of the cosmos, where each star and planet plays a part in the grand tapestry of existence.

As they gaze up at the night sky, Lili is filled with a renewed sense of purpose and determination. For in the celestial observatory, they find not only answers to their questions but also a sense of peace and belonging amidst the vastness of the cosmos.

Frank, the Agile Trickster, and the group uncover ancient star maps and celestial charts within the celestial observatory. These artifacts reveal hidden knowledge about the universe and their quest, unlocking secrets that have been hidden for eons.

As they explore the observatory, Frank and his friends stumble upon a collection of ancient scrolls and manuscripts, their pages yellowed with age and filled with cryptic symbols and diagrams. With a sense of excitement, they pore over the texts, eager to unravel the mysteries they contain.

The star maps and celestial charts offer glimpses into the vastness of the cosmos, detailing the movements of the stars and planets and the patterns that govern their orbits. Frank and his friends marvel at the intricacy of the charts, realizing that they hold the key to unlocking the secrets of their quest.

With each revelation, they feel a sense of awe and wonder, their minds racing with the possibilities that lie before them. The cosmic secrets they uncover offer clues to their

journey and shed light on the path that lies ahead, guiding them towards their ultimate destination.

In the celestial observatory, Frank is filled with a renewed sense of purpose and determination. Armed with the knowledge they have gained, they are ready to continue their quest, confident that they are one step closer to unraveling the mysteries of the universe.

Silvia, the Majestic Hippo, stands under the canopy of stars within the celestial observatory. Here, they strengthen their bonds of friendship and resolve, united by the vastness of the cosmos.

As they gaze up at the shimmering tapestry of stars above, Silvia feels a sense of awe and wonder wash over them. The twinkling lights above serve as a reminder of the interconnectedness of all things, binding them together in a shared journey through the mysteries of the universe.

In the quiet serenity of the observatory, Silvia reflects on the adventures they have shared and the challenges they have overcome. They share stories and laughter, their spirits buoyed by the friendship and camaraderie that have sustained them through their trials.

Under the watchful gaze of the stars, Silvia reaffirms their commitment to one another and to their quest. They pledge to stand by each other's side through thick and thin, drawing strength from the bonds of friendship and resolve that unite them.

As they stand together beneath the starlit sky, Silvia is filled with a sense of gratitude and determination. For in the vastness of the cosmos, they have found not only answers to their questions but also a sense of belonging and purpose that will guide them on their journey into the unknown.

The group ventures into the Whispering Caves, where the walls seem to echo with the whispers of ages past.

As they step into the darkness of the cavernous depths, the air grows thick with anticipation. The sound of their footsteps reverberates against the stone walls, bouncing back to them in eerie echoes that seem to carry secrets untold.

The group moves forward cautiously, guided by the faint glow of their torches as they navigate the labyrinthine passages of the caves. With each twist and turn, the whispers grow louder, filling their ears with a chorus of voices that speak of forgotten tales and ancient mysteries.

Despite the darkness that surrounds them, they press on, their curiosity piqued by the promise of discovery that lies hidden within the depths of the Whispering Caves. With each step they take, they feel the weight of history pressing down upon them, urging them onward in their quest for knowledge.

As they delve deeper into the caves, the whispers grow louder, their words becoming clearer with each passing moment. The group listens intently, their hearts racing with excitement as they unravel the secrets that have been concealed within the depths of the earth for countless generations.

They navigate through labyrinthine tunnels and passages, each leading deeper into the heart of the earth.

The group's torches cast flickering shadows upon the uneven walls as they wind their way through the labyrinth of tunnels. The air grows colder and more oppressive, and the faint echoes of their footsteps are swallowed by the vastness of the caverns.

With each turn they take, the passages seem to twist and warp, leading them ever deeper into the unknown. Yet, despite the disorienting maze of tunnels, they press onward, their determination unwavering in the face of the darkness that surrounds them.

As they navigate the labyrinth, they encounter obstacles and challenges at every turn. But with their resolve strengthened by their shared purpose, they push forward, trusting in their instincts to guide them through the maze-like passages.

Though the journey through the cavernous labyrinths is fraught with peril, they find solace in the knowledge that they are not alone. Together, they face the unknown with courage and determination, their bonds of friendship serving as a beacon of hope amidst the darkness that threatens to consume them.

They confront echoes of their own fears and doubts within the caves, forced to confront their innermost selves.

As they venture deeper into the heart of the Whispering Caves, the whispers around them take on a more sinister tone. Shadows dance along the walls, and the air grows heavy with a sense of unease as they are confronted with echoes of their own fears and doubts.

Each member of the group is forced to confront their innermost selves, facing the shadows that lurk within their own hearts. Memories and regrets echo through the caverns, casting doubt upon their resolve and threatening to undermine their confidence.

Yet, in the face of adversity, they find strength in one another, drawing courage from the bonds of friendship that unite them. With each step they take, they confront their fears head- on, determined to overcome the obstacles that stand in their way.

As they delve deeper into the darkness, they begin to unravel the tangled web of emotions that has plagued them, finding solace in the knowledge that they are not alone in their struggles. Together, they face their fears with courage and determination, knowing that only by confronting their inner demons can they hope to find peace within the Whispering Caves.

Lili emerges from the depths of the caves, their spirits strengthened by the trials they have faced.

After navigating the labyrinthine tunnels and confronting their innermost fears, Lili finally sees a glimmer of light ahead. With perseverance and determination, they press forward, their hearts filled with hope as they emerge from the darkness into the light.

As they step out into the open air, they are greeted by the warm embrace of sunlight, their eyes blinking in the brightness after so long in the darkness of the caves. The weight of their journey hangs heavy upon them, but they stand tall, their spirits lifted by the knowledge that they have faced their fears and emerged victorious.

Together, they take a moment to bask in the glow of their achievement, the air alive with the sound of their laughter and the flutter of Lili's wings. Though they know that more challenges lie ahead, they face the future with renewed confidence and determination, ready to continue their journey wherever it may lead.

The group enters the Blossoming Fields, where vibrant flowers stretch out as far as the eye can see, painting the landscape in a riot of color.

As they step into the fields, they are greeted by a kaleidoscope of hues, with flowers of every shade imaginable carpeting the ground beneath their feet. The air is filled with the sweet fragrance of blossoms, and the gentle hum of bees as they flit from flower to flower.

Lili pauses to admire the beauty of their surroundings, their hearts lifted by the sight of so much natural splendor. They wander through the fields, their hands trailing through the petals as they drink in the intoxicating scent of the flowers.

In the Blossoming Fields, they find solace and tranquility, a respite from the trials and tribulations of their journey thus far. Here, amidst the beauty of nature, they find renewal and strength, their spirits buoyed by the vibrant energy of the flowers that surround them.

As they continue on their way, they carry with them the memory of the Blossoming Fields, their hearts filled with gratitude for the fleeting moment of peace and beauty that they have found amidst the chaos of their quest.

Frank wanders alone through the Blossoming Fields. Here, he hears the whispers of nature in the rustling of leaves and the gentle sway of the flowers, feeling a deep connection to the natural world.

As Frank walks through the fields, he feels the soft breeze caress his skin and hears the gentle rustling of leaves overhead. The flowers sway in the wind, their petals dancing in a graceful rhythm that seems to echo the heartbeat of the earth itself.

In this tranquil oasis, Frank finds himself lost in the beauty of nature, his senses alive with the sights and sounds of the Blossoming Fields. He pauses to listen to the whispers of the wind and the song of the birds, feeling a sense of peace wash over him.

In the embrace of nature, Frank feels a deep connection to the world around him, a reminder of the interconnectedness of all living things. He closes his eyes and breathes in the sweet scent of the flowers, letting the beauty of the moment wash over him like a gentle wave.

As he continues his journey through the Blossoming Fields, Frank carries with him the memory of this tranquil oasis, his heart filled with gratitude for the brief respite it has provided amidst the chaos of their quest.

As Manny arrives in the Blossoming Fields, he joins Frank in witnessing the harmony of life that permeates the fields. Here, creatures big and small coexist in peaceful balance with their surroundings.

Together, Manny and Frank observe the bustling activity of the fields. Bees buzz lazily from flower to flower, collecting pollen as they go. Butterflies flit through the air, their delicate

wings painting streaks of color against the blue sky. In the distance, a family of rabbits nibbles on tender grass shoots, while birds chirp merrily from their perches in the trees.

In this vibrant tapestry of life, Manny and Frank marvel at the intricate web of relationships that sustains the ecosystem of the Blossoming Fields. Each creature plays its part, contributing to the delicate balance of nature in its own unique way.

As they watch, they feel a sense of reverence for the beauty and complexity of the natural world. They are reminded of the importance of living in harmony with their surroundings, of respecting the delicate balance of life that exists all around them.

In the Blossoming Fields, Manny and Frank find inspiration and renewal, their spirits uplifted by the sight of so much life flourishing in the heart of nature. With a renewed sense of purpose, they continue their journey, carrying with them the memory of the harmony they have witnessed and the lessons it has taught them.

Inspired by the beauty of the fields, Manny and Frank find renewal and growth within themselves as they stand amidst the vibrant flowers.

The splendor of the Blossoming Fields fills them with a sense of wonder and awe, igniting a spark of inspiration deep within their hearts. They feel the stirring of new beginnings, a sense of possibility blossoming like the flowers around them.

In the gentle embrace of nature, Manny and Frank reflect on their journey thus far and the challenges that lie ahead. They draw strength from the beauty that surrounds them, finding solace in the knowledge that they are part of something greater than themselves.

With renewed determination, they set their sights on the path ahead. Their spirits lifted by the beauty of the fields, they step forward with confidence, knowing that they are capable of overcoming any challenge that crosses their path.

As they bid farewell to the Blossoming Fields, Manny and Frank carry with them the memory of this tranquil oasis, their hearts filled with gratitude for the renewal and growth it has inspired within them. With each step they take, they move ever closer to their destiny, guided by the beauty and wisdom of the natural world.

In the Elemental Nexus, Silvia and her friends reach a place where the forces of nature converge in a dazzling display of power.

As they step into the Nexus, they feel a palpable energy coursing through the air. The ground beneath their feet thrums with the pulse of the earth, and they can hear the crackling of lightning in the distance. Around them, the air seems to shimmer with the heat of fire and the coolness of water, each element vying for dominance in the ever-shifting landscape.

Together, they marvel at the sight before them, awestruck by the raw power of the Elemental Nexus. Flames dance in intricate patterns, water cascades in shimmering curtains, and gusts of wind whip through the air with breathtaking force. It is a place of both beauty and danger, where the balance of the elements hangs in delicate equilibrium.

In the heart of the Nexus, Silvia and her friends feel a sense of reverence for the natural world and its boundless power. They know that within the swirling chaos of the elements lies the key to unlocking the mysteries of their quest, and they are determined to harness that power for the greater good.

With steady hearts and clear minds, Silvia and her friends prepare to venture further into the Elemental Nexus, ready to confront the challenges. For in this convergence of elements, they sense the potential for both peril and enlightenment, and they are determined to see their journey through to its conclusion.

In the Elemental Nexus, Silvia stands alone, witnessing the delicate balance between the elements, each working in harmony to sustain the world around them.

As she observes, Silvia is struck by the intricate dance of the elements, each one complementing and counterbalancing the others in a delicate symphony of power. Fire crackles and roars, but its flames are tempered by the soothing flow of water. Earth stands firm and resolute, while the gentle breeze of air whispers through the landscape.

Silvia marvels at the beauty of this balance, realizing the profound interconnectedness of all things. She understands that it is this delicate equilibrium that sustains life itself, and she feels a deep sense of reverence for the forces at play.

In the quiet of the Nexus, Silvia reflects on the lessons of balance and harmony, knowing that they hold the key to unlocking the mysteries of their quest. With newfound clarity, she prepares to delve deeper into the Elemental Nexus.

For in this convergence of elements, Silvia sees not only the raw power of nature but also the potential for enlightenment and growth. And she knows that by embracing the balance of forces within herself, she can harness the true power of the Elemental Nexus and fulfill her destiny.

Alone in the Elemental Nexus, Silvia faces elemental trials that test her mastery over the forces of nature, challenging her to prove her worthiness.

As she navigates through the Nexus, Silvia encounters obstacles that embody the essence of each element. She must navigate through scorching flames that threaten to engulf her, plunge into icy waters that chill her to the bone, withstand ferocious winds that threaten to sweep her away, and traverse treacherous terrain that threatens to crumble beneath her feet.

With each trial, Silvia draws upon her inner strength and resilience, calling upon the lessons she has learned throughout her journey. She must adapt and overcome, proving herself worthy of mastering the elements and unlocking the secrets of the Nexus.

Though the trials are daunting, Silvia faces them with courage and determination, knowing that they are a necessary step on the path to fulfilling her destiny. She is determined to emerge from the Elemental Nexus stronger and wiser.

As she faces the final trial, Silvia summons all of her strength and resolve, determined to prove herself worthy of the power that lies within the Nexus. With a steady heart and unwavering determination, she presses forward.

As Lili joins Silvia in the Elemental Nexus, they embark on a journey to restore balance to the Elemental Nexus, ensuring the continued harmony of the world.

Together, Silvia and Lili combine their strengths and abilities, working in unity to overcome the challenges that lie before them. They call upon the elements, harnessing their power to mend the fractures in the delicate balance of the Nexus.

With each step they take, Silvia and Lili draw closer to their goal, their determination unwavering in the face of adversity. They understand that restoring balance to the Elemental Nexus is essential to preserving the harmony of the world, and they are willing to do whatever it takes to succeed.

As they work together, Silvia and Lili forge a deep bond of understanding and friendship, their shared purpose driving them forward. They complement each other's strengths and weaknesses, relying on each other's support as they navigate the challenges of the Nexus.

In the end, their efforts are rewarded as they restore balance to the Elemental Nexus, ensuring that harmony is once again preserved. With a sense of accomplishment and fulfillment, Silvia and Lili emerge from the Nexus, knowing that their actions have made a difference in the world. And as they continue on their journey, they carry with them the knowledge that unity and understanding are the keys to restoring balance and harmony to all things.

As Manny and Frank approach the Crystal Spire, a towering structure that gleams with refracted light and crystalline beauty, they feel a sense of awe wash over them.

The Crystal Spire rises majestically before them, its surface shimmering with a myriad of colors as light dances through its crystalline structure. Each facet of the spire catches the sunlight, casting prismatic rainbows across the landscape.

Manny and Frank marvel at the beauty of the Crystal Spire, its radiance filling them with a sense of wonder and anticipation. They know that within its depths lie untold mysteries and challenges, but they are undeterred in their determination to explore its secrets.

With each step they take towards the towering structure, Manny and Frank feel a sense of excitement building within them. They are ready to face whatever trials may await them within the Crystal Spire, knowing that their friendship and camaraderie will see them through any obstacle.

Manny and Frank begin their ascent of the spire, their determination strong as they climb higher and higher towards its shimmering apex.

With each step, they feel the pull of the Crystal Spire's energy, drawing them closer to its radiant summit. They navigate the winding pathways and spiral staircases, their progress steady and resolute.

As they climb, Manny and Frank encourage each other, offering words of support and motivation to keep pushing forward. They know that reaching the summit is no easy task, but they are determined to see their journey through to the end.

Together, they press on, their spirits buoyed by the anticipation of what lies ahead. With each passing moment, they draw closer to their goal, their determination unwavering in the face of adversity.

As Manny and Frank continue their ascent, they encounter mirrors that reflect their true selves, forcing them to confront their innermost desires and fears.

The mirrors reveal aspects of themselves that they may have long buried or ignored, bringing their deepest thoughts and emotions to the surface. Manny and Frank are faced with the stark reality of their own reflections, forcing them to confront the truths that lie within.

Despite the discomfort and uncertainty that these reflections bring, Manny and Frank stand firm in their resolve. They recognize that facing their inner demons is a necessary step on their journey towards enlightenment and self-discovery.

With courage and determination, Manny and Frank confront their reflections head-on, embracing the truths that they reveal. They emerge from this trial stronger and more self- aware, ready to continue their ascent towards the summit of the Crystal Spire.

Lili and Manny, united in their journey, continue their ascent together, encountering mirrors that reflect their true selves. These mirrors force them to confront their innermost desires and fears.

As they gaze into the mirrors, Lili and Manny see reflections of their past, their present, and their possible futures. They are confronted with aspects of themselves that they may have long buried or ignored, making the face their deepest thoughts and emotions.

Despite the discomfort and uncertainty that these reflections bring, Lili and Manny stand together, offering each other support and encouragement. They recognize that facing their inner demons is a necessary step on their journey towards enlightenment and self-discovery.

With courage and determination, Lili and Manny confront their reflections side by side, embracing the truths that they reveal. They emerge from this trial stronger and more self- aware, their bond deepened by the shared experience. Together, they continue their ascent towards the summit of the Crystal Spire.

As the group enters the Shadowed Vale, a land cloaked in perpetual darkness, where shadows seem to dance and weave, a sense of unease settles over them.

The air is heavy with an oppressive darkness, obscuring their surroundings and casting everything into shadow. The landscape is shrouded in a thick mist, through which eerie shapes and silhouettes shift and move.

Despite the darkness that surrounds them, the group presses forward, their determination unwavering. They know that within the depths of the Shadowed Vale lie answers to their questions and challenges they must overcome.

With each step they take, they can feel the weight of the darkness pressing down upon them, but they refuse to be consumed by fear. Instead, they steel themselves for the trials that lie ahead, ready to confront the danger within the shadows of the vale.

As Manny and the group journey deeper into the Shadowed Vale, they hear echoes of sorrow and despair in the whispers of the wind. The melancholic cries seem to reverberate through the darkness, weighing heavily on their hearts.

With each gust of wind, the echoes grow louder, carrying with them the weight of centuries of sorrow and anguish. Manny and his friends feel the oppressive darkness pressing down upon them, threatening to engulf them in its suffocating embrace.

Despite the despair that surrounds them, Manny stands strong, a beacon of hope amidst the shadows. He offers his friends words of comfort and encouragement, reminding them that even in the darkest of times, there is always a glimmer of light to guide them forward.

Together, they press on, their spirits bolstered by their unity and determination. They refuse to let the echoes of sorrow consume them, instead choosing to focus on the hope that lies ahead. With Manny leading the way, they continue their journey through the Shadowed Vale.

As Manny and the group journey through the Shadowed Vale, they confront the darkness within themselves, facing their deepest fears and doubts.

In the oppressive gloom of the vale, shadows seem to take on a life of their own, twisting and contorting into grotesque shapes that mirror the darkness within their hearts. Manny and his friends feel the weight of their fears pressing down upon them, threatening to consume them in its cold embrace.

But Manny refuses to succumb to the darkness. With unwavering resolve, he leads his friends through the vale, guiding them with a steady hand and a steadfast heart. He encourages them to confront their fears head-on, reminding them that only by facing their inner demons can they hope to overcome them.

Together, they navigate through the vale, each step bringing them closer to the heart of the darkness that lurks within. With Manny's guidance, they find the strength to confront their deepest fears and doubts, emerging from the vale stronger and more resilient than before.

Though the shadows may still linger, Manny walks with newfound confidence, knowing that they have faced the darkness and emerged victorious. With their spirits uplifted and their resolve renewed, they continue their journey through the Shadowed Vale.

As Lili and Silvia lead the group forward, they encounter a powerful guardian that bars their path, challenging them to prove their worthiness to continue their quest.

The guardian looms before them, a formidable figure cloaked in shimmering armor and wielding a weapon of untold power. Its eyes blaze with an otherworldly light as it assesses the group, its presence radiating an aura of strength and authority.

Lili and Silvia exchange a determined glance, knowing that they must face this challenge head-on if they are to continue their journey. With steely resolve, they step forward to confront the guardian, ready to prove their worthiness through courage and determination.

As the guardian speaks, its voice resonates with the weight of ages, laying bare the trials that await those who seek to pass. Lili and Silvia listen intently, their hearts filled with a fierce determination to overcome whatever any challenge.

With a nod of silent agreement, Lili and Silvia prepare themselves for the trial ahead, knowing that their friendship and unity will be their greatest strengths in the face of adversity. Together, they stand ready to face the guardian's challenge and prove themselves worthy of continuing their quest.

Lili and Silvia lead the group through a series of trials that test their physical strength and endurance, pushing them to their limits.

With each trial, the group faces obstacles that demand unwavering determination and resilience. They must navigate treacherous terrain, overcome formidable obstacles, and endure physical challenges that push their bodies to the brink.

Lili and Silvia encourage their friends every step of the way, offering words of encouragement and support as they face each trial together. They know that it is not just physical strength that will see them through, but also the strength of their bond and the unity of their purpose.

As they press forward, the group draws upon their inner reserves of strength and determination, refusing to give in to fatigue or despair. Together, they overcome each trial, emerging stronger and more determined than ever before.

With Lili and Silvia leading the way, the group proves themselves worthy. They know that their strength, both physical and emotional, will carry them through the trials of the Guardian's Gauntlet and beyond.

As Lili and Silvia lead the group through the Guardian's Gauntlet, they encounter puzzles and riddles that test their intelligence and wit, challenging them to think creatively and strategically.

The trials of the mind are as formidable as any physical challenge they have faced, requiring them to unravel mysteries, solve complex puzzles, and decipher enigmatic riddles. Each trial demands careful thought and keen observation, pushing them to their mental limits.

Lili and Silvia encourage their friends to approach each puzzle with an open mind and a spirit of innovation. They know that success lies not only in brute strength, but also in the ability to think critically and solve problems creatively.

Together, they pool their knowledge and skills, working as a team to unravel the secrets of each trial. They draw upon their collective intelligence and intuition, supporting each other every step of the way.

As they progress through the trials of the mind, Lili and Silvia lead by example, demonstrating the power of intellect and determination. They inspire their friends to rise to the challenge, knowing that together, they can overcome any obstacle that stands in their way.

With unwavering determination and the power of teamwork, Lili and Silvia lead the group to triumph over the Guardian's Gauntlet.

Despite the formidable challenges they faced, including physical trials, mental puzzles, and the daunting presence of the guardian itself, they stood united and resolute. Through their combined efforts and unwavering resolve, they overcame each obstacle that stood in their path.

With Lili and Silvia guiding them, the group worked together seamlessly, drawing strength from each other's courage and support. They tackled each trial with tenacity, refusing to falter in the face of adversity.

As they emerged victorious from the gauntlet, a sense of accomplishment filled their hearts. They knew that they had proven themselves worthy of continuing their quest, their bond stronger than ever before.

The group sails into the waters where the Sirens dwell, their ship cutting through the waves with determination and caution. The air is thick with anticipation, each member of the group keenly aware of the dangers that lurk beneath the surface.

As they draw nearer to the Sirens' domain, the air becomes filled with the enchanting melodies that are the hallmark of these mythical creatures. The haunting songs weave through the air, their allure undeniable yet treacherous, beckoning sailors to their doom. Despite the danger, the group presses on, their resolve unwavering as they navigate the perilous waters. They know that succumbing to the Sirens' song could mean certain destruction, yet they are determined to face the challenge head-on.

With their hearts fortified against the lure of the Sirens' melodies, the group sails ever closer to their destination, their minds focused on the task at hand. They know that only by staying strong and united can they hope to emerge unscathed from the clutches of the Sirens' song.

Silvia and Frank, their hearts heavy with caution, hear the irresistible call of the Sirens. The enchanting melody echoes across the waves, its haunting beauty tugging at their very souls.

Despite their best efforts to resist, Silvia and Frank feel the pull of the Sirens' song growing stronger with each passing moment. Its allure is impossible to ignore, weaving a spell of enchantment that threatens to ensnare them completely.

As the melody washes over them, Silvia and Frank exchange worried glances, knowing that they must steel themselves against the temptation to succumb. They cling to their resolve, their minds racing with thoughts of the dangers that lie ahead if they were to give in to the Sirens' call.

With grim determination, Silvia and Frank fight to maintain their focus, their willpower the only defense against the seductive power of the Sirens' song. They steel themselves for the trials that lie ahead, knowing that their strength and unity will be tested like never before in the face of such overwhelming temptation.

Both of them struggle to resist the overwhelming allure of the Sirens' song, fighting against its hypnotic spell with all their might. Every note pulls at their senses, threatening to cloud their judgment and lead them astray from their quest.

With each passing moment, the temptation grows stronger, testing their resolve and determination. They exchange glances filled with silent reassurance, drawing strength from each other as they battle against the seductive power of the Sirens' song.

Despite the overwhelming odds, they cling to their purpose with unwavering determination, refusing to let the enchanting melodies sway them from their path. They focus their minds on the task at hand, their hearts set on overcoming the allure of the Sirens' call and emerging victorious.

With every ounce of willpower they possess, Silvia and Frank push back against the temptation, their determination shining like a beacon of light amidst the darkness of the Sirens' song. They know that their strength lies in their unity and resolve, and they stand firm against the enchantment that seeks to ensnare them.

Silvia, Frank, and the rest of the group summon every ounce of their willpower and inner strength to break free from the Sirens' enchantment. With sheer determination, they resist the allure of the mesmerizing song, their minds focused on their quest and their friends by their side.

Despite the overwhelming temptation, they refuse to yield, fighting against the hypnotic spell with unwavering resolve. With each moment, their determination grows stronger, fortified by the bonds of friendship and the shared purpose that unites them.

As the enchantment begins to weaken, Silvia, Frank, and their friends feel a surge of triumph swell within their hearts. With one final push, they break free from the Sirens' grasp, their ship sailing on towards safer waters.

Though the ordeal has tested them to their limits, they emerge from the encounter stronger and more determined than ever before. Their resolve hardened by the experience, they continue their journey with renewed vigor, knowing that they can overcome any challenge that lies ahead with unity, courage, and unwavering determination.

Silvia, the wise hippopotamus, leads the group as they arrive at the Astral Observatory, a place where they can peer into the depths of the cosmos and unlock the mysteries of the universe.

As they approach the observatory for the second time around, a sense of awe washes over them, its towering spires reaching towards the stars like fingers seeking to grasp the secrets of the cosmos. Silvia's eyes gleam with anticipation, her knowledge of the celestial realms guiding them towards this pivotal moment in their journey.

With each step, they draw closer to the observatory's entrance, the air alive with the hum of ancient magic and the whispers of distant stars. Silvia's friends look to her for guidance, their hearts filled with a mixture of excitement and trepidation at what they may discover within.

As they pass through the observatory's gates, they feel a shift in the very fabric of reality, as if they are stepping into a realm where time and space converge. Silvia leads them forward to a known place her, with quiet confidence, her gaze fixed on the wonders that await them beyond.

Silvia and her friends marvel at the celestial wonders visible through the observatory's telescopes. They gaze in awe at distant galaxies and nebulae, their eyes widening with wonder as they witness the vastness of the cosmos unfolding before them.

Each member of the group takes turns peering through the telescopes, their breath catching as they catch glimpses of swirling galaxies, sparkling star clusters, and ethereal nebulae. Silvia explains the significance of each celestial phenomenon, her voice filled with reverence for the mysteries of the universe.

As they gaze upon the stars, a sense of wonder fills their hearts, reminding them of the infinite possibilities that exist beyond the confines of their own world. Silvia's friends are captivated by the beauty and grandeur of the cosmos, their minds expanding with each new discovery.

In this moment of stargazer's delight, Silvia and her friends feel a profound connection to the universe, their spirits lifted by the awe-inspiring beauty of the celestial realm. They know that they are but small beings in a vast and wondrous cosmos, yet they feel a sense of unity and belonging amidst the stars.

They uncover ancient star charts and celestial maps within the observatory, revealing hidden knowledge about their quest and the forces they must confront.

As they study the intricate patterns of the stars and the alignments of the planets, a sense of clarity descends upon the group. They begin to understand the significance of their journey in their personal lives and the challenges that lie ahead, guided by the ancient wisdom contained within the celestial maps.

Silvia pores over the star charts with a focused intensity, her keen insight unlocking the secrets hidden within the celestial patterns. Her friends gather around her, their minds buzzing with anticipation as they piece together the clues that will lead them towards their ultimate goal.

With each revelation, the group's resolve is strengthened, their determination to succeed in their quest burning brighter than ever before. They know that they are on the cusp of uncovering truths that will shape the fate of their world, and they stand ready to face whatever challenges may come their way.

From the vantage point of the observatory, Silvia and her friends gain a broader perspective on their journey and their place within the vastness of the universe.

As they gaze out into the cosmos, their minds expand to encompass the infinite possibilities that stretch out before them. They contemplate the interconnectedness of all things, the ebb and flow of cosmic energies that shape the fabric of reality.

Silvia's friends feel a sense of awe wash over them as they consider the scale of the universe and their own place within it. They realize that their journey is but a small part of a much larger tapestry, a thread woven into the intricate design of the cosmos.

Yet, even as they contemplate the vastness of the universe, Silvia and her friends feel a sense of purpose burning within them. They know that they are destined for greatness, their actions guided by the wisdom of the stars and the boundless potential that lies within each of them.

With renewed determination, they set their sights on the challenges that lie ahead, ready to embrace the journey with open hearts and steadfast resolve. From the observatory's lofty heights, they chart a course towards their destiny, guided by the eternal perspective that only the cosmos can provide.

They arrive at the Shattered Citadel, a once-great fortress now in ruins, haunted by echoes of its former glory.

As they step through the crumbling archways and weathered stone corridors, they feel the weight of history pressing down upon them. The air is heavy with the whispers of forgotten tales and the lingering presence of those who once called this place home.

They tread carefully through the ruins, their eyes scanning the crumbling walls for any sign of what once was. They marvel at the intricate carvings and faded tapestries that adorn the ancient stone, each telling a story of a bygone era.

Despite the decay and destruction that surrounds them, they sense a power lingering within the ruins, a spark of magic that refuses to be extinguished. They know that there are secrets hidden within these walls, waiting to be uncovered by those brave enough to seek them out.

With each step they take, they draw closer to unlocking the mysteries of the Shattered Citadel, their hearts filled with a mixture of trepidation and excitement for the adventures that lie ahead.

As they continue their exploration of the Shattered Citadel, they hear echoes of ancient battles that once raged within its walls. The clang of swords, the shouts of warriors, and the thunder of siege engines reverberate through the corridors, filling the air with a palpable sense of tension and strife.

They pause to listen, their hearts heavy with the weight of history pressing down upon them. Each echo carries with it the stories of those who fought and died within these hallowed halls, their memories etched into the very stones of the fortress.

Despite the passage of time, the echoes of battle linger on, a reminder of the struggles that have shaped the destiny of the citadel and those who once dwelled within it. Silvia and her friends feel a sense of reverence for the fallen, their spirits humbled by the sacrifices made in the name of honor and duty.

As they press on through the ruins, they cannot help but wonder what secrets lie hidden beneath the scars of war. With each step, they draw closer to uncovering the truth about the citadel's turbulent past and the role it plays in their own quest for knowledge and enlightenment.

They continue their journey through the citadel's crumbling halls and shattered chambers, their eyes keenly searching for clues that will lead them closer to their goal.

Amidst the rubble and debris, they uncover fragments of ancient manuscripts and faded tapestries, each offering glimpses into the citadel's storied past. They piece together the puzzle of history, tracing the rise and fall of empires that once vied for dominance within these walls.

They sift through the remnants of the past, their fingers tracing the intricate carvings and weathered inscriptions that adorn the stone. Each discovery brings them closer to unlocking the secrets that lie hidden within the citadel's depths.

With determination and perseverance, they press on, undeterred by the challenges that confront them. They know that the answers they seek are within reach, waiting to be uncovered by those bold enough to venture into the heart of the Shattered Citadel.

As they delve deeper into the ruins, they can feel the pulse of ancient magic stirring in the air, guiding them ever closer to their destiny. With each step forward, they draw nearer to the truth, their spirits buoyed by the promise of discovery that lies just beyond the next crumbling archway.

With each step they take and each secret they uncover, they begin to restore honor to the citadel. Piece by piece, they reclaim its lost legacy, breathing new life into its ancient halls and preparing it for the battles yet to come.

The group work tirelessly, their hands and hearts united in a common purpose. They repair crumbling walls, polish tarnished armor, and hoist tattered banners high, restoring the citadel to its former glory.

As they toil, they feel the weight of responsibility upon their shoulders, knowing that they are the custodians of a legacy that stretches back through the annals of time. They are

determined to honor the sacrifices of those who came before them, ensuring that the citadel stands as a beacon of hope and resilience in the face of adversity.

With each stroke of their hammers and each sweep of their brooms, they breathe new life into the ancient fortress, infusing it with the strength and vitality it needs to face the challenges of the future. And as the sun sets on another day at the Shattered Citadel, they stand proud, knowing that they have restored honor to a place that was once lost to the ravages of time.

Lili takes the lead as the group confronts the Oracle once more, seeking answers to the questions that still linger in their minds.

With determination etched upon her face, Lili steps forward, her voice steady as she addresses the enigmatic figure before them. She demands clarity, her words echoing through the chamber as she seeks to unravel the mysteries that have plagued them since the beginning of their journey.

The Oracle, shrouded in shadows, regards them with an inscrutable gaze, her eyes seeming to pierce through the very fabric of reality. She speaks in cryptic riddles and half-truths, her words weaving a tapestry of fate and destiny that leaves Lili and her friends grasping for understanding.

But Lili refuses to be deterred. With courage and conviction, she presses the Oracle for answers, her determination unwavering in the face of uncertainty. She knows that the key to their quest lies within the Oracle's words, and she will not rest until she unlocks the secrets that lie hidden within.

As the confrontation unfolds, tensions rise within the chamber, the air crackling with anticipation. Lili and her friends stand united, ready to face whatever revelations the Oracle's gambit may bring, their faith in each other and their cause unwavering as they prepare to confront their destiny head-on.

Lili, displaying her characteristic toughness, listens intently as the Oracle delivers cryptic prophecies that hint at the challenges and trials that lie ahead. The group gathers around her, their brows furrowed in concentration as they try to decipher the enigmatic words spoken by the Oracle.

Each prophecy is like a puzzle piece, offering glimpses of the future yet shrouded in ambiguity. Lili's determination only grows stronger as she refuses to be daunted by the veiled nature of the Oracle's words. She knows that the key to unlocking their meaning lies in perseverance and unity.

With a resolute expression, Lili leads her friends in a concerted effort to unravel the mysteries hidden within the Oracle's prophecies. They pour over ancient texts and consult with each other, piecing together fragments of knowledge in their quest for understanding.

Despite the challenges posed by the cryptic nature of the prophecies, Lili remains steadfast, her unwavering resolve serving as a beacon of hope for her friends.

Together, they face each riddle with determination and courage, knowing that their journey is far from over and that the answers they seek lie just beyond the next cryptic verse.

Silvia takes over as they plot their next moves carefully, using the Oracle's guidance to plan their strategy and outmaneuver their enemies. With a steady hand and a keen mind, she leads the group in crafting a plan that will allow them to navigate the challenges ahead with precision and skill.

Drawing upon the wisdom imparted by the Oracle, Silvia formulates a strategy that capitalizes on their strengths and exploits the weaknesses of their adversaries. Each decision is made with careful consideration, each move calculated to maximize their chances of success.

As they prepare to set their plan into motion, they call upon the guidance of the divine, seeking answers from the gods themselves. Silvia's voice rings out in prayer, her words filled with reverence and determination as she beseeches the divine for guidance and protection.

In the stillness of the chamber, they feel a presence, a whisper of divine wisdom that fills them with clarity and resolve. The gods answer their call, offering guidance and strength as they prepare to face the challenges that lie ahead.

With the Oracle's guidance and the blessings of the gods, they stand ready to embark on the next leg of their journey, their spirits buoyed by the knowledge that they are not alone in their quest. Together, they will face it, fortified by their faith and their unwavering determination to see their mission through to its end.

As they embark on the next leg of their journey, they realize that they are players in a larger game of fate, where every move could determine the outcome of their quest and the most important is self awareness. Silvia and her friends exchange knowing glances, a silent acknowledgment passing between them as they contemplate the weight of their destiny.

In this intricate game of fate, they understand that every decision carries significance, every action a ripple that reverberates through the tapestry of their lives. They steel themselves for the challenges ahead, their resolve strengthened by the knowledge that they hold their fate in their hands.

With each step forward, they move with purpose and determination, navigating the twists and turns of their journey with care and precision. They know that they cannot control the hand they've been dealt, but they can choose how to play it, seizing every opportunity and facing every challenge with courage and conviction.

As they venture forth into the unknown, they do so with a sense of purpose and clarity, their hearts filled with the determination to shape their own destiny. Whatever trials may lie ahead, they will meet them head-on, ready to defy fate itself in pursuit of their quest.

The group enters the Labyrinthine Library, a vast repository of knowledge and wisdom spanning countless volumes and scrolls. Lili leads the way, her eyes wide with wonder as she takes in the endless rows of books that line the shelves, each one holding the promise of untold secrets and revelations, not only of the past but for the future as well.

As they navigate the labyrinthine corridors of the library, they are surrounded by the hushed whispers of ancient texts and the faint scent of parchment. Silvia and her friends move with reverence, their footsteps echoing softly against the polished marble floors as they explore the hidden depths of the library.

With each book they peruse and each scroll they unfurl, they uncover new insights and revelations that deepen their understanding of the world around them. They lose themselves in the vast expanse of knowledge contained within the library's walls, each page turned bringing them closer to the answers they seek.

Despite the overwhelming magnitude of the library, they press on, their thirst for knowledge driving them ever forward. They know that within these hallowed halls lie the keys to unlocking the mysteries of their quest, and they are determined to uncover them, no matter the cost.

Manny and his friends hear whispers of the ancients as they wander through the library's labyrinthine corridors, each filled with secrets and hidden truths. The ancient tomes seem to come alive as they pass, their pages rustling with the weight of centuries of knowledge.

As they delve deeper into the heart of the library, the whispers grow louder, echoing off the towering shelves and reverberating through the air. Manny and the group pause to listen, their ears attuned to the faint murmurings of forgotten lore and ancient wisdom.

With each whisper, they catch fleeting glimpses of the past, piecing together fragments of history that shed light on the mysteries of their quest. They marvel at the wisdom of those

who came before them, their spirits buoyed by the knowledge that they walk in the footsteps of giants.

Driven by curiosity and a thirst for understanding, the group press on, their minds alive with the possibilities that lie within the pages of the library's vast collection. They know that within these whispers of the ancients lie the answers they seek, and they are determined to uncover them, no matter the obstacles that lie in their path.

Manny carefully sift through the dusty tomes and ancient scrolls, searching for clues that will unlock the mysteries of the past and illuminate their path forward. Each book they examine is a treasure trove of knowledge, its pages filled with the stories of civilizations long gone and the secrets of ages past.

With painstaking care, they pour over the faded text and intricate illustrations, their fingers tracing the lines of ancient script as they seek to decipher their meaning. Manny's keen eyes scan the shelves, his mind racing as he absorbs the wealth of information contained within the library's walls.

As they delve deeper into the annals of history, Manny and his friends uncover tales of heroism and betrayal, of triumphs and tragedies that shaped the world as they know it. They marvel at the resilience of those who came before them, their hearts filled with a deep sense of reverence for the wisdom of the ages.

Despite the daunting task before them, Manny and the group press on, their determination unwavering in the face of adversity. They know that within these ancient texts lie the keys to unlocking the secrets of their quest, and they are prepared to search every corner of the library until they find them.

As Manny delves deeper into the library, they encounter guardians of knowledge, enigmatic beings who test their intellect and wisdom, challenging them to prove their worthiness.

These guardians, shrouded in mystery and ancient wisdom, stand as sentinels of the library's most precious secrets, guarding them with unwavering determination.

With each encounter, Manny and his friends are faced with riddles and puzzles that test their wit and cunning. They must rely on their collective knowledge and intuition to unravel the mysteries presented to them, drawing upon the lessons they have learned throughout their journey.

The guardians watch silently as the group navigate the challenges before them, their eyes gleaming with a mixture of curiosity and intrigue. They offer no assistance, allowing the group to forge their own path through the trials that lie ahead.

With each challenge overcome, Manny grows stronger and more confident in their abilities. They prove themselves worthy of the knowledge contained within the library's walls, earning the respect of the guardians and unlocking new depths of understanding along the way.

Silvia and her friends stepped into the Enchanted Grove, a sanctuary of tranquility and magic where nature flourished in all its splendor. As they crossed the threshold, the world around them transformed. The air grew cooler, infused with the sweet scent of blooming flowers and fresh pine. A gentle breeze rustled the leaves of ancient trees, creating a soothing symphony that calmed their weary spirits.

The trees stood tall and majestic, their thick trunks wrapped in vines and adorned with luminescent blossoms that glowed softly in the twilight. Sunlight filtered through the dense canopy above, casting dappled patterns on the ground and highlighting the vibrant greenery that carpeted the forest floor. Bioluminescent mushrooms dotted the path ahead, their gentle glow illuminating the way forward.

The ground was soft beneath their feet, covered in a thick layer of moss that muffled their footsteps. Birds with iridescent feathers flitted from branch to branch, their melodic songs

adding to the grove's enchanting ambiance. Small woodland creatures peeked curiously from behind bushes and tree trunks, their eyes wide with wonder but without fear.

At the heart of the grove, they found a large crystalline pond. The water was so clear that it mirrored the sky and the surrounding trees, creating a surreal, double-image effect. A circle of ancient stones stood at the water's edge, each stone covered in intricate runes that pulsed with a gentle, magical glow.

The group paused to take in the breathtaking beauty of the grove. It was a place untouched by time and the outside world, a sanctuary where the essence of life was celebrated and preserved. As they stepped further into the grove, a profound sense of peace washed over them. The worries and fears that had plagued them seemed to melt away, replaced by a deep connection to nature and the universe.

This was not just a place of beauty; it was a place of healing and reflection. They could feel the grove's magic working on them, mending their spirits and rejuvenating their bodies. They knew that this was a moment to pause, to breathe, and to gather their strength for the challenges that lay ahead in their lives.

The Enchanted Grove welcomed them with open arms, offering its tranquility and wisdom to those who sought its refuge. Here, amidst the splendor of nature, Silvia and her friends found a moment of respite and a reminder of the profound beauty and interconnectedness of all things.

As they ventured deeper into the Enchanted Grove, they began to hear the gentle whispers of the ancient trees. It started as a soft murmur, almost imperceptible, but gradually grew clearer as they attuned their senses to the grove's magic. The trees, it seemed, had stories to tell, tales of the grove's history and the creatures that dwelled within its bounds.

The whispers wove a tapestry of images and sounds in their minds. They learned of the grove's origins, a place born of pure magic where the natural world flourished in harmony.

The trees spoke of a time when great druids had walked these grounds, their powers intertwined with the essence of the grove, ensuring its protection and nurturing its growth.

Silvia could almost see the druids, their robes flowing as they tended to the grove, their hands glowing with healing light. She felt a connection to these ancient caretakers, a sense of kinship and shared purpose. The whispers conveyed not just the grove's history but also its deep wisdom, a reminder of the delicate balance that sustained all life.

The trees also shared tales of the creatures that called the grove home. They spoke of the shy deer that roamed the clearings, their coats dappled with sunlight filtering through the leaves. They described the mischievous foxes that played near the pond, their eyes gleaming with curiosity and intelligence. The birds, with their iridescent feathers, were messengers of the grove, carrying news and maintaining the harmony of this enchanted sanctuary.

Each story was a thread in the rich tapestry of the grove's existence. Silvia and her friends listened in awe, their hearts swelling with reverence for the ancient wisdom being imparted to them. They felt privileged to be part of this living history, to hear the voices of the trees that had stood witness to countless cycles of growth and change.

Amidst the whispers, they also sensed a gentle warning. The grove had faced threats before, from those who sought to exploit its magic for their gain. It had survived because of the resilience of its inhabitants and the guardianship of those who loved it. The trees urged Silvia and the group to be vigilant, to protect the grove and its secrets from those who would harm it.

In the heart of the grove, by the crystalline pond and the circle of ancient stones, Silvia felt a profound connection to the natural world. The whispers of the trees were a gift, a reminder of the interconnectedness of all life and the importance of preserving the harmony of nature. As the whispers faded, the group stood in silent contemplation. They had been entrusted with the grove's stories, its wisdom, and its warnings. With renewed determination, they

vowed to honor the grove's legacy, to protect its magic, and to carry its lessons with them as they continued their journey.

As Silvia wandered alone through the vibrant flora and fauna of the Enchanted Grove, she felt a deep sense of connection to her surroundings. The air was filled with the sweet scent of blooming flowers, and the gentle rustling of leaves created a soothing symphony that seemed to whisper words of comfort and peace.

While her friends explored other parts of the grove, Silvia took this moment to reflect on the journey they had shared. She thought about the trials they had faced, the victories they had won, and the losses they had endured. Each memory was like a petal of a flower, delicate and beautiful, contributing to the overall beauty of their shared experience.

As she walked, Silvia's thoughts turned to the bonds of friendship that had grown between her and her friends. They had started as a group of individuals, each with their own goals and dreams, but the journey had woven their lives together inextricably. The grove, with its serene beauty and ancient wisdom, seemed to amplify these feelings, making her acutely aware of the strength they drew from each other.

She paused by a cluster of vibrant wildflowers, their petals glowing in the soft light. Silvia knelt down, touching one of the blossoms gently. The flower responded to her touch, unfurling further as if in greeting. She smiled, feeling a sense of friendship even with the plants around her.

As if on cue, a small, iridescent bird landed on a nearby branch. Its melodic song filled the air, a sweet and joyous tune that seemed to celebrate the harmony of the grove. Silvia listened, her heart swelling with gratitude for the friendships she had forged. She knew that just as the grove's inhabitants thrived together, so too did she and her friends.

The bird's song seemed to carry a message of hope and unity, a reminder that they were not alone on their journey. Silvia closed her eyes, letting the music wash over her, and felt a

profound sense of peace. In that moment, she knew that the bonds of friendship she shared with her friends were unbreakable, forged in the fires of their shared adventures and strengthened by their mutual respect and trust.

As she stood up and continued her walk, Silvia felt a renewed sense of purpose. The grove had reminded her of the importance of life friendship and camaraderie, and she was determined to carry this lesson with her. She knew that whatever challenges lay ahead, they would face them together, drawing strength from their unity and the deep bonds they had formed.

Silvia made her way back to where her friends were gathered. As they shared stories and laughter amidst the vibrant flora and fauna, she felt a profound sense of belonging. In the heart of the Enchanted Grove, surrounded by nature's splendor, their friendship blossomed anew, providing them with the solace and strength they needed to continue their journey.

The grove had not only healed their bodies but had also nurtured their spirits, deepening their connections and reaffirming their commitment to each other. With their bonds of friendship stronger than ever.

As Silvia and her friends spent more time within the Enchanted Grove, they felt the grove's magical aura working its wonders on them. The air seemed to shimmer with an ethereal glow, and the vibrant colors of the flora and fauna around them pulsed with life and energy. This place was a sanctuary not just for the body but for the spirit as well.

Silvia could feel the tension and fatigue of their long journey melting away. The grove's magic seeped into her being, washing over her like a gentle, refreshing wave. She closed her eyes and took a deep breath, letting the tranquil energy of the grove fill her lungs. With each inhalation, she felt more alive, more connected to the world around her.

Her friends experienced the same rejuvenation. Lili, who had been carrying the weight of their struggles on her shoulders, visibly relaxed, her face softening into a serene smile.

Manny, usually brimming with restless energy, found a peaceful stillness within himself. The grove's magic touched each of them differently, but the result was the same: a profound sense of renewal and vitality.

The group gathered by the crystalline pond, where the ancient stones stood as silent sentinels. They sat in a circle, feeling the energy of the grove flow through them, linking their spirits in a web of light and harmony. Silvia began to speak, her voice soft but filled with conviction.

"This place is a gift," she said. "It's a reminder of why we started this journey in the first place. To find beauty, to seek wisdom, and to protect what is precious. We are more than just travelers; we are guardians of something greater."

Her words resonated deeply with everyone. They had all been through so much, faced so Manny challenges, but here in the Enchanted Grove, they remembered their true purpose. The grove's magic did more than heal their bodies; it reignited the flame of determination within their hearts.

They spent the rest of the day exploring the grove, each discovery filling them with wonder and joy. They marveled at the bioluminescent mushrooms that glowed brighter as night approached, creating a fairy-tale landscape that seemed to come alive in the twilight. They watched the iridescent birds as they settled into their nests, their songs blending into a lullaby that soothed their souls.

As night fell, they gathered around a small campfire, its flames dancing in harmony with the stars that began to twinkle overhead. The grove, even under the blanket of night, was a place of light and life. The soft glow of the bioluminescent plants and the gentle hum of nocturnal creatures created an ambiance of serenity and magic.

Silvia looked around at her friends, their faces illuminated by the firelight and the soft glow of the grove. She felt a surge of gratitude for their friendship and the strength they gave each

other. In this moment of quiet reflection, she knew that they were ready for whatever lay ahead.

"The grove has given us its blessing," Silvia said, her voice filled with a newfound resolve. "We have been renewed, and we carry its magic within us. Let's honor this gift by continuing our journey with even greater determination."

Her friends nodded in agreement, their eyes shining with the same resolve. The Enchanted Grove had rejuvenated their spirits, filling them with the energy and determination they needed to face the challenges ahead. As they settled in for the night, their hearts were light, and their spirits were strong.

In the morning, they would leave the grove behind, but its magic would stay with them, a source of strength and inspiration. The Enchanted Grove had reminded them of their purpose and rekindled their inner fire. With renewed energy and determination, they were ready to continue their journey with confidence.

They stood at the edge of the Shadowed Sanctuary, a place unlike any they had encountered before. The air was thick with an oppressive darkness that seemed to swallow the light, leaving the path ahead shrouded in mystery. The trees here were twisted and gnarled, their branches reaching out like skeletal hands, and the ground was covered in a thick layer of mist that clung to their ankles as they moved forward.

The transition from the vibrant, life-filled Enchanted Grove to the eerie, foreboding Shadowed Sanctuary was stark and unsettling. Silvia felt a chill run down her spine as they stepped into the sanctuary, the air growing colder with each step. The silence was deafening, broken only by the occasional rustle of unseen creatures moving in the shadows.

"Lili, stay close," Silvia whispered, her voice barely more than a breath. Lili nodded, her eyes scanning their surroundings with a mixture of caution and curiosity. Manny took up the rear, his hand resting on the hilt of his sword, ready for any potential threats.

The darkness seemed to have a life of its own, shifting and swirling as if reacting to their presence. Silvia could feel the weight of the sanctuary's secrets pressing down on them, an invisible force that seemed to seep into their very bones. She knew they had to stay vigilant, for danger could lurk in any corner, hidden by the veil of darkness.

As they ventured deeper, they began to notice the remnants of a once-grand structure, now reduced to ruins. Ancient stone pillars, covered in moss and ivy, stood as silent sentinels, marking the path forward. The walls, where they still stood, were adorned with faded carvings and cryptic symbols that hinted at the sanctuary's storied past.

"This place feels... ancient," Manny muttered, his voice echoing softly in the gloom. "Like it's been waiting for something, or someone, for a long time."

Silvia nodded, her eyes fixed on a particularly intricate carving of a serpent winding its way around a tree. "There's a power here, something old and powerful. We need to be careful."

As they pressed on, the darkness seemed to grow thicker, the shadows deeper. They moved cautiously, their senses heightened, every sound and movement scrutinized. The oppressive atmosphere weighed heavily on their spirits, but they drew strength from each other, their bond a source of light in the surrounding gloom.

Suddenly, a faint glimmer caught Silvia's eye. She motioned for the group to stop and pointed ahead. In the distance, a soft, flickering light broke through the darkness, casting eerie shadows on the surrounding walls. It seemed to beckon them forward, a beacon of hope in the otherwise impenetrable darkness.

"Let's check it out," Lili suggested, her voice barely a whisper.

They approached the light with caution, each step deliberate and silent. As they drew closer, they realized the light emanated from a small, intricately carved lantern hanging from a rusted hook on one of the ancient pillars. The lantern's flame flickered weakly, but its light was enough to reveal a hidden passageway leading deeper into the sanctuary.

"This must be the way," Silvia said, her voice filled with determination. "But we need to be on guard. There's no telling what lies ahead."

With renewed resolve, they stepped into the passageway, leaving the flickering lantern behind. The darkness closed in around them once more, but they pressed on, guided by their shared purpose and the faint hope that somewhere in the depths of the Shadowed Sanctuary, they would find the answers they sought.

The air grew colder and more oppressive as they ventured further, the silence punctuated only by their soft footsteps and the occasional distant echo. The passageway twisted and turned, a labyrinth of stone and shadow that seemed to go on forever.

Despite the pervasive darkness, Silvia felt a sense of determination burning within her. They had come this far, faced countless trials and challenges, and they would not be deterred now. With each step, they moved closer to unraveling the mysteries of the Shadowed Sanctuary and discovering the secrets hidden within its depths.

The labyrinthine halls of the Shadowed Sanctuary seemed to stretch endlessly, each turn leading them deeper into a maze of darkness and mystery. The air grew colder, the silence more oppressive, and an unsettling feeling of being watched settled over them like a heavy cloak. Silvia could sense the presence of unseen eyes, tracking their every move from the shadows.

Their footsteps echoed softly against the stone floor, the sound magnified by the stillness of the sanctuary. The walls, covered in ancient carvings and faded murals, seemed to tell stories of a bygone era, their cryptic messages lost to time. Silvia ran her fingers along the cool rough surface of the stone, feeling the history embedded in each groove and indentation.

"Lili, do you feel that?" Silvia whispered, her voice barely audible.

Lili nodded, her eyes scanning the darkness. "Yes, it's like we're being watched. But I can't see anything."

Manny, walking slightly ahead, turned back to face them. "Stay close and keep your wits about you. We don't know what might be lurking in these shadows."

As they moved through the sanctuary's winding corridors, the sensation of being watched grew stronger. Shadows danced on the walls, their shapes twisting and contorting as if alive. The faintest whisper of movement, too quiet to be certain, kept them on edge. Every creak and groan of the ancient structure seemed amplified, echoing through the halls like ghostly murmurs.

They passed through a series of archways, each more elaborate than the last, adorned with symbols and figures that seemed to shift and change in the flickering light. Silvia could almost feel the weight of the history pressing down on them, the stories of those who had walked these halls before them lingering in the air.

"Look at these carvings," Lili said, pointing to a particularly intricate mural. "It's like they're trying to tell us something."

The mural depicted a grand scene: a gathering of robed figures around a central altar, their faces hidden in shadow. Above them, a constellation of stars formed a pattern that seemed familiar, yet just out of reach in Silvia's memory. She traced the lines with her finger, trying to make sense of the imagery.

"These symbols," Manny said, studying another part of the mural, "they look like constellations. Could they be a map or a guide of some sort?"

Silvia nodded thoughtfully. "It's possible. The sanctuary might have been a place of great importance, where they studied the stars and sought guidance from the cosmos. But we need to stay focused. Whatever secrets this place holds, we have to be ready for anything."

As they pressed on, the feeling of being watched intensified. The darkness seemed to close in around them, thickening with each step. Silvia could feel the hairs on the back of her neck standing up, a primal warning of unseen danger. She glanced at her friends, seeing the same wariness reflected in their eyes.

Suddenly, a faint, ghostly light flickered ahead of them, casting long shadows that danced eerily on the walls. They paused, unsure of what lay ahead. The light seemed to beckon them forward, yet carried with it an air of foreboding.

"We have to keep moving," Silvia said, her voice steady despite the tension in the air. "Whatever that light is, it might lead us to answers."

They moved cautiously toward the light, each step taken with the utmost care. The air grew colder, the silence more profound. As they approached, the source of the light became clear: an old, ornate candelabrum standing in the center of a large chamber. The candles flickered with an otherworldly glow, casting an eerie illumination over the room.

The chamber was vast, its ceiling lost in shadow. Along the walls, ancient tapestries hung in tatters, their once vibrant colors faded and worn. The air was thick with the scent of decay and the faintest hint of something metallic, like old blood.

As they stepped into the room, the sensation of being watched reached its peak. The shadows seemed to coalesce, forming vague shapes that hovered at the edge of their vision. Silvia felt a shiver run down her spine, her instincts screaming that they were not alone.

"Stay together," Manny warned, his voice low and tense. "And be ready for anything."

Silvia and her friends moved to the center of the chamber, their eyes scanning the shadows for any sign of movement. The weight of the unseen eyes bore down on them, a silent testament to the secrets and dangers that lurked within the Shadowed Sanctuary. They knew they had to remain vigilant, for the haunted halls of this ancient place held more than just memories of the past.

Silvia the Majestic, a hippopotamus known for her wisdom, led her friends deeper into the Shadowed Sanctuary. The oppressive atmosphere weighed heavily on their spirits, and the sense of being watched by unseen eyes grew stronger. Each step brought them closer to the heart of the sanctuary, where they would have to confront the shadows both around them and within themselves.

As they moved forward, the corridor opened into a vast chamber. The room was filled with an eerie glow that seemed to come from nowhere and everywhere at once. The walls were adorned with faded murals depicting scenes of struggle and triumph, their meanings lost to time. The atmosphere was thick with a palpable sense of foreboding, and the air felt colder than ever.

"Lili the Melodic Butterfly, what is this place?" whispered Lili, her sharp eyes scanning the surroundings.

Silvia the Majestic, tilted her head, listening to the faint echoes that seemed to whisper from the walls. "This is a place of trials, Lili. We must be prepared to face our deepest fears and confront the darkness within ourselves."

Manny, known as the lion, always alert, sensed something more in the air. "Stay close, everyone. I have a feeling this room is more than it seems."

As they ventured further into the chamber, the shadows seemed to grow thicker, almost tangible. Suddenly, the shadows began to shift and take form, rising from the ground and walls to confront the group. Each animal saw a different shape before them, each shadow representing their deepest fears and insecurities.

Lili faced a shadow that resembled a larger, more powerful predator. Its eyes gleamed with malice as it stalked towards her. She felt a surge of fear, remembering her own moments of doubt and vulnerability. But she steeled herself, spreading her delicate wings and standing her ground.

"You are not real," Lili declared, her voice steady. "I am stronger than my fears."

The shadow paused, flickering uncertainly before dissipating into the air. Lili took a deep breath, her confidence bolstered by the victory.

Manny, known as the lion, was confronted by a shadow that took the form of a massive, coiling snake, its fangs bared and eyes filled with a predatory gleam. Manny's heart raced as he remembered past encounters with such predators, but he forced himself to remain calm.

"This is just a trick," Manny said firmly, facing the shadow with unwavering resolve. "I have faced worse and survived."

The snake shadow hesitated, then melted away, leaving Manny standing tall and unshaken.

Silvia the Majestic faced a different challenge. The shadow before her took the form of a mirror image, reflecting all her doubts and fears about leading her friends into danger. The shadow hippopotamus's eyes were filled with the same wisdom and uncertainty that Silvia often felt within herself.

"Am I truly capable of guiding them?" Silvia asked herself, the weight of responsibility heavy on her shoulders.

The shadow hippopotamus did not respond, but Silvia knew the answer lay within. She took a deep breath, letting the memories of their journey and the bonds they had formed fill her with strength.

"I may not have all the answers, but I will not let fear rule me," Silvia declared. "Together, we are strong."

The shadow hippopotamus flickered and vanished, leaving Silvia standing resolute and confident.

As each animal confronted and overcame their personal shadows, the darkness in the chamber began to recede. The oppressive weight lifted, replaced by a renewed sense of purpose and camaraderie. They had faced their inner demons and emerged stronger for it.

Silvia the Majestic looked around at her friends, seeing the determination and strength in their eyes. "We have conquered our fears and proven our resilience. Now, let's continue our journey and uncover the secrets of the Shadowed Sanctuary."

With their spirits rejuvenated and their bonds strengthened, Silvia and her friends pressed on, ready to face whatever challenges lay ahead. The shadows of the sanctuary no longer held the same power over them, and they moved forward with a renewed sense of hope and determination.

With courage and determination, Silvia the Majestic and her friends emerged from the shadows of the sanctuary. The oppressive atmosphere began to dissipate, replaced by a gentle glow that grew stronger with each step they took. They had faced their inner demons and emerged victorious, their spirits strengthened by the ordeal they had faced.

As they stepped out of the chamber and into the light, a sense of relief washed over them. The weight that had pressed down upon their shoulders lifted, replaced by a newfound sense of freedom and clarity. They had confronted the darkness within themselves and emerged stronger for it, their bonds of friendship forged in the fires of adversity.

"We did it," exclaimed Lili the Melodic Butterfly, her voice filled with pride. "We faced our fears and emerged victorious."

Manny, known as the lion, nodded in agreement. "Indeed, we have proven our resilience and strength. There is nothing we cannot overcome when we stand together."

Silvia the Majestic smiled, her heart filled with gratitude for her friends. "Thank you all for your courage and determination. Together, we are unstoppable."

With renewed spirits and a sense of purpose, they continued their journey, ready to face whatever challenges lay ahead. The shadows of the sanctuary no longer held sway over them, for they had emerged into the light stronger and more determined than ever before.

As they ventured forth into the unknown, their hearts filled with hope and anticipation. Whatever trials may come, they knew they would face them together, united in their quest for truth and enlightenment. And as they journeyed onwards, the light of friendship and camaraderie illuminated their path, guiding them towards their ultimate destiny.

As they stepped into the Eternal Garden, a collective gasp escaped the lips of Silvia the Majestic, Lili the

Melodic Butterfly, and Manny, known as the lion. The sight before them was beyond compare - a kaleidoscope of colors greeted their eyes as flowers of every shape and hue stretched out as far as the eye could see.

Lili's wings fluttered with excitement as she took in the breathtaking sight. "I've never seen anything like this! It's like a dream!"

Manny's eyes widened in wonder as he surveyed the endless expanse of blooms. "Truly, this place is a marvel. It's as if time itself has stopped here."

Silvia nodded in agreement, her heart filled with awe at the beauty that surrounded them. "Indeed, the Eternal Garden lives up to its name. It's a realm of perpetual beauty and tranquility."

As they ventured further into the garden, they were greeted by the sweet scent of blossoms and the gentle hum of bees. Each step revealed new wonders - towering sunflowers reaching towards the sky, delicate orchids hidden amongst the foliage, and vibrant roses that seemed to glow with an inner light.

For a moment, they forgot the trials and tribulations of their journey, lost in the wonder of the Eternal Garden. Here, amidst the beauty of nature, they found a sense of peace and serenity that washed away the weariness of their travels.

"This place is like a sanctuary," remarked Lili, her voice soft with reverence.

Manny nodded, his gaze lingering on a particularly stunning display of irises. "Indeed, it feels as though we've stumbled upon a hidden paradise."

Silvia smiled, her heart filled with gratitude for the chance to experience such beauty. "Let us take a moment to appreciate this gift and draw strength from its tranquility. We have faced Manny challenges on our journey, but here in the Eternal Garden, we can find solace and renewal."

And so, surrounded by the timeless beauty of the Eternal Garden, they paused to revel in the splendor of nature. In this realm of eternal beauty, they found respite from the trials of their quest, drawing strength from the boundless wonders that surrounded them.

Lili the Melodic Butterfly's eyes sparkled with wonder as she flitted from flower to flower, marveling at the garden's magical flora. "Can you believe it? Each of these flowers possesses properties of immortality and eternal youth!"

Manny, known as the lion, nodded in agreement, his curiosity piqued by the mystical properties of the blooms. "Indeed, it's fascinating. Imagine the possibilities if we could harness such power."

Silvia the Majestic approached a cluster of lilies, their petals shimmering with an otherworldly glow. "The legends were true. The Eternal Garden holds wonders beyond our wildest dreams."

Together, they explored the garden, each flower revealing new secrets and mysteries. Amidst the blooms of immortality, they found hope and wonder, their spirits buoyed by the possibility of everlasting beauty and life.

As they ventured deeper into the Eternal Garden, they encountered guardians who stood watch over the garden's secrets. These ethereal beings, with eyes that gleamed with ancient wisdom, tested the group's resolve and determination to prove their worthiness.

Lili's wings fluttered nervously as the guardians approached, their presence imposing yet serene. "Who are you?" she asked, her voice trembling slightly.

Manny stood tall, his gaze meeting the guardians' with unwavering determination. "We seek knowledge and enlightenment. We mean no harm to this sacred place."

Silvia, her heart steady, addressed the guardians with reverence. "We humbly ask for your guidance and wisdom, noble guardians. We are but travelers on a quest for truth."

The guardians regarded them silently, their eyes searching the depths of their souls for sincerity and purpose. After a moment that seemed to stretch into eternity, the guardians nodded in acknowledgment.

"You have shown courage and humility," one of the guardians spoke, their voice echoing like distant chimes. "But to prove yourselves worthy of the garden's secrets, you must first pass our trials."

With that, the guardians vanished, leaving behind a series of challenges that tested the group's resolve and determination. They faced each trial with courage and perseverance, their bonds of friendship and unity strengthening with every obstacle overcome.

In the end, they emerged victorious, their spirits lifted by the knowledge that they had proven themselves worthy of the garden's mysteries. As they continued their journey, guided by the wisdom of the guardians, they knew that they were one step closer to unlocking the secrets that lay hidden within the Eternal Garden.

They worked tirelessly to overcome the challenges presented by the guardians of the Eternal Garden. With each trial they faced, their bond grew stronger, their determination unwavering in the face of adversity.

As they emerged victorious, the garden seemed to sigh with relief, its vibrant blooms shimmering with newfound vitality. The air hummed with a sense of peace and tranquility, and the guardians returned, their eyes softening with approval.

"You have proven yourselves worthy," one of the guardians spoke, their voice gentle like a summer breeze. "Through your actions, you have restored harmony to the Eternal Garden, ensuring its beauty remains preserved for generations to come."

Silvia bowed her head in gratitude, her heart filled with a sense of fulfillment. "It has been an honor to serve this sacred place. We will cherish the memories of our time here forever."

Lili smiled, her wings fluttering with joy. "May the Eternal Garden continue to thrive, a testament to the beauty of nature and the power of friendship."

Manny nodded in agreement, his gaze sweeping over the garden with reverence. "Let us carry the lessons we have learned here with us on our journey, knowing that we have made a difference in the world."

And so, with harmony restored and their spirits uplifted, they bid farewell to the Eternal Garden, their hearts light with the knowledge that they had played a part in preserving its timeless beauty for all eternity.

Frank bounded ahead, his agile movements leading the way as the group ascended to the Phoenix's Roost. The path was treacherous, winding its way up the mountainside amidst swirling clouds and billowing smoke.

With each leap and bound, Frank's heart raced with excitement. The prospect of encountering the mythical phoenix filled him with a sense of exhilaration and anticipation. He knew that this journey would test not only his physical prowess but also his cunning and wit.

As they climbed higher, the air grew thick with the scent of smoke, and the distant crackle of flames echoed through the mist. Frank pressed on, his determination unwavering despite the challenges that lay ahead.

At last, they reached the summit, and before them stood the Phoenix's Roost - a towering perch surrounded by swirling flames and billowing ash. Frank's eyes widened with wonder as he beheld the majestic sight before him.

"This is it," he exclaimed, his voice filled with awe. "The Phoenix's Roost."

With a sense of purpose burning in his heart, Frank prepared to face whatever trials awaited him on this sacred ground. He knew that the journey ahead would be perilous, but he was ready to confront the challenges head-on, guided by his quick wit and unwavering determination.

As Frank the Agile Trickster and his friends approached the Phoenix's Roost, they were enveloped by a haunting melody that seemed to echo through the very air itself. The song of the phoenix filled their hearts with a sense of awe and wonder, its power resonating deep within their souls.

Frank's ears twitched as he listened to the ethereal music, his heart stirred by its haunting beauty. He knew that the phoenix's song held secrets beyond imagining, and he felt a surge of anticipation as he prepared to delve deeper into its mysteries.

Lili's wings fluttered in time with the melody, her spirit lifted by the otherworldly tune. "It's so beautiful," she whispered, her voice barely audible over the melodic strains.

Manny, nodded in agreement, his eyes shining with reverence. "Indeed, it is a song of power and majesty. We are truly in the presence of greatness."

With each note that filled the air, the group felt a connection to something greater than themselves. The phoenix's song seemed to speak to their very souls, stirring emotions long dormant and awakening a sense of purpose deep within their hearts.

Frank closed his eyes, letting the melody wash over him, its notes weaving a tapestry of wonder and magic. In that moment, he felt a kinship with the mythical bird whose song echoed through the ages, knowing that their destinies were intertwined in ways he could scarcely comprehend.

As they stood on the threshold of the Phoenix's Roost, Frank and his friends were filled with a sense of anticipation for the journey that lay ahead. Guided by the haunting melody of the phoenix's song, they prepared to venture deeper into the heart of the roost, ready to unlock its secrets and discover the truth that lay hidden within.

With hearts ablaze and spirits ignited by the haunting melody of the Phoenix's song, Frank the Agile Trickster and his friends stood at the precipice of destiny. As the melody reached its crescendo, a fiery phoenix emerged from the flames, its majestic form towering above them.

Without hesitation, Frank spread his wings, feeling the heat of the flames lick at his feathers as he prepared to take flight. Beside him, Lili and Manny followed, their determination shining in their eyes as they embraced their newfound purpose and destiny.

With a mighty cry, the phoenix took to the skies, its radiant plumage illuminating the darkness with a brilliant glow. Frank and his friends followed close behind, their hearts filled with awe and wonder as they soared towards the horizon, propelled by the power of the phoenix's wings.

As they flew, a sense of liberation washed over them, their worries and fears falling away with each beat of their wings. They were no longer bound by the constraints of the earth, but free to roam the skies as guardians of the eternal flame.

Together, they journeyed onwards, guided by the wisdom of the phoenix and the strength of their unbreakable bond. With wings outstretched and spirits soaring, they embraced the limitless possibilities that lay before them, ready to face whatever challenges the future may hold.

As they disappeared into the distance, their silhouettes against the setting sun, Frank and his friends knew that their flight marked the beginning of a new chapter in their journey. With the phoenix as their guide, they would chart a course towards redemption and enlightenment, their hearts filled with hope and determination as they embraced the boundless expanse of the skies.

As they ventured into the dense fog of the Mystic Marshlands, Frank the Agile Trickster and his friends found themselves enveloped in an eerie silence. The mist clung to their fur and feathers, obscuring their vision and casting strange shadows upon the murky waters below.

Frank's keen eyes scanned the surroundings, alert for any sign of danger lurking in the shadows. The marshlands were a labyrinth of twisting pathways and tangled vegetation, and he knew that they would need to tread carefully if they were to navigate their way through the mist.

Lili's wings quivered with unease as she surveyed their surroundings. "I don't like the feel of this place," she murmured, her voice barely audible over the muffled sounds of the marsh.

Manny, nodded in agreement, his senses on high alert for any sign of movement in the fog. "We must proceed with caution. The Mystic Marshlands are known for harboring mysterious creatures and hidden dangers."

With each step they took, the mist seemed to grow thicker, obscuring their surroundings and disorienting their senses. Strange noises echoed through the marsh, the calls of unseen creatures sending shivers down their spines.

Despite the oppressive atmosphere, the group pressed on, their determination unwavering in the face of adversity. They knew that they were walking into the unknown, but they also knew that they were not alone - together, they would brave the perils of the Mystic Marshlands and emerge victorious on the other side.

Liliy shivered as eerie whispers echoed through the mist, sending a chill down her spine. "Did you hear that?" she asked, her voice trembling.

Frank's ears twitched as he strained to listen, his senses on high alert. "It sounds like voices in the mist. But who— or what— are they?"

Manny, frowned, his brow furrowing with concern. "I fear we're not alone in these marshlands. We must stay vigilant."

The whispers grew louder, their words indistinct yet filled with an ominous undertone. Silvia the Majestic, usually composed, glanced nervously around them. "I don't like this. It feels as though the marsh itself is alive and watching us."

Frank nodded in agreement, his gaze darting from shadow to shadow. "We need to keep moving, but stay close together. We won't let whatever's out there catch us off guard."

With apprehension gnawing at their hearts, the group pressed onward, their steps quickening as they sought to escape the unsettling whispers that haunted the mist-shrouded marshlands.

Lili's wings trembled as they navigated through the treacherous swamps, the murky waters threatening to ensnare them at every turn. "This is more difficult than I imagined," she exclaimed, her voice tinged with worry.

Frank's keen eyes scanned their surroundings, searching for a safe path through the tangled vegetation and hidden pitfalls. "Stay close, everyone," he called out, his voice firm with determination. "We'll find our way through this quagmire together."

Manny nodded, his senses on high alert for any sign of danger lurking beneath the murky waters. "Watch your step," he warned, his voice echoing through the mist. "The marsh is full of hidden traps and obstacles."

Silvia's powerful legs propelled her forward, her movements steady despite the uneven terrain. "We must keep moving," she urged, her eyes fixed on the path ahead. "The longer we linger, the greater the danger."

With each step, they forged ahead, their hearts filled with determination to overcome whatever obstacles the marshlands threw their way. Together, they braved the treacherous swamps, their bond of friendship guiding them through the darkest of times.

As they forged onward through the mist-shrouded marshlands, Lili, Frank, Manny, and Silvia encountered one obstacle after another, each more daunting than the last. Yet, with determination and perseverance, they pressed forward, refusing to be deterred by the dangers that lurked in the shadows.

Frank, ever the agile trickster, leaped across treacherous patches of sinking mud, his movements fluid and precise. "Stay close, everyone," he called out, his voice a beacon of reassurance in the darkness. "We're almost through."

Lili's wings beat steadily as she soared above the murky waters, her keen eyes scanning the horizon for signs of danger. "We can do this," she encouraged, her voice unwavering despite the uncertainty that hung in the air.

Manny, known for his sage wisdom, guided them with steady resolve, his instincts honed by years of experience. "Keep your wits about you," he cautioned, his words a reminder to stay vigilant in the face of adversity.

Silvia, with her majestic strength, led the way through tangled thickets and treacherous bogs, her determination unyielding in the face of the marsh's grasp. "We will emerge from this stronger than before," she declared, her voice a beacon of hope amidst the darkness.

And emerge they did, their spirits undaunted by the challenges they had faced. With each obstacle overcome, their bond grew stronger, their resolve unshakeable in the face of adversity. As they stepped out of the mystic marshlands unscathed, they knew that together, there was no challenge they could not overcome.

As they approached the crumbling walls of the Forgotten Fortress, Lili the Melodic Butterfly took the lead, her wings fluttering with a sense of purpose. The fortress loomed before them, its weathered stones bearing the scars of ancient battles long forgotten.

Lili's eyes swept over the ruins, her gaze lingering on the faded banners and broken battlements. "This place holds untold secrets," she murmured, her voice tinged with reverence for the history that lay hidden within its walls.

Frank, Manny, and Silvia followed close behind, their footsteps echoing through the silent courtyard. "It's a somber sight," Frank observed, his eyes scanning the dilapidated structures with a mixture of curiosity and caution.

Manny nodded in agreement, his keen intellect already at work as he assessed the fortress's defenses. "We must tread carefully," he cautioned, his voice a solemn reminder of the dangers that lurked within.

Silvia's powerful presence filled the air, her majestic form a symbol of strength and resilience. "Let us proceed with caution," she declared, her voice steady despite the weight of the fortress's history pressing down upon them.

With Lili leading the way, they ventured deeper into the heart of the Forgotten Fortress, their hearts filled with anticipation for the secrets that awaited them within its ancient halls.

As Lili and her friends delved deeper into the heart of the Forgotten Fortress, they were met with a haunting cacophony of echoes - the residual whispers of past conflicts that still lingered within its walls. The air was heavy with the weight of history, pressing down upon them like a suffocating blanket.

Lili's wings trembled as she listened to the echoes of war reverberating through the fortress, her heart heavy with the knowledge of the suffering that had taken place within its walls. "The echoes of the past are strong here," she whispered, her voice barely audible over the din. Frank's ears twitched as he strained to discern the faint sounds of battle echoing through the corridors. "It's as if the fortress itself is haunted by the memories of those who once fought and died here," he remarked, his voice tinged with solemnity.

Manny's brow furrowed in thought as he contemplated the significance of the echoes. "We must be cautious," he warned, his eyes scanning their surroundings for any sign of danger. "The past may be long gone, but its echoes still hold power."

Silvia's gaze swept over the crumbling walls, her heart heavy with the weight of the fortress's history. "Let us proceed with reverence," she suggested, her voice a solemn reminder of the need to respect the sacrifices made by those who came before them.

With each step they took, the echoes of war grew louder, their voices a haunting reminder of the fortress's turbulent past. Yet, despite the darkness that surrounded them, Lili and her friends pressed on, their spirits unbroken by the echoes of history that reverberated through the Forgotten Fortress.

As they explored the depths of the Forgotten Fortress, they stumbled upon relics of a bygone era - faded tapestries and weathered manuscripts that spoke of valor and heroism from the fortress's glory days. These tales of bravery and sacrifice stirred something deep within them, inspiring them to continue their own quest with renewed resolve.

Lili's eyes sparkled with wonder as she gazed upon the ancient tapestries, each thread woven with stories of knights and warriors who had once called the fortress home. "These tales remind us that even in the darkest of times, there is still light to be found," she mused, her voice filled with determination.

Frank's agile mind absorbed the stories with keen interest, his admiration for the heroes of old evident in his expression. "Their courage serves as a beacon for us," he remarked, his tone thoughtful. "If they could overcome such adversity, then surely we can do the same."

Manny nodded in agreement, his eyes alight with the fire of inspiration. "We must honor their legacy by continuing our own journey with courage and conviction," he declared, his voice ringing out with determination.

Silvia's powerful presence seemed to swell with pride as she listened to the tales of valor and heroism, her own resolve strengthened by the example set by those who had come before them. "Let us carry their spirit with us as we press onward," she proclaimed, her voice echoing through the fortress's halls.

With newfound determination burning in their hearts, they resolved to continue their quest, guided by the tales of valor that had inspired them within the walls of the Forgotten Fortress. As they prepared to face whatever challenges lay ahead, they knew that the heroes of old would be watching over them, their legacy living on through the courage of those who dared to follow in their footsteps.

With hearts heavy with the weight of history, they gazed upon the dilapidated walls of the Forgotten Fortress. Yet, amidst the ruins, they saw not just decay, but the potential for renewal. Determined to honor the fortress's fallen defenders, they embarked on the arduous task of restoring it to its former glory.

Lili's eyes shimmered with determination as she surveyed the crumbling battlements. "We cannot let the sacrifices of those who came before us be in vain," she declared, her voice echoing through the silent courtyard.

Frank nodded in agreement, his agile mind already formulating plans for reconstruction. "It won't be easy, but with teamwork, anything is possible," he remarked, his gaze unwavering despite the enormity of the task ahead.

Manny's keen intellect was put to work as he assessed the structural integrity of the fortress. "We'll need supplies and manpower," he observed, his mind already calculating the logistics of the restoration effort.

Silvia's powerful presence filled the air as she surveyed the ruins, her determination unwavering in the face of adversity. "Together, we will reclaim the fortress's legacy and honor its fallen defenders," she proclaimed, her voice resonating with strength and conviction.

With their resolve steeled, they set to work, their hands and hearts united in a common purpose. They repaired crumbling walls, cleared overgrown vegetation, and polished tarnished armor, breathing new life into the ancient fortress with each passing day.

As the days turned into weeks, the Forgotten Fortress began to transform before their eyes, its once-dreary halls now filled with the sounds of hammering and laughter. Through their tireless efforts, they restored the fortress to its former glory, ensuring that its legacy would endure for generations to come. And as they stood amidst the newly-restored battlements, they knew that their bond of friendship had grown even stronger, forged in the fires of adversity and tempered by the shared determination to honor the heroes of the past.

Frank and Lili stood at the entrance of the Crystal Labyrinth, their eyes wide with awe as they took in the breathtaking sight before them. The maze was a dazzling spectacle, with shimmering crystals reflecting and refracting light in an array of colors that danced across the walls and floor.

Frank's agile mind was immediately at work, analyzing the intricate patterns of light. "This place is incredible," he murmured, his voice tinged with excitement. "But it's also a challenge. We need to be careful not to get lost in here."

As Frank and Lili continued their journey through the Crystal Labyrinth, they found themselves surrounded by an ever-changing kaleidoscope of colors and light. The shimmering crystals not only refracted light but also began to show images— reflections of themselves, more vivid and intense than any mirror could produce.

Frank paused in front of a particularly large crystal, his reflection staring back at him with startling clarity. "It's... me," he whispered, his voice filled with a mix of curiosity and apprehension.

Lili approached another crystal nearby, her own reflection gazing back at her with equal intensity. "These aren't just reflections," she said softly. "They're showing us our true selves."

Frank nodded, his agile mind racing to understand the significance of the images. "We have to confront whatever these reflections reveal," he said, his voice steady. "It's the only way to move forward."

As they stood before their reflections, the crystals began to shift and change, showing them scenes from their pasts, their dreams, and their deepest fears.

Frank saw himself as a young, inexperienced trickster, struggling to prove his worth. He watched as he made mistakes, faced ridicule, and doubted his abilities. But he also saw his determination, his relentless pursuit of excellence, and the moments of triumph that defined his journey.

"I've always feared not being good enough," Frank admitted, his voice barely above a whisper. "But I see now that every failure was a step towards becoming who I am today."

Lili's reflection showed her as a timid, quiet butterfly, afraid to use her voice and talents. She saw the times she held back, fearing judgment, and the moments she let her insecurities control her. But she also saw the times she chose to be brave, to sing and inspire others, and the joy that came from embracing her true self.

"I've always feared being judged," Lili said, her voice strong despite the emotions swirling within her. "But I see now that my voice has power, and it's okay to be heard."

They stood together, facing their reflections, and felt a profound sense of acceptance and understanding. The labyrinth had forced them to confront their innermost desires and fears, but in doing so, it had also shown them their strengths and the beauty of their true selves.

With renewed determination, Frank and Lili turned away from their reflections, ready to continue their journey. The Crystal Labyrinth had tested them, but it had also strengthened their bond and their resolve.

"Let's keep moving," Frank said, his voice filled with newfound confidence. "We have a path to follow, and a destiny to fulfill."

Lili nodded, her melodic voice filled with resolve. "Together, we can face anything," she said. "Let's see where the light leads us next."

With their spirits buoyed by the revelations they had faced, Frank and Lili ventured deeper into the Crystal Labyrinth, ready to embrace whatever challenges lay ahead.

Lili nodded, her melodic voice filled with determination. "We have to stay focused and work together," she said, her eyes scanning the maze for any clues that might help them navigate its twists and turns. "These crystals might be beautiful, but they can also be deceiving."

As they ventured deeper into the labyrinth, the light grew more intense, creating a kaleidoscope of colors that made it difficult to see clearly. Frank and Lili moved cautiously, their senses heightened as they relied on each other to find their way through the maze.

"Look at this," Frank said, pointing to a cluster of crystals that seemed to glow with a different light. "I think these might be a guide. If we follow the pattern, it might lead us to the center."

Lili studied the crystals, her keen eyes picking up on the subtle differences in the light. "You're right," she agreed, her voice filled with confidence. "Let's follow the path and see where it takes us."

Together, they navigated the labyrinth, their bond of friendship and trust guiding them through the dazzling maze of light. As they followed the trail of glowing crystals, they felt a sense of unity and purpose, knowing that they could overcome any challenge as long as their hearts disires to do so.

With each step they took, the colors grew more vibrant, illuminating their path and filling them with a renewed sense of wonder and determination. The Crystal Labyrinth was a test of their resolve, but Frank and Lili were ready to face it head-on, their spirits shining as brightly as the crystals that surrounded them.

As they ventured deeper into the Crystal Labyrinth, the dazzling reflections began to shift and warp, forming visions that encircled them. The air grew thick with an ethereal mist, and the labyrinth's walls of shimmering crystal seemed to pulse with a life of their own.

Lili's steps faltered as the crystals around her started to glow brighter, projecting scenes that felt both familiar and disorienting. "Frank, something's wrong," she said, her voice echoing strangely in the confined space.

Frank turned to respond, but his words were lost as he too became surrounded by swirling images. They both stood transfixed, unable to distinguish reality from illusion. The labyrinth had ensnared them in a world of its own making.

Lili saw herself in her childhood home, a place of warmth and safety. She was a young butterfly again, fluttering among the flowers in the garden, her wings vibrant and new. She heard her parents' voices calling out to her, and for a moment, she felt a deep, aching longing to stay in this serene vision forever.

"Lili, come play with us," the familiar voices beckoned. She turned, seeing the comforting faces of her family, and felt tears welling up in her eyes. "Is this real?" she wondered aloud, reaching out towards the vision.

Meanwhile, Frank found himself standing in the middle of a bustling city, a place of endless opportunities and challenges. He saw his future self, a master trickster, renowned and respected by all. Crowds cheered his name, and he felt the rush of adrenaline as he performed daring feats. The vision was intoxicating, filling him with a sense of pride and fulfillment.

"Is this what I'm destined to become?" Frank asked, mesmerized by the grandeur of the scene. "Is this my future?"

The illusions grew more intense, their pull stronger. Lili and Frank were each trapped in their own world of visions, struggling to break free. The line between reality and fantasy blurred, and they felt themselves slipping further into the depths of the labyrinth's enchantment.

"Lili!" Frank's voice finally broke through the haze, echoing distantly. "We have to snap out of it!"

Lili heard Frank's call, her heart pounding as she tried to focus on his voice. "Frank, where are you?" she shouted, her eyes scanning the shifting scenes for any sign of him.

"Lili, this isn't real!" Frank's voice came closer, filled with urgency. "We have to break free!"

Summoning all her willpower, Lili tore her gaze away from the vision of her family and focused on the shimmering crystals around her. She remembered the reflections of their true selves, the strength they had discovered together. With a determined shake of her head, she shattered the illusion, the images dissipating like mist in the wind.

Frank did the same, breaking free from the vision of his future and reorienting himself to the reality of the labyrinth. "Lili, are you okay?" he asked, rushing to her side.

"I'm fine," Lili replied, breathing heavily. "That was... intense. We can't let these illusions trap us."

"Agreed," Frank said, his voice firm. "We have to stay focused and keep moving. The labyrinth is testing us, but we won't let it win."

Together, they pressed on, their determination renewed. The Crystal Labyrinth had tried to ensnare them in illusions, but Frank and Lili's bond and resolve had seen them through. With

each step, they grew more resilient, ready to face whatever challenges the labyrinth might throw their way next.

With the illusions shattered and their minds clear, Frank and Lili pressed forward through the Crystal Labyrinth, determined to find their way out. The shimmering walls still dazzled with refracted light, but the two friends moved with purpose, their steps sure and confident.

"Lili, do you see that?" Frank pointed ahead, where a faint glow seemed to emanate from deeper within the labyrinth.

"I see it," Lili replied, her eyes narrowing with focus. "Let's head that way. It might be the exit." They navigated through the twisting corridors, their reflections constantly shifting and changing with the crystals' light. Despite the disorienting environment, they relied on each other to stay grounded and oriented.

"Remember what we've learned," Lili said, her voice steady. "The labyrinth feeds on our fears and desires. We have to stay true to ourselves."

Frank nodded, glancing at the intricate patterns etched into the crystalline walls. "And we have to trust each other. We'll find the way out together."

As they moved deeper into the labyrinth, the glow grew brighter, casting long shadows against the crystal surfaces. The path seemed to narrow, funneling them towards a single point of light. They walked in silence, their breaths synchronized, their resolve unwavering.

Finally, they reached a large, open chamber where the light source became apparent. At the center stood a massive crystal, its surface smooth and polished, radiating a serene, otherworldly glow. The light it emitted was warm and inviting, dispelling the shadows that had plagued their journey.

"This must be it," Frank said, awe in his voice. "The heart of the labyrinth."

Lili stepped forward, placing her hand on the crystal's surface. "I think this is our way out," she said softly. "The labyrinth wanted to test us, and we've proven ourselves."

The crystal pulsed gently under her touch, and a pathway began to form, the walls parting to reveal a clear exit. Frank and Lili exchanged a look of relief and triumph.

"We did it," Lili said, a smile breaking across her face. "We found our way."

Together, they stepped onto the path, following it towards the exit. As they walked, they felt a sense of accomplishment and enlightenment wash over them. The challenges they had faced within the labyrinth had not only tested their resolve but also deepened their understanding of themselves and each other.

Emerging from the depths of the labyrinth, Frank and Lili were greeted by the sight of their friends waiting for them, concern etched on their faces. The sunlight outside was bright and welcoming, a stark contrast to the labyrinth's dim interior.

"Frank! Lili!" Manny called out, rushing to meet them. "Are you both alright?"

"We're fine," Lili assured him, her smile unwavering. "We made it through, and we've learned so much."

Silvia nodded, her eyes filled with pride. "I knew you two could do it."

As they stood together, the group felt a renewed sense of unity and purpose. The Crystal Labyrinth had been a formidable challenge, but they had emerged from it stronger and more resolved than ever. With newfound wisdom and an unbreakable bond, they were ready to face whatever lay ahead in their journey.

The air grew tense as the group ventured deeper into the ancient forest, their path suddenly blocked by a towering figure. The guardian, a majestic and imposing creature with an aura of ancient power, stood resolute in their way. Its eyes, glowing with an otherworldly light, assessed them with an intensity that sent shivers down their spines.

"This must be the Guardian's Gauntlet," Silvia murmured, her voice filled with awe and apprehension.

The guardian's voice resonated like the rumble of distant thunder, filling the clearing. "To proceed, you must prove your worth. Show me the strength of your hearts and the purity of your intentions."

Frank stepped forward, his posture confident. "We seek to continue our quest for the greater good. We've faced Manny trials and emerged stronger each time. We're ready for whatever challenge you set before us."

The guardian nodded solemnly. "Very well. To prove your worth, you must each face a trial of spirit and courage. Only then will you be deemed worthy to continue."

Silvia, Manny, Lili, and Frank exchanged determined glances, their resolve unwavering.

"I'll go first," Silvia said, stepping up. "I'm ready."

The guardian raised one massive hand, and a beam of light enveloped Silvia, transporting her to a secluded part of the forest where her trial would begin.

Silvia's Trial

Silvia found herself in a tranquil glade, the air filled with the sweet scent of blooming flowers. At first, it seemed peaceful, but soon the atmosphere changed. Shadows began to gather, and she felt a growing sense of unease.

"Face your deepest fear," the guardian's voice echoed around her.

Suddenly, she was surrounded by images of her friends in peril, their cries for help piercing the air. Her heart raced, and she felt a surge of panic. But then, she remembered their journey, their bond, and their trust in each other.

"This is an illusion," she said firmly. "We stand together, always."

With that declaration, the shadows dissipated, and the glade returned to its serene state. Silvia felt a sense of calm wash over her as the light transported her back to the clearing.

Manny's Trial

Next, Manny stepped forward. He was transported to a vast desert, the sun beating down mercilessly. The endless expanse of sand seemed daunting, and he felt a wave of hopelessness.

"Find your way through the desert," the guardian's voice instructed.

Manny took a deep breath, recalling the wisdom he'd gained over their journey. "I must trust in myself and my instincts," he said.

He began walking, using the position of the sun and the wind's direction to guide him. As he focused on the journey rather than the destination, he found his way through the desert, feeling more confident with each step.

Returning to the clearing, Manny's resolve was stronger than ever. Lili's Trial

Lili's turn came next. She was transported to a dark cave, the only light coming from faintly glowing crystals embedded in the walls. The oppressive silence was broken only by the sound of her own footsteps.

"Uncover the truth within," the guardian's voice challenged.

Lili's heart pounded, but she remembered her melodic voice's power. She began to sing, her voice resonating through the cave. The crystals glowed brighter, illuminating hidden paths and revealing the cave's beauty.

Her song led her to a hidden chamber where a radiant crystal pulsed with light. Touching it, she felt a rush of understanding and insight. The cave dissolved around her, and she returned to the clearing with newfound clarity.

Frank's Trial

Finally, Frank stepped forward. He was whisked away to a forest, its trees towering and dense. The path was obscured, and he felt the weight of the unknown pressing down on him.

"Trust in your agility and wit," the guardian's voice urged.

Frank navigated the forest, using his agility to leap over obstacles and his wit to solve the puzzles nature presented. Each step forward built his confidence, and soon he emerged from the dense forest, his spirit unbroken.

Back in the clearing, the guardian regarded them with a newfound respect. "You have faced your trials with courage and integrity. You are worthy to continue your quest."

The path ahead cleared, and the group felt a renewed sense of purpose. Together, they had proven their worth, ready to face whatever lay ahead in their extraordinary journey.

Frank, breathing heavily, grinned. "We did it. Together."

Silvia nodded, her eyes shining with pride. "We can face anything as long as we stand together."

Manny and Lili exchanged smiles, their bond strengthened by the ordeal. Emerging Victorious.

The path ahead cleared, revealing the continuation of their journey. The guardian stepped aside, granting them passage.

"You have earned the right to continue your quest. Go forth with my blessing," the guardian declared.

As they moved forward, the group felt a renewed sense of purpose and strength. They had proven their worth and were ready to face whatever lay ahead in their extraordinary journey. With unwavering determination, they marched on, united by their trials and the unbreakable bonds of friendship.

Manny led the group cautiously into the Veiled Sanctuary, a realm shrouded in mist and mystery. The air was thick with a sense of secrecy, and an almost palpable silence enveloped them as they moved forward.

"This place feels... different," Lili whispered, her wings fluttering softly as she hovered beside Manny.

"Yeah, it's like the air itself is holding its breath," Frank added, his agile form tense with anticipation.

Silvia, her large frame moving with surprising grace, nodded. "We need to stay alert. There are hidden truths here, waiting to be uncovered."

Manny, known for his wisdom and calm demeanor, took a deep breath, his eyes scanning the surroundings. "Let's proceed carefully. We need to be open to whatever this place is trying to tell us."

As they ventured deeper into the sanctuary, the mist seemed to part before them, revealing glimpses of ancient structures and shadowy figures that moved just out of sight.

"Do you think we're being watched?" Frank asked, his eyes darting around nervously.

"I don't just think it, I feel it," Lili replied, her voice a hushed whisper. "But we can't let that stop us. We need to find the hidden truths this place holds."

Silvia, always the source of strength for the group, gave a reassuring nod. "Together, we can face whatever lies ahead. Let's keep moving."

With Manny leading the way, the group pressed on, their senses heightened and their resolve unwavering. The Veiled Sanctuary held Manny secrets, but they were determined to uncover them all.

As Manny and his friends ventured deeper into the Veiled Sanctuary, the air grew heavier with an almost tangible sense of history. Faint whispers began to echo through the mist, the voices of ancient guardians who once protected this sacred place.

"Do you hear that?" Frank asked, his ears twitching as he strained to catch the elusive sounds.

Lili fluttered closer to Manny. "It sounds like whispers, but I can't make out the words."

Silvia's large ears perked up, her eyes narrowing in concentration. "They're voices from the past. Guardians who once watched over this sanctuary."

Manny nodded, his wise eyes scanning the mist. "The ancients are trying to communicate with us. We need to listen carefully."

The whispers grew more distinct, though still enigmatic, as if the guardians were speaking in a forgotten language. The group paused, standing still in the midst of the swirling mist, trying to discern the messages being conveyed.

"Maybe they're trying to tell us something important," Lili suggested, her wings gently beating the air. "Something about the sanctuary or our journey."

Frank, ever the cautious one, looked around warily. "Or they could be warning us about dangers ahead."

Silvia took a deep breath, her voice steady. "Whatever it is, we need to pay attention. These whispers carry the weight of ages."

Manny closed his eyes, focusing intently on the whispers. "I think they're guiding us, showing us the way forward. We just have to trust in their wisdom."

With renewed determination, the group continued their journey through the Veiled Sanctuary, guided by the whispers of the ancient guardians. The presence of those who had come before filled them with a sense of purpose and reverence, their spirits bolstered by the connection to the past.

Together, they moved forward, ready to uncover the hidden truths and face whatever challenges lay ahead.

Navigating through the sanctuary's labyrinthine corridors, Manny and his friends felt the weight of secrecy that shrouded its innermost chambers. The whispers of the ancients grew fainter, leaving them to rely on their own instincts to find their way.

Frank led the way, his keen eyes scanning for any sign of danger. "These corridors all look the same. We need to find some kind of marker or clue to guide us."

Lili fluttered above the group, her delicate wings brushing against the stone walls. "There must be something hidden here, something that will show us the path."

Silvia, ever the steady presence, ran her hand along the ancient carvings etched into the walls. "Look for symbols or patterns. Anything that seems out of place."

Manny, the sage of the group, paused at an intersection, studying the pathways before them. "The ancients built this sanctuary to protect something. We need to think like them. Where would they hide their most precious secrets?"

As they moved deeper into the sanctuary, the corridors became more intricate, the walls adorned with cryptic symbols and faded murals. Each turn seemed to lead them further into a maze of history and mystery.

Lili landed on Manny's shoulder, her voice a whisper. "Do you think the whispers were trying to tell us something about this place? Maybe there's a hidden door or a secret passage."

Manny nodded thoughtfully. "It's possible. We need to pay close attention to the details. The ancients were masters of subtlety."

Frank stopped abruptly, his sharp eyes catching a faint glow emanating from behind a tapestry. "Over here! There's something behind this."

Silvia and Manny joined Frank, carefully pulling back the tapestry to reveal a hidden door, its surface covered in intricate carvings. The door seemed to pulse with a soft light, beckoning them forward.

"This must be it," Silvia said, her voice filled with awe. "The entrance to the innermost chambers."

Manny placed a hand on the door, feeling the ancient magic that resonated from it. "We've come this far. Let's see what secrets the ancients have been protecting."

With a collective breath, they pushed the door open, revealing a passageway that led deeper into the sanctuary. The air was thick with anticipation as they stepped through, ready to unravel the veil of secrecy that had shrouded this place for centuries.

As they ventured further into the passageway, the corridor opened into a grand chamber, illuminated by a soft, ethereal glow. The walls were lined with ancient tomes and relics, each one a testament to the sanctuary's hidden wisdom.

"Look at all this," Frank murmured, his eyes wide with wonder. "It's like a treasure trove of knowledge."

Lili fluttered to a nearby pedestal, her gaze fixed on a beautifully ornate scroll. "This must be what the ancients were protecting. We need to understand its significance."

Manny stepped forward, his heart swelling with pride and reverence. "We've done it. We've unraveled the veil and uncovered the sanctuary's deepest secrets. Now, we must honor this place and the wisdom it holds."

Silvia nodded, her voice filled with determination. "Let's take this knowledge and use it to guide us on our journey. The ancients have shown us the way."

Together, they stood in the heart of the Veiled Sanctuary, their spirits united by the bond they had forged and the secrets they had uncovered. With newfound wisdom and resolve, they prepared to face whatever challenges lay ahead, knowing that the ancients' guidance would light their path.

Manny, Lili, Frank, and Silvia stood at the precipice of the Echoing Abyss, a yawning chasm that seemed to swallow all light and sound. The air was thick with an oppressive darkness, and the echoes of past trials reverberated through the depths, creating an unsettling atmosphere.

Manny gazed into the abyss, his eyes narrowing as he tried to discern what lay below. "This is unlike anything we've encountered before. It feels... ominous."

Lili fluttered nervously, her wings quivering with unease. "I can sense something down there. Something ancient and powerful."

Frank cracked his knuckles, his agility ready to face whatever challenges awaited. "Whatever it is, we'll face it together. No abyss is too deep for us."

Silvia, ever the stalwart leader, nodded in agreement. "Let's proceed with caution keep in mind we have been in the abyss before. We must be prepared for anything."

With a collective breath, they began their descent into the Echoing Abyss. The walls of the chasm were jagged and uneven, casting eerie shadows that danced in the faint light they carried with them. The echoes grew louder with each step, filling the void with a haunting chorus of forgotten voices and distant footsteps.

"Do you hear that?" Lili whispered, her voice barely audible over the echoing din.

Manny nodded, his brow furrowed in concentration. "It's like the abyss is trying to speak to us, to warn us."

Frank scanned their surroundings, his senses heightened. "Stay close, everyone. We don't know what's waiting for us down here."

The descent felt endless, the darkness pressing in on them from all sides. Yet, they pressed on, driven by their determination to unravel the mysteries that lay hidden within the depths of the abyss.

As they descended further, the air grew colder, and the echoes grew more pronounced. Shadows flickered on the walls, their forms twisting and contorting as if alive with unseen energy.

Silvia tightened her grip on her staff, her senses alert for any sign of danger. "Keep your wits about you. We must remain vigilant."

Suddenly, the ground beneath them shifted, causing them to stumble. The abyss seemed to come alive, its darkness swirling around them like a malevolent force.

"This place is alive," Frank muttered, his voice tinged with awe and apprehension. Lili shivered, her wings beating nervously. "I don't like this. It feels... wrong."

Manny glanced around, his mind racing with possibilities. "We can't turn back now. We must find out what awaits us at the bottom."

With renewed resolve, they continued their descent, navigating through the shifting shadows and echoing whispers. Each step brought them closer to the heart of the abyss, where they knew the true challenge awaited.

The echoes grew louder, their voices overlapping and intertwining in a cacophony of sound. Visions flickered at the edges of their perception, fleeting glimpses of faces and landscapes lost to time.

Finally, after what felt like an eternity, they reached the bottom of the Echoing Abyss. The ground was firm beneath their feet, but the air was heavy with anticipation.

"We made it," Silvia murmured, her voice filled with relief and determination.

Frank scanned their surroundings, his eyes narrowing in search of any threat. "Now what?"

Manny took a deep breath, his gaze steady. "Now, we find out what this abyss is hiding. There must be a reason we were led here again."

As they stood together at the bottom of the chasm, they prepared themselves for the challenges that lay ahead, knowing that the true test of their courage and strength was yet to come.

~As Manny, Lili, Frank, and Silvia stood at the bottom of the Echoing Abyss, the darkness seemed to press in on them from all sides. The echoes of past trials still reverberated through the chasm, a haunting reminder of the challenges they had faced and those that lay ahead.

Manny clenched his fists, his brow furrowed in concentration. "There's something unsettling about this place. It's like it's trying to show us something."

Lili nodded, her eyes darting nervously around the abyss. "I feel it too. It's as if the abyss is reflecting our own fears and doubts back at us."

Frank adjusted his stance, his agile frame poised for action. "We've come this far together. Whatever's down here, we face it together."

Silvia tightened her grip on her staff, her eyes scanning the shadows warily. "Let's stay focused. We can't afford to let our fears get the better of us."

As they moved deeper into the abyss, the darkness seemed to take on a life of its own. Shadows danced on the walls, twisting and contorting into grotesque shapes that mirrored the group's inner turmoil.

Manny suddenly stopped, his voice echoing in the silence. "Do you hear that?"

Lili strained to listen, her heart pounding in her chest. "It sounds like… whispers." Frank stepped forward, his senses on high alert. "Whispers of what?"

Silvia closed her eyes, concentrating on the faint sounds echoing through the abyss. "Whispers of our fears, The echoes remind us that because we didn't face our fears when we had the chance, we must confront them again. The abyss is trying to show us our darkest thoughts."

The whispers grew louder, swirling around them like a vortex of doubt and uncertainty. Visions flickered in the corners of their vision, memories and fears laid bare in the shifting shadows.

"I see... my failures," Manny admitted, his voice tinged with regret.

Lili shivered, her wings trembling. "I see... the uncertainty of the future."

Frank clenched his jaw, his fists tightening. "I see... the battles we've yet to face."

Silvia took a deep breath, her voice steady despite the turmoil around them. "These are our inner demons, manifesting in the darkness. But we are stronger than our fears."

With renewed determination, they faced their inner demons head-on, confronting their doubts and insecurities with courage and resolve. Each step forward was a battle against the shadows that threatened to overwhelm them.

"We've faced worse," Manny declared, his voice firm with conviction.

Lili nodded, her eyes shining with determination. "Together, we can overcome anything."

Frank cracked a smile, his confidence returning. "Let's show this abyss what we're made of."

Silvia led the way, her staff glowing faintly with inner strength. "Onward, friends. We have a quest to complete."

With their spirits united and their resolve unshaken, they navigated through the abyss, pushing back against the darkness that sought to consume them. Each moment of doubt was met with a moment of clarity, each fear confronted with unwavering courage.

As they journeyed deeper into the abyss, they began to sense a shift in the air. The whispers faded, replaced by a sense of calm resolve. The darkness seemed to recede, giving way to a faint light that beckoned them forward.

"Look," Lili whispered, her voice filled with wonder.

Ahead of them, a faint glow illuminated a path through the abyss. It was as if the darkness had been waiting for them to confront their fears before revealing the way forward.

Manny glanced back at his friends, a smile spreading across his face. "We did it. We faced the abyss and emerged stronger."

Frank nodded, his gaze following the path ahead. "Let's not waste any more time. We've got a quest to finish."

Silvia placed a reassuring hand on Manny's shoulder, her eyes reflecting pride in their journey. "We've come this far together. There's nothing we can't handle."

With a shared sense of accomplishment and renewed determination, they followed the glowing path, eager to discover what awaited them next in their adventure.

~Emerging from the depths of the Echoing Abyss, Manny, Lili, Frank, and Silvia found themselves bathed in a gentle glow of ethereal light. The oppressive darkness of the abyss began to dissipate, replaced by a serene radiance that lifted their spirits.

Manny looked around, marveling at their surroundings. "It's as if we've stepped into another realm entirely."

Lili's wings fluttered with relief, the tension of the abyss melting away. "I feel... lighter. Whatever darkness we faced down there, it feels like a distant memory now."

Frank stretched his limbs, a grin spreading across his face. "That was one intense descent. But hey, we made it."

Silvia nodded, her gaze sweeping over the landscape before them. "We're not out of the woods yet, though. There's more to this place than meets the eye."

As they moved forward, they noticed the terrain changing around them. Soft grasses underfoot gave way to shimmering pools of crystal-clear water that reflected the light above. Trees with leaves that seemed to shimmer like silver lined their path, their branches reaching skyward in a silent salute to the heavens.

"What is this place?" Lili asked in wonder, her voice filled with awe.

Manny stroked his chin thoughtfully. "It feels... sacred. Like we've stumbled upon a realm untouched by time."

Frank surveyed their surroundings, his eyes keen for any signs of movement. "Let's keep moving. We need to find out why we were drawn here."

They continued onward, guided by an invisible force that seemed to beckon them deeper into the ethereal summit. The air hummed with an otherworldly energy, and a sense of tranquility settled over them like a comforting embrace.

Suddenly, they came upon a clearing where a figure stood bathed in a halo of light. It was a majestic creature with wings that glimmered like opal and eyes that held the wisdom of ages. "Welcome, travelers," the creature's voice echoed softly, yet it resonated deep within their souls.

Silvia stepped forward, her expression a mixture of reverence and curiosity. "Who are you?"

The creature inclined its head gracefully. "I am the Guardian of the Ethereal Summit, keeper of the balance between light and darkness."

Lili approached cautiously, her wings still trembling slightly. "What is this place? Why were we led here?"

The Guardian's gaze softened, a hint of sadness flickering in its eyes. "You have been chosen to restore the harmony that has been disrupted. The Echoing Abyss was but a trial to test your resolve."

Frank folded his arms, his demeanor resolute. "What do you need us to do?"

The Guardian spread its wings, its form glowing brighter. "You must venture forth into the heart of the summit, where the forces of light and darkness converge. There, you will find the key to restoring balance."

Manny nodded, understanding dawning on his face. "We accept this challenge."

With a gentle nod, the Guardian gestured toward a path that led deeper into the summit. "Go forth, brave souls. The fate of this realm rests in your hands."

As they embarked on their new quest, their hearts filled with determination. The ethereal summit held mysteries and challenges yet to be faced, but together, they were ready to confront whatever lay ahead.

Let's reflect on the characters and their roles in the story so far:

1. **Manny (The lion):**

~Manny embodies wisdom and leadership among the group. As the lion, he brings a calm and insightful perspective to their adventures. He often analyzes situations deeply and provides guidance to his friends, drawing from his knowledge and experience.

2. **Lili (The Melodic Butterfly):**

~Lili is characterized by her gentle and intuitive nature. She possesses a keen sense of empathy and often serves as the emotional center of the group. Her melodious voice and delicate wings symbolize her connection to beauty and harmony, which she seeks to preserve in their journey.

3. **Frank (The Agile Trickster):**

~Frank is known for his agility, quick thinking, and mischievous spirit. He adds a sense of humor and lightness to their trials, often using his cleverness to navigate challenges. Despite his playful nature, Frank is fiercely loyal and dependable when it comes to protecting his friends.

4. **Silvia (The Majestic Hippo):**

~Silvia stands as the stalwart leader of the group. Her majestic presence and strength serve as a pillar of support for her friends. She embodies courage, determination, and a deep sense of responsibility, always putting the well-being of the group above her own concerns.

Together, they form a balanced team, each bringing their unique strengths and qualities to complement one another. Their journey through various challenges and mystical realms not only tests their individual abilities but also strengthens their bond as friends facing adversity together.

Silvia gazed around the Emerald Enclave, the verdant sanctuary bathed in the gentle hues of morning light. Lush foliage surrounded them, vibrant flowers in full bloom, and the air carried the sweet scent of blossoms.

"Friends," Silvia began, her voice steady yet tinged with concern, "we have come so far, faced countless challenges together. Perhaps it is time we return to where we came from."

Manny looked at Silvia with a furrowed brow, his wise eyes reflecting the shimmering green of the enclave. "Silvia, we've journeyed together through trials and tribulations. Turning back now would diminish all that we've achieved."

Lili, perched delicately on a nearby branch, nodded in agreement. "We've seen wonders and faced our deepest fears. To return now would be to deny the purpose that brought us here."

Frank, leaning against a moss-covered rock, crossed his arms thoughtfully. "The journey has changed us, made us stronger. I'm not ready to leave it all behind just yet."

Silvia sighed, understanding their sentiments. "But what lies ahead may be even more perilous. Are we prepared to face it?"

"We've faced darkness and emerged stronger," Manny reassured her. "Whatever lies ahead, we face it together."

Lili fluttered down to stand beside Silvia. "The Enclave holds mysteries and wonders. I believe there is more here for us to discover."

Frank pushed off from the rock, his expression resolute. "I didn't come this far to turn back now. Let's see where this path leads."

Silvia nodded slowly, her determination reignited by her friends' steadfast resolve. "Then onward we go, into the heart of the Emerald Enclave. Together."

With renewed purpose, they set forth deeper into the sanctuary, ready to uncover more of its secrets and face whatever challenges awaited them.

Silvia gazed around the Emerald Enclave, the verdant sanctuary bathed in the gentle hues of morning light. Lush foliage surrounded them, vibrant flowers in full bloom, and the air carried the sweet scent of blossoms.

As the group ventured deeper into the heart of the Emerald Enclave, the verdant surroundings seemed to come alive with an ethereal glow. The air hummed with an unseen energy, and the foliage whispered secrets carried on the gentle breeze.

Suddenly, they found themselves at the edge of a majestic grove, where ancient trees stood sentinel in a circular formation, their branches intertwined like guardians protecting a sacred sanctuary. Light filtered through the canopy in dappled patterns, casting a serene glow over the clearing.

Manny, ever the sage, approached the grove with reverence. "These trees must hold great significance. They seem to pulse with an ancient power."

Silvia nodded in agreement, her eyes scanning the grove for any signs of movement. "I sense a presence here, watching us."

Lili, her wings trembling slightly with anticipation, spoke softly. "The guardians of this grove. They must be the keepers of its mysteries."

Frank, always ready for a challenge, stepped forward boldly. "Let's approach them. We must prove ourselves worthy to proceed."

As they entered the grove, the atmosphere shifted subtly. Shadows danced among the trees, and a faint murmuring filled the air, like the rustling of leaves in a gentle breeze. Then, from the shadows emerged figures cloaked in shimmering green robes, their faces obscured by hoods.

The lead guardian, their voice carrying a wisdom earned through centuries, spoke with authority. "Travelers of the celestial odyssey, you stand before the guardians of the Emerald Enclave. To proceed, you must prove your worthiness."

Manny stepped forward, his demeanor calm yet resolute. "We seek only to understand the mysteries of this place, to learn from its wisdom."

The guardians exchanged a knowing glance, their eyes penetrating yet benevolent. "Knowledge is earned through trials," they replied in unison, their voices echoing through the grove.

With that, the guardians unleashed a series of challenges upon the group. They faced tests of strength and agility, puzzles that required wit and wisdom, and trials that tested their bonds of friendship and unity.

Through each challenge, Manny, Silvia, Lili, and Frank demonstrated their courage, resilience, and unwavering determination. They relied on each other's strengths, offering support and encouragement in moments of doubt.

Finally, as the last challenge was overcome, the guardians nodded in approval. "You have proven yourselves worthy," they intoned, their voices resonating through the grove.

Silvia, her heart filled with gratitude, bowed respectfully. "Thank you for this opportunity. We will honor the trust you have placed in us."

The lead guardian stepped forward, placing a hand on Silvia's shoulder. "The path forward is yours to tread, travelers. May the wisdom of the Emerald Enclave guide you on your celestial odyssey."

With that, the guardians receded into the shadows of the grove, leaving the group to continue their journey deeper into the mysteries of the Emerald Enclave, their spirits emboldened and their resolve strengthened by the challenges they had faced.

Through their actions, they restore harmony to the Emerald Enclave, ensuring its beauty remains preserved for generations to come. The guardians' challenges had not only tested their resolve but also imparted wisdom that resonated deep within them.

With newfound understanding, Manny, Silvia, Lili, and Frank worked tirelessly alongside the guardians of the grove. Together, they nurtured the sacred land, tending to the flora and fauna that thrived within its boundaries. They repaired ancient pathways, revitalized mystical springs, and honored the spirits that dwelled there.

Silvia, with her innate connection to nature, led the efforts to heal the wounds inflicted upon the enclave over centuries of neglect. Her gentle touch coaxed life back into withered plants, while her wisdom guided the group in preserving the delicate balance of the ecosystem.

Lili, with her melodious voice that could calm even the wildest of storms, sang songs of renewal and growth.

Her songs echoed through the grove, bringing harmony and peace to all who listened, human and creature alike.

Frank, ever the agile and resourceful trickster, used his skills to rebuild what had been lost. With boundless energy, he constructed shelters for weary travelers, carved intricate symbols of protection into the bark of ancient trees, and ensured that the enclave would remain a sanctuary for all who sought solace within its embrace.

Manny, the lion, shared his knowledge of celestial lore and ancient wisdom with the guardians. Together, they unearthed forgotten rituals and rites, restoring the spiritual essence that permeated every corner of the Emerald Enclave.

As seasons passed and years turned into decades, the Emerald Enclave flourished once more. Its once-fading beauty now radiated with an ethereal glow, drawing travelers from distant lands who sought the wisdom and tranquility that only the enclave could offer.

And so, the celestial odyssey continued, guided by the lessons learned and the bonds forged in the heart of the Emerald Enclave. Each member of the group carried with them the spirit of harmony and the determination to preserve the sanctity of all realms they encountered on their journey.

The group arrives at the Sanctuary of Stars agian, a place where the night sky stretches out in all its splendor, adorned with countless stars. The air is crisp and tinged with a hint of magic, as if the very essence of the cosmos swirls around them.

Manny, known as the lion, gazes up at the heavens with awe, his eyes reflecting the twinkling stars above. "This place is truly remarkable. It feels as though we've stepped into a realm where time and space converge."

Silvia, the majestic hipo, nods in agreement, her eyes scanning the horizon where constellations form intricate patterns. "The stars hold secrets and stories untold. It's as if each one is a beacon guiding us on our celestial odyssey."

Lili, the melodic butterfly, hovers gracefully, her wings shimmering in the starlight. "I've never seen such beauty. It's as if the stars themselves sing a song of infinite possibilities."

Frank, the agile trickster, grins mischievously, his eyes twinkling like the distant stars. "I wonder what adventures await us here. Perhaps the stars have tales to share and challenges to test our mettle."

As they stand together beneath the celestial canopy, a sense of wonder and anticipation fills their hearts. The Sanctuary of Stars beckons them forward again, promising mysteries waiting to be unraveled and destinies waiting to be fulfilled once and for all.

Lili floated gracefully through the Sanctuary of Stars, her wings shimmering in the gentle starlight that bathed the celestial refuge. Each step she took seemed to resonate with the whispers of the cosmos, the echoes of distant galaxies and celestial bodies.

"These stars," Lili mused softly, her voice barely above a whisper, "they hold stories older than time itself. Each one a beacon of light in the vastness of the universe."

Manny, walking beside her, nodded in agreement, his gaze fixed upon the constellations above. "They speak of journeys taken and destinies fulfilled. We are but small parts in their grand tapestry."

Silvia, her eyes scanning the horizon where the sky met the distant horizon, felt a sense of awe wash over her. "To think that we are here, amidst such cosmic beauty... It's humbling." Frank, ever the agile explorer, leaped from one stone to another, his movements reflecting the grace of the stars above. "These echoes, they remind us of our place in the universe. Small, yet significant."

As they wandered deeper into the sanctuary, the stars seemed to dance around them, painting the night sky with hues of blue, silver, and gold. Each twinkling light carried with it a promise of infinite possibilities, a reminder that even in the darkest of times, there was light to guide their way.

Lili paused beneath a particularly bright cluster of stars, her wings fluttering with excitement. "Do you think we'll find answers here, among the stars?"

Manny placed a comforting hand on her shoulder, his expression serene. "Perhaps not answers in the conventional sense, but understanding. Each star holds a story just like our hearts, and together they form the fabric of our journey."

Silvia glanced at her friends, a smile touching her lips. "Let's embrace this moment, this sanctuary of stars. Together, we will find our way."

And so they continued their journey through the Sanctuary of Stars, guided by the echoes of eternity that whispered through the cosmos, each step bringing them closer to the truths they sought and the destinies that awaited them.

Under the shimmering canopy of stars, the group gathered in a circle, their eyes turned upwards in quiet contemplation. Around them, the celestial sanctuary radiated with a serene energy, as if the stars themselves were listening.

Lili spoke first, her voice soft yet filled with determination. "Stars of the cosmos, ancient guides of the night, we seek your wisdom. Show us the path we must take to fulfill our quest."

A gentle breeze stirred the air, causing the leaves of nearby trees to rustle softly. The stars twinkled in response, casting their light upon the assembled friends as if in acknowledgment of their plea.

Manny closed his eyes briefly, as if communing with unseen forces. "Guide us through the trials that await, reveal to us the strength we must harness within ourselves."

Silvia raised her staff towards the heavens, a symbol of their unity and purpose. "Illuminate our hearts with clarity, that we may discern truth from illusion on our journey."

Frank, ever pragmatic, spoke with unwavering resolve. "Grant us the resilience to face adversity, and the courage to stand strong in the face of darkness."

As they stood together, their words and intentions mingled with the cosmic energies that surrounded them. The stars seemed to pulse in response, aligning themselves into patterns that spoke of challenges and triumphs yet to come.

Lili opened her eyes, a serene smile gracing her features. "Thank you, stars of the sanctuary, for your guidance and light. We are ready to face what lies ahead."

With renewed determination, they continued their exploration of the Sanctuary of Stars, each step imbued with the quiet assurance that they were on the right path.

The echoes of eternity whispered around them, a reminder that their journey was not just about reaching their destination, but about embracing the lessons and growth along the way.

The night deepened, and the stars above shone with a brilliance that seemed to encompass the entire sanctuary. Manny, Lili, Frank, and Silvia stood together in a clearing, their faces upturned towards the celestial canvas that stretched endlessly overhead.

Lili closed her eyes and took a deep breath, feeling the gentle caress of starlight on her face. "It's as if the stars themselves are blessing our journey," she murmured softly.

Frank nodded in agreement, his eyes sparkling with awe. "I've never felt such peace and serenity. It's like the weight of our quest has lifted for this moment."

Manny, his gaze thoughtful, spoke up next. "The stars have a way of reminding us of our place in the universe, of our connection to something greater than ourselves."

Silvia, holding her staff upright, felt a renewed sense of purpose wash over her. "Let this moment of tranquility strengthen our resolve. We carry the hopes of Manny on our shoulders."

Together, they stood in silent reverence, allowing the radiance of the stars to envelop them in a cocoon of calmness and clarity. The worries and uncertainties that had plagued them momentarily faded, replaced by a deep-seated confidence that they were on the right path.

As they basked in the celestial glow, a sense of unity and determination settled within their hearts. Each star above seemed to whisper secrets of perseverance and courage, urging them onward in their celestial odyssey.

"We should rest here for the night," Manny suggested gently, breaking the peaceful silence. "Tomorrow, we continue our journey with renewed strength."

Lili nodded, a serene smile gracing her features. "Yes, a moment of rest under the stars will do us good."

With a shared understanding, they settled down in the tranquil embrace of the Sanctuary of Stars, their dreams intertwined with the echoes of eternity that surrounded them.

The journey led Manny, them to the Ethereal Nexus, a place where the very fabric of reality seemed to shimmer and waver. They stood at the threshold, their senses tingling with anticipation as they gazed upon the shifting landscapes that lay beyond.

"This place…" Lili breathed, her voice hushed with reverence. "It feels like we're standing at the edge of the universe."

Frank nodded, his eyes scanning the horizon where the boundaries between realms blurred. "It's like the

Nexus is a gateway to countless possibilities, realms we've only imagined."

Manny adjusted his spectacles, his gaze fixed on the swirling energies that danced around them. "The Nexus is said to connect worlds, bridging the mundane and the fantastical."

Silvia, gripping her staff tightly, felt a mixture of excitement and caution. "Let's proceed carefully. The Ethereal Nexus holds mysteries we may not fully comprehend."

They ventured forth into the Nexus, each step echoing softly against the ethereal ground beneath their feet. The air hummed with unseen energies, shifting and coalescing in patterns that defied earthly logic.

As they delved deeper, the boundaries between realms became even more pronounced. They caught glimpses of landscapes that defied description— vast plains of swirling colors,

floating islands adorned with crystalline structures, and skies alive with luminescent creatures.

"This place challenges everything we know," Lili mused, her wings fluttering nervously. "It's both exhilarating and unsettling."

Frank surveyed their surroundings with a keen eye, his senses attuned to the subtle shifts in energy. "We must tread carefully. The Nexus doesn't abide by our rules."

Manny nodded in agreement, his expression thoughtful. "Every step here could lead us deeper into the unknown. We must stay focused."

Silvia led the way with determination, her instincts guiding them through the ever-changing landscapes. "Our quest has brought us here for a reason. We must find what we seek."

They pressed on through the swirling energies of the Ethereal Nexus, each passing moment bringing them closer to the heart of its mysteries. With each step, they felt the boundaries of their reality expand, opening their minds to the infinite possibilities that awaited beyond the Nexus.

It had been years since Lili the melodic butterfly, Silvia the majestic hippo, Frank the agile trickster, and Manny the sage of sands escaped the confines of the Zoo of wonders. Their adventures had taken them across realms and through epochs, exploring the mysteries of ancient mystic times that lay hidden from ordinary eyes.

In a forgotten corner of the world, they stumbled upon an abandoned observatory, its weathered stones whispering tales of forgotten stars and lost civilizations. Here, under the vault of the night sky, they once more, drawn by a familiar sensation— a soft murmur that danced on the edges of their perception.

Lili, with her wings shimmering with remnants of the cosmic melodies she had once danced to in distant galaxies, was the first to catch wind of the whispers. They spoke of realms where time flowed like a river, carrying with it the echoes of civilizations long vanished.

Silvia, her memories of the zoo pond now mingled with visions of celestial waters, felt the whispers resonate deep within her ancient soul. They called to her with promises of wisdom and enlightenment, urging her to plunge into the depths of the unknown.

Frank, ever the agile explorer of mysteries, scaled the observatory's crumbling walls with grace that defied his bulky form. From the highest vantage point, he scanned the stars through a makeshift telescope fashioned from relics of their past journeys, deciphering constellations that held clues to gateways between worlds.

Manny, the sage whose journeys through ancient sands had honed his understanding of cosmic truths, sat in quiet contemplation beneath the observatory's dome. The whispers, he realized, were not just echoes of distant beings but threads in the tapestry of creation itself, weaving together past, present, and future in a cosmic symphony.

As they delved deeper into the mysteries of the observatory, they unearthed artifacts left behind by forgotten astronomers and mystics. Ancient scrolls and star charts hinted at portals that bridged the gap between worlds, while inscriptions etched into stone spoke of beings whose forms transcended mortal comprehension.

Silvia, her curiosity piqued by the whispers' call, ventured into caverns beneath the observatory where echoes of ancient chants reverberated through crystalline stalactites. There, amidst the glow of bioluminescent fungi, she communed with spirits who spoke of a time when hippos walked among gods and goddesses.

Lili, her wings brushing against the pages of a tome filled with celestial harmonies, conducted symphonies of light that echoed the whispers' melodies across the observatory grounds.

Each note she played resonated with the vibrations of distant stars, drawing forth memories of a time when butterflies danced across galaxies.

Frank, perched atop the observatory's dome with stars reflected in his eyes, pieced together fragments of a cosmic puzzle that spanned millennia. He traced the paths of comets and asteroids that carried messages from civilizations that had once sought answers to the same mysteries they now pursued.

Manny, with sand from ancient deserts still clinging to his fur, meditated amidst the observatory's ruins, his mind reaching out across the cosmos. In visions that transcended time and space, he glimpsed the faces of beings who whispered secrets of creation and destruction, of cycles that spanned eons.

But with each revelation came a deeper understanding of their place in the universe— a butterfly, a hippo, a trickster, and a sage, bound together by the whispers that echoed through the annals of time. Their escape from the zoo had been but the beginning of a journey that now stretched beyond the limits of mortal existence.

United by their shared quest for knowledge and their unbreakable bond forged through countless adventures, Lili, Silvia, Frank, and Manny embraced the whispers of otherworldly beings. For in the mysteries they unraveled and the truths they unearthed, they found not just answers but a purpose that transcended the boundaries of any single world or time.

Having delved deep into the mysteries whispered by ancient observatories and cosmic gateways, Lili the melodic butterfly, Silvia the majestic hippo, Frank the agile trickster, and Manny the sage of sands found themselves at the threshold of the astral crossroads. This nexus of ethereal pathways existed beyond the confines of any single realm, where beings of pure energy and consciousness dwelled— entities that defied mortal comprehension.

Guided by whispers that echoed through their memories, the four friends ventured into the heart of the astral crossroads. The pathways shimmered with iridescent hues, their essence

woven from threads of starlight and cosmic dust. Each step carried them further from the known and deeper into the unknown, where the boundaries between reality and imagination blurred like ripples on a pond.

Lili, her wings aglow with the echoes of celestial melodies, floated effortlessly along the pathways. Here, amidst the ethereal currents, she encountered beings whose forms shifted like reflections in a kaleidoscope— creatures of pure light and sound that communicated through harmonies that resonated with the very fabric of the cosmos.

Silvia, her massive form navigating these astral pathways with grace born of ancient wisdom, communed with entities whose presence filled the void with a sense of serenity and awe. They spoke to her of epochs when galaxies were born from the breath of cosmic giants, and of the eternal dance of creation and destruction that shaped the tapestry of existence. Frank, ever the agile explorer, bounded from one pathway to another, his laughter echoing through the astral realms. He encountered trickster spirits who tested his wit and wisdom, challenging him to decipher riddles that spanned dimensions and timelines. Through these encounters, he gleaned insights into the nature of perception and reality that expanded his understanding beyond mortal limits.

Manny, the sage whose journeys through ancient sands had prepared him for the revelations of the astral crossroads, walked with measured steps that resonated with the heartbeat of the universe itself. He conversed with cosmic guardians whose gaze pierced through time and space, offering glimpses of civilizations that rose and fell like waves upon an infinite shore.

As they navigated the astral crossroads, the friends discovered that time flowed differently here— a river that twisted and turned, carrying with it echoes of past and future. They witnessed visions of worlds where possibilities unfolded like petals of a cosmic flower, each choice branching into new realities that stretched across the multiverse.

Yet, amidst the wonders and challenges of the astral crossroads, they also encountered shadows— echoes of their own doubts and fears that lurked in the corners of their consciousness. Visions haunted their dreams— of trials that tested their resolve, of temptations that threatened to ensnare their souls in illusions spun from starlight and shadow.

But through their trials and triumphs, Lili, Silvia, Frank, and Manny remained steadfast in their quest for knowledge and understanding. They embraced the teachings of beings whose existence transcended mortal comprehension, finding solace in the realization that they were but threads in the tapestry of creation— a butterfly, a hippo, a trickster, and a sage, bound together by the ethereal pathways of the astral crossroads.

And so, guided by the whispers that had led them from the confines of a zoo to the farthest reaches of cosmic consciousness, they continued their journey. For in navigating the astral crossroads, they discovered not only the secrets of the universe but also the boundless potential that lay within each of them— a potential to shape destinies and weave new stories amidst the stars.

Silvia and Lili floated together through the shimmering pathways of the astral nexus, their forms illuminated by the soft glow of distant stars and the radiant energies that pulsed through the ethereal currents.

Silvia: (gazing out into the vast expanse) Lili, do you ever wonder about the stars? How they seem to hold stories of worlds beyond our own?

Lili: (flitting gracefully beside Silvia) All the time, Silvia. They sing to me in whispers of ancient times and distant places. It's as if each twinkling light is a thread weaving together the tapestry of the universe.

Silvia: (nodding thoughtfully) I used to think our world was just the zoo, and then the observatory. Now, here we are, amidst pathways that connect everything. It's like the boundaries between us and the cosmos have dissolved.

Lili: (pausing to catch a gentle breeze of cosmic energy) Exactly, Silvia. These pathways, they're not just routes through space— they're connections between realities. Every step we take here, it's like touching the essence of countless worlds and beings.

Silvia: (a sense of wonder in her voice) And the beings we've encountered— pure energy, consciousness unbound by flesh or form. They understand the universe in ways we can only glimpse.

Lili: (smiling softly) Yet, they also seem to recognize something in us, Silvia. A spark of curiosity, perhaps, or a longing for understanding. They speak to us in harmonies and light, inviting us to dance with the cosmos.

Silvia: (her eyes reflecting the distant glow of a passing comet) We've come so far from the zoo, Lili. From our enclosures to these pathways where time bends and realities converge. It's humbling and exhilarating all at once.

Lili: (reaching out to touch a faint ripple in the astral fabric) I think that's the beauty of it, Silvia. In this vastness, we're not just observers— we're participants. Each thought, each step, shapes the currents of existence around us.

Silvia: (nodding in agreement) We're part of something grander than we ever imagined. Our journey has shown us that the boundaries between us and the universe are illusions. We are intertwined with the cosmos in ways that defy our understanding.

Lili: (her wings shimmering with the echoes of distant harmonies) And yet, here we are, embracing the mysteries and revelations that unfold with every moment. Together, Silvia, we're navigating the convergence of realities with courage and curiosity.

Silvia: (a gentle smile spreading across her face) Courage and curiosity— qualities that have guided us from the zoo to these celestial pathways. Who knew that two creatures from such different worlds could share this journey and find such kinship?

Lili: (gazing at Silvia with warmth) Perhaps it's because, at our core, we're all made of stardust and dreams. In this nexus, we're reminded that we are not alone— we are connected to each other and to the vastness of the universe.

Silvia: (her voice filled with awe) Yes, Lili. Connected, intertwined, and forever changed by the wonders we've encountered. Let's continue to explore, to learn, and to cherish this convergence of realities that surrounds us.

As Silvia and Lili floated onward through the astral nexus, their voices joined the cosmic symphony that resonated through the pathways of stars and dreams. Together, they embraced the interconnectedness of all things and the boundless expanse of the universe that awaited their discovery.

The Arcane Archives stood as a bastion of knowledge amidst the swirling mists of the astral nexus, its towering spires reaching toward the starlit heavens. Lili the melodic butterfly and Silvia the majestic hippo approached its ancient gates with a sense of reverence, their hearts fluttering with anticipation at the mysteries that awaited within.

Lili: (her wings trembling with excitement) Silvia, look at this place! It's as if the whispers led us here, to the heart of all knowledge.

Silvia: (nodding, her eyes wide with wonder) It's magnificent, Lili. Imagine the stories these halls hold— of civilizations that rose and fell, of beings that walked among the stars long before us.

Together, they crossed the threshold into the grand foyer of the Arcane Archives, where shelves upon shelves of scrolls, tomes, and artifacts stretched into infinity. The air hummed

with the residual energies of centuries past, a testament to the wisdom and curiosity that had brought the ancients to this sacred repository.

Lili: (floating closer to a shelf adorned with ancient manuscripts) Each scroll here could hold secrets of the cosmos, Silvia. Stories of creation, of cosmic journeys, and of beings whose names have faded into myth.

Silvia: (running a gentle hoof along the spine of a massive tome) And these artifacts— carvings, crystals, and relics that seem to pulse with the very essence of the stars. I can feel the weight of their history.

As they ventured deeper into the labyrinthine corridors of the library, they encountered chambers dedicated to different realms of knowledge. Astronomical charts depicted constellations that guided ancient travelers through the vastness of space, while alchemical experiments were chronicled in dusty manuscripts that spoke of transmutation and transformation.

Lili: (tracing intricate patterns on a celestial map) Silvia, look at this! It's a map of the cosmos, charting the pathways between stars and galaxies. I wonder if the beings we've encountered in the astral nexus knew of these routes.

Silvia: (studying a mural depicting celestial beings in cosmic dance) Perhaps they did, Lili. These murals— depictions of beings whose forms transcend mortal understanding. They seem to be woven into the very fabric of creation itself.

Their journey through the Library of the Ancients continued, each step revealing new wonders and revelations. They discovered chambers where time flowed differently, where echoes of past conversations and future prophecies whispered through the air. In one hall, Manny the sage of sands joined them, his presence adding a depth of wisdom to their exploration.

Manny: (his voice resonating with the wisdom of ages) Lili, Silvia— this place holds more than just knowledge. It's a gateway to understanding the fundamental truths of existence. The scrolls and artifacts here are keys that unlock the mysteries of the cosmos.

Lili: (turning to Manny with a smile) Manny, you're right. These texts— they're not just words on parchment. They're echoes of voices that sought to grasp the same truths we seek now.

Silvia: (nodding in agreement) And the beings we've encountered in the astral nexus— they must have drawn upon this repository of wisdom in their own journeys.

The interconnectedness of all things becomes clearer with each scroll we unravel.

Together, the three friends— Lili, Silvia, and Manny— delved deeper into the Library of the Ancients, their quest for knowledge intertwined with the stories of those who had come before. They unearthed prophecies that spoke of cosmic alignments and cycles of renewal, and they deciphered glyphs that hinted at gateways to realms beyond mortal comprehension.

Manny: (as they reached the central chamber adorned with a pulsating crystal) Here, at the heart of the archives, we find the culmination of millennia of exploration and discovery. This crystal— it resonates with the energies of creation itself.

Lili: (captivated by the crystal's shimmering light) It's as if the cosmos is speaking to us, Manny. Whispering secrets that have been guarded by time and space.

Silvia: (her gaze reflecting the crystal's glow) And we, in turn, become custodians of these truths. Guardians of knowledge that spans the ages and reaches into the infinite expanse of the universe.

In the Library of the Ancients, amidst the hallowed halls of wisdom and the shimmering depths of cosmic understanding, Lili, Silvia, and Manny embraced their role as seekers of truth. They were bound together not only by their quest for knowledge but also by the realization that they were part of a vast tapestry of existence— a tapestry woven with threads of starlight and the echoes of ancient whispers.

Deep within the labyrinthine corridors of the Arcane Archives, Lili the melodic butterfly, Silvia the majestic hippo, and Manny the sage of sands stood before a collection of ancient tomes and scrolls. The air was thick with the scent of aged parchment and the faint hum of residual magical energies that lingered within the chambers.

Lili: (her wings trembling with anticipation) Silvia, Manny— look at these scrolls! They seem to radiate with a power that transcends time itself.

Silvia: (nodding, her gaze fixed on a particularly ornate tome) These writings— they hold the secrets of ancient magics, the kind that shape reality and bend the elements to one's will.

Manny: (his eyes alight with curiosity) Indeed, my friends. These tomes are more than just repositories of knowledge. They are conduits through which the mysteries of magic reveal themselves.

Together, they began to sift through the scrolls and manuscripts, each one adorned with glyphs and sigils that shimmered with arcane energy. They uncovered spells of elemental manipulation, incantations that could summon beings from distant realms, and rituals that promised to unveil hidden truths obscured by the veils of time and space.

Lili: (tracing a delicate finger over a rune inscribed on a weathered scroll) Manny, these runes— they're like keys that unlock the essence of magic itself. What do you make of them?

Manny: (studying the scroll with a scholar's eye) Each rune represents a concept— a force of nature, a cosmic principle, or a fundamental truth. Together, they form a language that binds magic to the fabric of reality.

Silvia: (lifting a tome filled with illustrations of celestial alignments) And these illustrations— they depict rituals that harness the power of stars and planets. Imagine the possibilities, Lili, Manny— of wielding such cosmic forces in our own journeys.

As they delved deeper into the tomes of power, they uncovered ancient spells that had shaped civilizations long forgotten. They read of wizards who had traversed the astral planes, of enchantments that had fortified kingdoms against the ravages of time, and of potions that granted immortality to those who dared to seek it.

Manny: (turning a page in a tome bound in dragonhide) This text— it speaks of a ritual that bridges the realms between life and death. It's said to draw upon the energies of the cosmos to transcend mortal limitations.

The Celestial Odyssey: Journey Through Portals

Lili: (her voice filled with wonder) And these spells— they're not just words on paper. They resonate with the very essence of magic, waiting for those with the courage and wisdom to wield them.

Silvia: (her thoughts drifting to the possibilities) Imagine what we could accomplish with these powers, Manny. To heal, to protect, to understand the mysteries that have eluded us for so long.

Their exploration of the tomes of power led them deeper into the heart of arcane knowledge. They uncovered spells of illusion and enchantment, potions that granted visions of distant futures, and charms that bound spirits to the will of the caster. Each discovery expanded their understanding of magic and its role in shaping the destinies of worlds.

Manny: (as they reached a chamber filled with glowing crystals) Here, amidst these crystals, we find the convergence of magic and science. The ancients understood that magic is not separate from the natural order— it is woven into its very fabric.

Lili: (gazing at the crystals' pulsating light) It's as if these crystals are conduits for the energies of creation. They amplify the spells we've read about, bridging the gap between mortal and cosmic realms.

Silvia: (her gaze focused on a spell circle etched into the chamber floor) And these circles— they're focal points for channeling magical energies. With the right incantation, they could reshape landscapes or forge alliances with beings beyond our understanding.

In the presence of the tomes of power, Lili, Silvia, and Manny felt a profound connection to the ancient wizards and scholars who had penned these words centuries ago. They realized that magic was not merely a tool for wielding power but a means of unraveling the mysteries of existence itself— a journey that would forever change their perception of the world and their place within it.

As they continued to explore the depths of the Arcane Archives, their minds filled with visions of possibilities yet to be realized. Together, they embraced the secrets of magic and the responsibility that came with wielding such unimaginable potency in a universe brimming with wonders and dangers alike.

Deep within the sanctum of the Arcane Archives, Lili the melodic butterfly and Manny the sage of sands found themselves face to face with guardians who stood vigil over the repository's most sacred texts. These guardians, beings of ethereal light and ancient wisdom, regarded the intruders with eyes that seemed to pierce through time and space.

Lili: (her wings fluttering nervously) Manny, look at them. They're like beings out of the myths we've read—

guardians of knowledge who test those who seek the secrets of the cosmos.

Manny: (calm and composed, meeting the guardians' gaze) Indeed, Lili. These guardians are keepers of the lore that spans epochs. They test not just our intellect but our resolve to honor the wisdom contained within these hallowed halls.

The guardians, their forms shimmering with the radiance of celestial energies, spoke in voices that echoed like distant thunder across the astral plains.

Guardian 1: (addressing Lili and Manny with a voice that resonated with authority) Travelers of the mortal realm, you stand before the guardians of lore. To gain passage to the deepest truths, you must prove yourselves worthy.

Lili: (stepping forward, her voice steady despite her nerves) We seek only knowledge and understanding, noble guardians. We wish to learn from the wisdom of the ancients and carry forth their teachings.

Guardian 2: (regarding Manny with a scrutinizing gaze) Wisdom is not bestowed lightly, sage of sands. It is earned through trials of intellect and challenges of spirit. Are you prepared to face the tests that await you?

Manny: (bowing respectfully) I am, honored guardians. My journeys through sands and stars have prepared me for the trials that lie ahead. I seek not only knowledge but the wisdom to wield it with respect and humility.

The guardians nodded in acknowledgement, their forms shifting like nebulae caught in a cosmic dance. They gestured toward a series of chambers adorned with symbols and glyphs that glowed with arcane significance.

Guardian 1: (motioning toward the first chamber) Within these chambers lie riddles and puzzles crafted by the ancient masters. Solve them, and you shall prove your intellect worthy of the secrets they guard.

Guardian 2: (indicating the second chamber) In the chamber beyond, trials of perception and insight await. You must see beyond the surface and grasp the deeper truths hidden within the illusions of reality.

Lili and Manny exchanged a determined glance, their resolve strengthened by the challenge laid before them. With steady steps, they entered the first chamber, where riddles etched into stone awaited their deciphering.

Lili: (examining the first riddle with furrowed brow) Manny, this riddle— it speaks of cycles and transformations. It's as if the answer lies not in words but in understanding the flow of cosmic energies.

Manny: (studying the symbols surrounding the riddle) Indeed, Lili. The ancients often encoded their wisdom in metaphors and allegories. We must look beyond the literal and seek the deeper meanings hidden within.

Together, they worked through each riddle, their minds attuned to the subtle nuances of ancient language and cosmic philosophy. They debated interpretations, tested hypotheses, and unraveled the mysteries that had confounded scholars for millennia.

Guardian 1: (as Lili and Manny emerged victorious from the first chamber) You have shown intellect and insight, travelers. But the path ahead holds trials of a different kind. Are you prepared to face the challenges of perception and truth?

Lili: (nodding with determination) We are ready, noble guardians. Lead us to the chamber where we shall prove our worthiness once more.

Guided by the guardians of lore, Lili and Manny ventured into the second chamber, where illusions and tests of perception awaited. They navigated through illusions that distorted reality and challenges that tested their ability to discern truth from falsehood.

Manny: (his voice echoing through the chamber) Lili, these illusions— they're reflections of our own fears and doubts. To see through them, we must trust in our bond and in the knowledge we've gained.

Lili: (her wings glowing with inner light) Together, Manny, we can overcome any challenge. These tests are not just about proving ourselves to the guardians but affirming our commitment to the pursuit of wisdom.

With each trial they faced, Lili and Manny grew closer to the core of the guardians' tests. They demonstrated not only their individual strengths but also the power of their partnership— a bond forged through countless adventures and shared discoveries.

Guardian 2: (as Lili and Manny emerged triumphant from the final trial) You have shown resilience and unity, travelers. You have proven yourselves worthy of the knowledge that awaits within the deepest chambers of the Arcane Archives.

Manny: (bowing respectfully) We are honored, noble guardians. Your tests have taught us the value of perseverance and the importance of humility in the face of wisdom.

Lili: (smiling gratefully) Thank you for guiding us, guardians. We will carry the lessons of this day with us as we continue our journey through the realms of magic and cosmic understanding.

And so, Lili the melodic butterfly and Manny the sage of sands stood as guardians of lore in their own right, entrusted with the ancient wisdom that had tested their intellect and resolve. Together, they embraced the challenges that had shaped their journey through the

Arcane Archives, knowing that their quest for knowledge had only just begun amidst the vastness of the cosmos.

In the quiet aftermath of their trials within the Arcane Archives, Silvia the majestic hippo and Manny the sage of sands found themselves drawn to a chamber secluded from the main halls— an alcove where forbidden knowledge lay veiled behind ancient wards and protective enchantments. Here, amidst the faint glow of glyphs and the hushed whispers of forgotten incantations, they stood poised to unlock secrets that had been safeguarded for ages untold.

Silvia: (her presence commanding yet reverent) Manny, this chamber— it feels different, as if the very air carries echoes of powers beyond mortal comprehension.

Manny: (his eyes reflecting the shimmering glyphs) Indeed, Silvia. These wards— they are not meant to keep intruders out but to protect the sanctity of what lies within. We tread upon ground where few have ventured.

Silvia nodded solemnly, her thoughts lingering on the responsibilities that came with delving into forbidden knowledge. Together, they approached a pedestal adorned with a pulsating crystal, its light casting intricate patterns on the walls adorned with tapestries depicting cosmic events and celestial beings.

Silvia: (studying the crystal with cautious curiosity) Manny, do you sense it? The energy emanating from this crystal— it's as if it holds the essence of stars within its core.

Manny: (placing a hand gently on the crystal's surface) This crystal is a conduit, Silvia. It channels energies that resonate with the very fabric of magic and creation. Through it, we may gain insights that transcend our mortal understanding.

With measured care, Manny began to unravel the protective wards surrounding the crystal, his fingers tracing ancient sigils that glowed faintly in response to his touch. The air around them hummed with anticipation, a palpable energy that hinted at revelations waiting to be unveiled.

Silvia: (her voice a whisper amidst the charged atmosphere) Manny, what do you think we will find here? What forbidden knowledge could be so potent that it requires such guardianship?

Manny: (his gaze fixed on the crystal as the wards dissolved) Legends speak of arcane truths that challenge the very boundaries of magic and mortality, Silvia. They are threads in the tapestry of existence, woven with the power to reshape reality itself.

As the final ward fell away, the crystal's glow intensified, casting a luminous aura around them. Shadows danced on the walls, reflections of beings and events that transcended time and space— a testament to the magnitude of what lay hidden within.

Silvia: (her breath catching as the crystal's light enveloped them) Manny, it's as if the cosmos itself is speaking to us through this crystal. What do you see?

Manny: (his voice resonating with awe) I see glimpses of realms beyond our own, Silvia. Beings of pure energy and consciousness, civilizations that span galaxies, and forces that bind the cosmos together in an intricate dance of balance and chaos.

Together, they immersed themselves in the revelations that unfolded before them, each revelation a fragment of a larger mosaic that painted a picture of universal truths. They learned of spells that defied the laws of physics, of rituals that summoned entities from the depths of astral realms, and of prophecies that foretold cataclysms and rebirths spanning eons.

Silvia: (her eyes wide with wonder) Manny, this knowledge— it's both exhilarating and daunting. To think that we hold within our grasp the understanding of powers that shape the very fabric of existence.

Manny: (nodding solemnly) With this knowledge comes great responsibility, Silvia. We must wield it wisely, mindful of the consequences that ripple through the cosmos with each incantation and revelation.

As they continued to unlock the forbidden knowledge hidden within the crystal, Silvia and Manny felt the weight of their discoveries settle upon their shoulders. They understood that with insight came the burden of choice— to use their newfound understanding for the greater good or risk unraveling the delicate balance that held the universe together.

Silvia: (her voice steady with resolve) Manny, we must share what we learn here with Lili and Frank. Together, we can harness this knowledge to protect the realms we hold dear and to nurture the growth of wisdom among all who seek it.

Manny: (placing a reassuring hand on Silvia's shoulder) Indeed, Silvia. Our journey through the Arcane Archives has brought us closer to the heart of magic and the forces that shape our destinies. Let us carry this responsibility with courage and humility as we forge ahead into the unknown.

In the quiet of the chamber, amidst the echoes of cosmic whispers and the radiant glow of forbidden knowledge, Silvia and Manny stood as guardians of insights that would forever alter their understanding of the universe. They knew that their journey was far from over— that with each revelation, they edged closer to the nexus where magic, knowledge, and destiny converged in a tapestry woven with threads of infinite possibilities.

As they ventured deeper into their explorations, they found themselves standing at the threshold of the Dreamer's Domain— a realm where dreams took on a life of their own, and the boundaries between imagination and reality blurred into a tapestry of shifting landscapes and ephemeral visions.

Frank: (his eyes bright with curiosity) Wow, look at this place! It's like stepping into a painting where the colors swirl and dance with every thought.

Lili: (her wings shimmering with anticipation) Frank, welcome to the Dreamer's Domain. Here, dreams are not just fleeting illusions but tangible realms shaped by the minds that wander within.

Silvia: (gazing around in awe) It's beautiful and haunting at the same time. I can feel the echoes of countless dreams that have woven this tapestry of realities.

Manny: (his voice carrying the weight of ancient wisdom) Dreams are the gateways to the subconscious, where fears, desires, and truths are laid bare. In this realm, we may uncover insights that elude us in waking life.

Together, they embarked on a journey through the Dreamer's Domain, where landscapes shifted like sand dunes in a desert wind, and whispers of forgotten memories drifted through the air like echoes of distant melodies.

Frank: (as they traversed a forest of floating trees) This place— it's like a playground for the imagination. I wonder if we can shape it with our thoughts, like lucid dreamers in control of their own destinies.

Lili: (smiling as she twirled through a field of glowing flowers) Perhaps, Frank. Dreams here are fluid, responding to the emotions and intentions of those who wander within. It's a realm where possibilities are limited only by the boundaries of our minds.

Silvia: (pausing to touch a waterfall that flowed with liquid stardust) And these dreamscapes— they hold memories and emotions, woven into the fabric of their existence. Each sight and sound tells a story of the dreamers who shaped them.

As they ventured deeper into the Dreamer's Domain, they encountered manifestations of their own subconscious thoughts and emotions— phantoms that danced on the edge of perception and reflections of fears and hopes long buried in waking life.

Manny: (contemplating a mirror that reflected alternate realities) Here, in the mirrors of dreams, we glimpse paths not taken and futures yet to unfold. It's a reminder that our choices shape not only our waking world but the dreamscape that surrounds us.

Frank: (his movements agile as he leaped between floating islands of thought) And these islands— they're like stepping stones across a river of imagination. Who knows what wonders or challenges await us as we navigate this realm?

Their journey through the Dreamer's Domain was a testament to the power of dreams as windows into the soul and as gateways to realms beyond mortal comprehension. They encountered beings of ephemeral light who whispered prophecies of futures intertwined with the threads of dreams.

Lili: (listening to a spectral being sing a haunting melody) This being— it's like a fragment of a forgotten dream, seeking to be remembered. Its song echoes through the corridors of time, a testament to the enduring power of dreams.

Silvia: (watching as the landscape shifted into a city of floating crystal towers) In this realm, dreams shape reality, and reality shapes dreams. It's a delicate balance that blurs the boundaries of what we perceive as possible.

Their exploration of the Dreamer's Domain led them to revelations about themselves and the interconnectedness of all things. They learned that dreams were not mere fantasies but reflections of inner truths and aspirations that guided their waking lives.

Manny: (as they reached the heart of the Dreamer's Domain, where a shimmering gateway awaited) Here, at the nexus of dreams, we find the convergence of realities. It is a place where the subconscious meets the conscious, and where visions of past, present, and future intertwine.

Frank: (standing at the threshold of the gateway, his gaze fixed on the horizon of dreams) What lies beyond, Manny? What mysteries await us as we step through this threshold of dreams?

Lili: (her wings glowing with the essence of starlight) Whatever awaits us, Frank, we face it together— as friends bound not only by our quest for knowledge but by the dreams that unite us in this ever-shifting tapestry of existence.

With courage and curiosity guiding their steps, they stepped through the gateway of dreams, ready to embrace the mysteries that awaited them beyond the boundaries of reality.

As Frank the agile trickster wandered alone through the ethereal landscapes of the Dreamer's Domain, he found himself immersed in visions that shimmered like mirages on the horizon of dreams. Each step through this realm of shifting realities brought him closer to glimpses of memories and desires woven into the fabric of time itself.

Frank: (his footsteps echoing softly on the crystalline ground) These visions— they're like echoes of lives lived long ago, lingering in the corridors of dreams. I wonder whose memories I am about to witness.

With each passing moment, the dreamscapes transformed, shifting from lush gardens bathed in moonlight to towering cities of glass and steel that reflected the stars above. Frank felt as though he were walking through the memories of countless souls who had left their mark on the tapestry of existence.

Frank: (pausing beneath a tree that whispered secrets on the wind) What stories do you hold, old friend? What tales of love, loss, and triumphs echo through your branches?

As he continued his journey, Frank encountered scenes that unfolded before him like scenes in a cosmic play. He witnessed lovers parting beneath a sky ablaze with comets, warriors forging alliances amidst fields of battle, and scholars unlocking mysteries that had baffled civilizations for centuries.

Frank: (watching a group of children chase after fireflies in a meadow of dreams) These moments— they're snapshots of lives lived with passion and purpose. In this realm, time flows like a river, carrying memories that shape the destinies of all who dare to dream.

Amidst the visions, Frank found himself drawn to a chamber where a solitary figure stood amidst swirling mists— a figure whose presence radiated with the weight of untold stories and unfulfilled dreams.

Figure: (turning to Frank with eyes that held the wisdom of ages) Wanderer of dreams, you seek truths that transcend the boundaries of mortal perception. What visions do you seek in the tapestry of time?

Frank: (bowing respectfully) I seek understanding, ancient one. These visions— they offer glimpses of lives lived and lessons learned. They speak of a tapestry woven with threads of courage, love, and the resilience of the human spirit.

Figure: (nodding knowingly) The past is a mirror, reflecting the choices and convictions that shape the present. Through these visions, you may uncover truths that resonate with your own journey through the realms of dreams.

Encouraged by the figure's words, Frank delved deeper into the visions that unfolded before him. He witnessed the forging of empires and the rise and fall of civilizations, each event leaving an indelible mark on the fabric of time.

Frank: (as he stood on the precipice of a cliff overlooking a sea of memories) These visions— they're not just about the past. They're about understanding how our choices today shape the futures of tomorrow. It's a reminder of our interconnectedness with all who have walked this path before us.

As the visions continued to reveal themselves, Frank's own reflections intertwined with those of the figures he encountered in the dream realm. He saw echoes of his own journey— of daring escapades and moments of camaraderie shared with Lili, Silvia, and Manny.

Frank: (smiling as he watched a constellation form in the night sky of dreams) These visions— they're reminders that our stories are woven together, each thread contributing to the tapestry of our shared experiences. In this realm, we are bound not only by dreams but by the courage to forge our own destinies.

With newfound clarity and a deeper appreciation for the echoes of the past, Frank continued to navigate through the Dreamer's Domain. Each vision offered him insights into the resilience of the human spirit and the enduring quest for meaning that transcended the boundaries of time and space.

Frank: (as he prepared to leave the Dreamer's Domain, his heart filled with gratitude) Thank you, dreamscape, for revealing truths that elude us in the waking world. Your visions have opened my eyes to the richness of our shared history and the infinite possibilities that lie ahead.

With a final glance back at the swirling mists of the dream realm, Frank the agile trickster stepped beyond its boundaries, carrying with him the lessons and revelations that would shape his journey through the realms of magic and cosmic understanding.

In the heart of the Dreamer's Domain, where dreams manifested as tangible realities shaped by the subconscious, Lili and Frank found themselves confronted with a daunting challenge. Here, amidst landscapes that shifted like mirages and shadows that whispered of forgotten fears, they were forced to confront the darkest corners of their own minds.

Lili: (her wings trembling slightly, radiating a soft glow in the dim light) Frank, these dreams— they're not just illusions. They're reflections of our deepest fears and desires, laid bare for us to confront.

Frank: (his expression serious, yet determined) Lili, I sense it too. This realm— it's like a mirror that shows us the parts of ourselves we'd rather keep hidden. But to navigate through it, we must face these shadows head-on.

As they ventured deeper into the dream realm, the landscapes around them twisted into surreal visions— nightmares that crawled from the depths of their subconscious minds. They encountered phantoms that whispered doubts and insecurities, and specters that mirrored their fears of failure and loss.

Lili: (as they passed through a forest of whispering trees) Frank, these voices— they're echoes of doubts that linger in the corners of our thoughts. Can we trust ourselves to overcome them?

Frank: (his voice steady despite the uncertainty) We must, Lili. These dreams— they challenge us not to succumb to our fears but to embrace them as part of who we are. Only then can we truly understand their hold over us.

Amidst the swirling mists of nightmares, Lili and Frank found themselves facing illusions that tested their resolve and their bond as friends on a journey through the realms of dreams. They navigated through labyrinths of uncertainty and illusions that distorted reality, each step a battle against the shadows that threatened to engulf them.

Lili: (as they stood before a mirror that reflected their greatest fears) Frank, look— this mirror, it shows us visions of what we fear most. It's as if our minds are projecting these nightmares onto the fabric of dreams.

Frank: (studying the mirror with a furrowed brow) These reflections— they're not just illusions, Lili. They're reminders of the vulnerabilities that make us human. But we have the power to shape our own destinies, even in the face of our darkest fears.

Together, they confronted the nightmares that loomed before them— manifestations of regrets and uncertainties that threatened to unravel their resolve. With each challenge they faced, Lili and Frank found strength in their shared determination to confront the shadows that lurked within their own minds.

Lili: (as they reached the heart of a storm of swirling shadows) Frank, these nightmares— they're relentless. But with you by my side, I feel a courage I didn't know I possessed.

Frank: (smiling reassuringly) And with you, Lili, I know we can navigate through any storm. These nightmares— they're tests of our resilience and our belief in ourselves.

As they stood amidst the tempest of nightmares, Lili and Frank found themselves transformed— not by the darkness that surrounded them, but by the light of courage and determination that burned within their hearts. They realized that confronting their fears was not just a test of their strength but a journey of self-discovery and acceptance.

Lili: (her wings glowing with inner light) Frank, these dreams— they've shown us that our fears do not define us. It's how we face them that shapes our destinies.

Frank: (nodding in agreement) Lili, together we've shown that even in the darkest dreams, there is light. We carry this courage with us as we continue our journey through the realms of magic and dreams.

With renewed resolve and a deeper understanding of themselves, Lili and Frank emerged from the depths of their nightmares, their bond strengthened by the trials they had faced together. As they ventured onward through the Dreamer's Domain, they knew that whatever challenges lay ahead, they would face them with courage, compassion, and the unwavering belief in the power of dreams to illuminate even the darkest paths.

In the quiet aftermath of their journey through the Dreamer's Domain, Silvia the majestic hippo and Manny the sage of sands found themselves standing at the threshold of awakening— a moment where the boundaries between dreams and reality blurred, and the truths they had uncovered in the dream realm resonated deeply within their spirits.

Silvia: (her presence calm yet resonant) Manny, these dreams— they have challenged us in ways we never expected. But through them, we've uncovered truths that have stirred the depths of our souls.

Manny: (his eyes reflecting the wisdom of ages) Indeed, Silvia. The dream realm is a mirror that reflects not just our fears and desires, but the truths we often overlook in the waking world. Our journey has tested our courage and our resolve to face these truths head-on.

As they stood amidst the lingering echoes of dreams, Silvia and Manny felt a profound sense of clarity and purpose wash over them. They had confronted illusions that masked deeper realities and navigated through challenges that tested their beliefs and convictions.

Silvia: (gazing out at the horizon where dreams met reality) Manny, what we've learned— it's more than just knowledge. It's a testament to the resilience of the human spirit and our capacity to grow through adversity.

Manny: (nodding thoughtfully) Silvia, in the dream realm, we confronted shadows that mirrored our own insecurities and doubts. But we emerged stronger, with a deeper understanding of ourselves and the interconnectedness of all things.

Their conversation was punctuated by a silence that spoke volumes— a silence filled with the echoes of dreams and the whispers of truths that had reshaped their perspectives on life and existence.

Silvia: (breaking the silence with a gentle smile) Manny, I feel as though we've awakened not just from dreams but from a slumber of complacency. These trials— they've ignited a fire within us, urging us to embrace our truths and live with purpose.

Manny: (placing a reassuring hand on Silvia's shoulder) Indeed, Silvia. Our awakening is a journey that continues beyond the dream realm. It's a commitment to honor the insights we've gained and to carry forward the wisdom that has illuminated our path.

As they prepared to leave the dream realm behind, Silvia and Manny carried with them the lessons and revelations that had shaped their journey. They knew that their spirits had been strengthened by the trials they had faced and the truths they had uncovered— their bond forged through shared experiences that transcended the boundaries of dreams and reality.

Silvia: (gazing back at the dream realm one last time) Farewell, dreamscape. Your challenges have been great, but the gifts of understanding and growth are greater still.

Manny: (his voice carrying the weight of newfound wisdom) Farewell, indeed. We depart with gratitude for the trials that have awakened us to the truths that define our journey through the realms of magic and cosmic understanding.

With hearts full of courage and spirits awakened to the truths that had unfolded in the dream realm, Silvia the majestic hippo and Manny the sage of sands stepped beyond the boundaries of dreams, ready to embrace the next chapter of their quest for knowledge and enlightenment. Together, they carried forward the light of understanding that had illuminated their path— a testament to the transformative power of dreams and the resilience of the human spirit.

In the heart of their journey through the realms of magic and cosmic understanding, Lili the melodic butterfly, Silvia the majestic hippo, Manny the sage of sands, and Frank the agile trickster arrived at the Celestial Crucible— a place where the tapestry of reality itself was woven and shaped by the hands of cosmic beings. Here, amidst the swirling energies of creation, they stood in awe of the monumental task that lay before them.

Lili: (her wings shimmering with anticipation) Look around, everyone. This place— it resonates with the essence of creation. I can feel the threads of reality weaving together in harmony. Silvia: (her presence commanding yet reverent) Indeed, Lili. The Celestial Crucible— it's where stars are born and galaxies take shape. We stand at the threshold of cosmic forces beyond mortal comprehension.

Manny: (his eyes reflecting the wisdom of ages) This forge of creation— it's a nexus where the dreams of cosmic beings intertwine with the fabric of existence. Every thought, every intention— woven into the tapestry of reality.

Frank: (his demeanor playful yet contemplative) Who would've thought we'd stumble upon the birthplace of galaxies? It's like a cosmic playground where the rules of reality are written in stardust and energy.

As they ventured deeper into the Celestial Crucible, the air hummed with the song of creation— a symphony of energies that pulsed with the rhythm of cosmic harmony. They witnessed celestial beings sculpting worlds with gestures of light and sound, each movement a testament to the power of their collective will and imagination.

Lili: (as they approached a crystalline structure that shimmered with iridescent hues) This structure— it's like a crystallization of thoughts and intentions. It holds the essence of dreams that shape the cosmos.

Silvia: (studying the cosmic architects at work) These beings— they are the weavers of reality, crafting galaxies and constellations with a precision that defies mortal understanding. It's a dance of creation that unfolds before our eyes.

Manny: (tracing patterns in the air with a finger of sand) Each gesture, each thought— it ripples through the fabric of reality, shaping the destiny of worlds yet to be born. We are witnessing the genesis of existence itself.

Their journey through the Celestial Crucible was a testament to the interconnectedness of all things— a realization that every action, every intention, resonated through the vast tapestry of creation. They beheld cosmic forces at play, shaping the universe with a delicate balance of chaos and order.

Frank: (as they stood beneath a cascade of cosmic energies) It's overwhelming, isn't it? To think that our actions, our dreams— they echo through the cosmos, leaving traces of our existence in the stars.

Lili: (her voice carrying the wonder of discovery) Frank, every thought, every dream— it's a brushstroke on the canvas of creation. Here, amidst the Celestial Crucible, we witness the tapestry of existence unfolding before us.

Silvia: (her gaze fixed on distant nebulae) And yet, for all its grandeur, creation is also a reflection of balance. For every star born, there is a supernova; for every galaxy, a black hole. It's a reminder of the cycles that govern the cosmos.

Manny: (his presence serene amidst the cosmic symphony) As we stand here, united in our awe of creation, let us remember that we too are threads woven into this tapestry. Our journey through the realms of magic has led us to this forge of existence, where we witness the infinite possibilities of cosmic imagination.

With hearts filled with reverence and minds open to the mysteries of creation, Lili the melodic butterfly, Silvia the majestic hippo, Manny the sage of sands, and Frank the agile trickster embraced the profound beauty of the

Celestial Crucible. Here, amidst the birthplace of galaxies and the sculpting of stars, they found inspiration and purpose in their quest for knowledge and understanding.

Lili: (raising her voice to the cosmos) To creation— to the forge where dreams take shape and destinies are written in stardust!

Silvia: (joining her voice with Lili's) To balance— to the dance of chaos and order that sustains the cosmos!

Manny: (his words a quiet prayer amidst the cosmic energies) To wisdom— to the journey of discovery that spans the realms of magic and beyond!

Frank: (his laughter echoing like celestial music) To adventure— to the infinite possibilities that await us as we navigate the tapestry of existence!

Together, they stood as friends bound not only by their quest for understanding but by the cosmic forces that connected them to the very essence of creation. In the presence of the Celestial Crucible, they knew that their journey was far from over— that with each revelation, they forged deeper connections to the mysteries that shaped the universe and their place within it.

In the luminous expanse of the Celestial Crucible, where cosmic energies swirled and galaxies were born from the dreams of celestial beings, Lili the melodic butterfly, Silvia the majestic hippo, Manny the sage of sands, and Frank the agile trickster stood ready to face trials that would test their ability to shape reality itself. Here, amidst the symphony of creation, they prepared to harness the power that pulsed through the fabric of existence.

Lili: (her wings shimmering with anticipation) Look at this place— it's like a canvas waiting for our intentions to paint upon it. What trials do you think await us, friends?

Silvia: (her presence commanding yet thoughtful) Lili, I sense that these trials— they will challenge us to channel our desires with clarity and purpose. In the Celestial Crucible, every thought has the potential to shape galaxies.

Manny: (his eyes reflecting the wisdom of ages) Indeed, Silvia. The trials of creation— they require not just power, but insight into the harmonies and balances that sustain the cosmos. We must approach them with respect for the forces we seek to wield.

Frank: (his demeanor playful yet focused) Trials, you say? I wonder if we'll be conjuring stars or shaping entire worlds. It's like a cosmic playground where the rules of reality are ours to bend.

As they prepared to embark on their trials, the Celestial Crucible responded to their presence, shimmering with energies that mirrored their intentions and desires. They each felt the weight of responsibility that came with wielding the power of creation— knowing that their actions could echo through the fabric of reality itself.

Lili: (as they approached the first trial, a crystalline structure that glowed with inner light) This trial— it resonates with the essence of dreams and aspirations. What do you wish to create, Silvia?

Silvia: (her gaze fixed on the structure with determination) Lili, I wish to create a sanctuary— a place where all creatures, great and small, can find solace and harmony amidst the chaos of existence.

Manny: (studying the intricate patterns etched into the structure) Silvia's vision— it's not just a creation, but a testament to balance and compassion. In the Celestial Crucible, such intentions hold great power.

Frank: (his eyes alight with curiosity) And what about you, Manny? What creation stirs within your heart as we stand on the threshold of cosmic possibility?

Manny: (smiling serenely) Frank, I seek to create a beacon of wisdom— a place where knowledge flows like rivers and illuminates the paths of those who seek enlightenment. In this realm, the power of creation is a gift to be wielded with humility and purpose.

With their intentions clear and their hearts aligned, Lili, Silvia, Manny, and Frank embarked on their trials within the Celestial Crucible. Each trial presented them with challenges that tested their ability to channel cosmic energies and shape them into tangible manifestations of their desires.

Lili: (as she wove melodies of light through the air) Music— it's the language of my soul. With each note, I seek to weave harmony and joy into the fabric of creation.

Silvia: (as she sculpted mountains and valleys from shimmering energies) Strength and resilience— they define my vision. Let these landscapes stand as a testament to the enduring spirit of all beings.

Manny: (as he inscribed ancient runes into the cosmic ether) Knowledge— it's the foundation of understanding. May these symbols unlock the mysteries of the universe for those who dare to seek wisdom.

Frank: (as he conjured illusions that danced like fireflies in the night) Trickery and laughter— they are my tools. Let these illusions remind us not to take ourselves too seriously amidst the grandeur of creation.

Each trial unfolded like a symphony of creation, with Lili, Silvia, Manny, and Frank weaving their intentions into the tapestry of reality. They faced challenges that tested their resolve and their understanding of the cosmic forces at play, each trial a step closer to mastering the art of shaping worlds and stars.

Lili: (as her melodies filled the Celestial Crucible with echoes of laughter and joy) These trials

— they're not just about creation, but about the intentions that drive our actions. In the end, it's the harmony we create that defines our journey.

Silvia: (as mountains rose and rivers flowed at her command) The power of creation— it flows through us like rivers of stardust. May our creations be reflections of the dreams that inspire us.

Manny: (as ancient runes glowed with ethereal light) In the Celestial Crucible, our intentions shape reality. Let us wield this power with reverence for the balance that sustains the cosmos.

Frank: (as illusions danced and sparkled like cosmic fireworks) Creation— it's a dance of light and shadow, laughter and wonder. Let us embrace the joy of shaping our own destinies.

With their trials completed and their creations infused with the essence of their intentions, Lili, Silvia, Manny, and Frank stood united in the Celestial Crucible. They had forged bonds of friendship and understanding amidst the cosmic forces that shaped their journey through the realms of magic and cosmic understanding.

Lili: (raising her voice to the cosmos) To creation— to the trials that have tested our spirits and forged our destinies!

Silvia: (joining her voice with Lili's) To intention— to the power that flows through us and shapes the worlds we dare to imagine!

Manny: (his words a quiet prayer amidst the cosmic energies) To balance— to the harmonies that sustain the cosmos and guide our path through the stars!

Frank: (his laughter echoing like celestial music) To adventure— to the trials that remind us of the joy and wonder in shaping our own realities!

Together, they stood as friends bound not only by their quest for knowledge and understanding, but by the bonds of camaraderie forged in the fires of creation. In the presence of the Celestial Crucible, they knew that their journey was far from over— that with each creation, they had woven their own destinies into the fabric of existence itself.

In the midst of the Celestial Crucible, where the echoes of creation reverberated through the cosmos, Lili the melodic butterfly, Silvia the majestic hippo, Manny the sage of sands, and Frank the agile trickster found themselves confronted with a profound challenge. Cosmic forces, unseen and ancient, stirred with intentions that threatened to disrupt the delicate balance of creation itself. Together, they stood united, ready to confront these forces and restore harmony to the universe.

Lili: (her wings glowing with determination) Friends, the energies here— they're shifting. It's as if the cosmos itself is in turmoil. What do you sense?

Silvia: (her presence steady and resolute) Lili, Manny, Frank— these cosmic forces, they resonate with power beyond mortal comprehension. We must be vigilant and united in our efforts to restore balance.

Manny: (his eyes scanning the celestial horizon) Indeed, Silvia. The ancient energies— they pulse with intentions that could tip the scales of creation. Our task is to protect the harmony that sustains the cosmos.

Frank: (his demeanor focused yet playful) Cosmic forces, huh? Sounds like a challenge worthy of our talents. Let's show these celestial troublemakers what we're made of!

As they prepared to confront the cosmic forces that threatened to disrupt the fabric of reality, the Celestial Crucible hummed with anticipation. Energies swirled around them, forming eddies of light and shadow that mirrored the cosmic struggle unfolding before their eyes.

Lili: (as she weaved threads of melody into a shield of harmonious resonance) Music— it's a language that transcends words. Let these melodies ward off discord and bring harmony back to the stars.

Silvia: (as she summoned the strength of mountains and rivers to fortify their position) Strength and resilience— they are our allies in this cosmic dance. May they stand firm against the tumultuous energies that threaten to unravel creation.

Manny: (as he inscribed ancient runes that glowed with protective light) Knowledge— it's a shield that guards against ignorance and chaos. Let these symbols harness the wisdom of ages to guide our path through the celestial storms.

Frank: (as he conjured illusions that danced and dazzled, distracting the cosmic forces) Trickery and laughter— they're the unexpected allies in any battle. Let these illusions sow confusion among our foes and buy us the time we need to restore balance.

Amidst the clash of cosmic energies, Lili, Silvia, Manny, and Frank fought with courage and determination. They faced adversaries whose intentions resonated with the echoes of ancient conflicts and cosmic struggles that spanned epochs of time.

Lili: (her voice rising above the cosmic tumult) These forces— they challenge us not just physically, but spiritually. Through music, let us remind them of the harmony that binds all existence.

Silvia: (her roar echoing across the celestial battlefield) Strength and resilience— we stand as guardians of balance, defenders of the cosmic order that sustains life across the universe.

Manny: (his words infused with the wisdom of ages) Knowledge— it's a beacon that guides us through the shadows of uncertainty. With these runes, let us illuminate the path to restoration and renewal.

Frank: (his laughter ringing like celestial bells) Trickery and laughter— it's a reminder that even in the midst of chaos, joy can be found. Let these illusions weave a tapestry of confusion that unravels our enemies' intentions.

Together, they fought with a unity born of shared purpose and unwavering resolve. Through melodies that transcended words, strength that fortified their spirits, knowledge that illuminated their path, and illusions that danced like fireflies in the night, they confronted the cosmic forces that sought to disrupt the balance of creation.

Lili: (as the cosmic forces began to falter beneath their combined efforts) Friends, we're doing it! We're restoring harmony to the cosmos.

Silvia: (her voice a triumphant roar) Together, we are unstoppable! Let the balance of creation be restored, and may the echoes of our victory resonate across the stars.

Manny: (his runes glowing with renewed vigor) The wisdom of ages guides us through the cosmic storms. With each moment, we bring order where chaos once threatened to reign.

Frank: (his illusions scattering like stardust in the wind) Cosmic troublemakers, consider yourselves outwitted! Laughter and trickery have their place in the cosmos, but harmony reigns supreme.

As the cosmic forces yielded to their combined efforts, the Celestial Crucible shimmered with renewed tranquility. The energies that had once churned with discord now settled into a symphony of cosmic harmony, their efforts to restore balance rewarded with the peace that comes from victory.

Lili: (her wings fluttering with relief) The balance— it's been restored. We did it, together.

Silvia: (her presence calming as the celestial energies subsided) Friends, in the face of cosmic turmoil, we stood united. Let this victory remind us of the strength we find in each other.

Manny: (his gaze reflecting the cosmos' serenity) Indeed, Silvia. Our journey through the realms of magic and cosmic understanding has taught us that unity and resolve can overcome even the greatest of challenges.

Frank: (his laughter echoing like cosmic music) And let's not forget the power of a well-timed illusion! Cosmic forces, beware— we're a force to be reckoned with.

In the aftermath of their confrontation with the cosmic forces, Lili, Silvia,, Manny, and Frank the agile trickster stood united in the Celestial Crucible. They had faced trials that tested their spirits and their bonds of friendship, emerging victorious with a renewed sense of purpose and unity.

Lili: (raising her voice to the cosmos) To harmony— to the balance that binds us to the cosmos and to each other!

After their victory over the cosmic forces in the Celestial Crucible, Lili the melodic butterfly, Silvia the majestic hippo, Manny the sage of sands, and Frank the agile trickster found themselves reflecting on their origins and the journey that had brought them to this pivotal moment. Amidst the cosmic energies that pulsed through the fabric of existence, they spoke of their past and the transformative power of their actions as they continued to explore the mysteries of the cosmos.

Lili: (her wings shimmering with a gentle glow) Remember where we came from, friends? From the confines of the zoo to the vast expanse of the celestial realms— we've come so far.

Silvia: (her presence calming yet resolute) Lili, Manny, Frank— our journey has been one of discovery and transformation. We've transcended our origins to become guardians of balance and agents of change in the cosmic dance of creation.

Manny: (his eyes reflecting the wisdom of ages) Indeed, Silvia. From our humble beginnings, we've embraced the challenges of the unknown, wielding the power of creation with reverence and purpose.

Frank: (his demeanor playful yet introspective) Zoo animals turned cosmic adventurers— now that's a tale worth telling! Who would've thought our escapades would lead us to shape the destiny of worlds and galaxies?

As they journeyed through the celestial realms, the echoes of their past adventures mingled with the cosmic energies that surrounded them. They spoke of the trials they had faced— the arcane archives, the dreamer's domain, and the Celestial Crucible— all milestones in their quest for knowledge and understanding.

Lili: (as they floated amidst nebulae that shimmered with iridescent hues) Each trial, each challenge— it has shaped us into who we are now. From melodies to mountains, we've learned to wield the power of creation with grace.

Silvia: (as celestial beings greeted them with reverence) Our actions— they ripple through the cosmos, shaping the destiny of worlds and galaxies. In every thought and deed, we are agents of change.

Manny: (as he traced constellations with a finger of sand) Knowledge— it's the thread that connects us to the tapestry of existence. Through our journey, we've become custodians of cosmic wisdom, guiding the dance of creation with insight and compassion.

Frank: (as illusions danced like stardust in the cosmic winds) And let's not forget the mischief along the way! Laughter and trickery— they're the spice that keeps our cosmic adventures lively.

Their reflections were punctuated by moments of awe and wonder as they navigated through realms where stars were born and galaxies took shape. Each step forward was a testament to their resilience and their commitment to embracing the mysteries that awaited them.

Lili: (her voice filled with gratitude) Friends, in the face of uncertainty, we've found strength in each other. Together, we've become more than zoo animals— we're cosmic adventurers, shaping the destiny of worlds with every heartbeat.

Silvia: (her roar echoing across cosmic horizons) Our journey— it's a testament to the transformative power of courage and conviction. Let us continue to explore, to learn, and to shape the cosmos with the wisdom we've gained.

Manny: (his words carrying the weight of cosmic understanding) As agents of change, we carry the responsibility to safeguard the balance of creation. Let us forge ahead with humility and purpose, knowing that our actions resonate through the stars.

Frank: (his laughter mingling with the cosmic symphony) To adventure— to the endless possibilities that await us in the cosmic dance of creation. Let's make every moment count, my friends!

In the presence of celestial beings and cosmic energies that spanned the vastness of time and space, Lili, Silvia, Manny, and Frank stood united. They had transcended their origins as zoo animals, embracing their roles as guardians of balance and agents of change in the ever-unfolding tapestry of existence.

Lili: (raising her voice to the cosmos) To transformation— to the journey that has shaped us into who we are destined to become!

Silvia: (joining her voice with Lili's) To unity— to the bonds that strengthen us and guide our path through the stars!

Manny: (his words a quiet prayer amidst the cosmic energies) To wisdom— to the knowledge that illuminates our journey and shapes our understanding of the universe!

Frank: (his laughter echoing like celestial fireworks) To mischief— to the joy and laughter that remind us of the lightness of being amidst the grandeur of creation!

Together, they stood as friends bound not only by their past but by the limitless potential of their future adventures. In the celestial realms where stars whispered secrets and galaxies spun tales of cosmic wonder, they knew that their journey as cosmic adventurers was just beginning— a testament to the transformative power of courage, unity, and the relentless pursuit of cosmic understanding.

Silvia: (joining her voice with Lili's) To unity— to the strength we find in our bonds and the resilience that guides our path through the stars!

Manny: (his words a quiet prayer amidst the cosmic energies) To wisdom— to the knowledge that illuminates our journey and shapes our understanding of the universe!

Frank: (his laughter echoing like celestial fireworks) To adventure— to the trials that remind us of the joy and wonder in shaping our own destinies amidst the grandeur of creation!

Together, they stood as friends bound not only by their quest for knowledge and understanding but by the bonds forged in the fires of cosmic confrontation. In the presence of the Celestial Crucible, they knew that their journey through the realms of magic and cosmic understanding was far from over— that with each victory, they had forged deeper connections to the mysteries that shaped the universe and their place within it.

The journey of Lili the melodic butterfly, Silvia the majestic hippo, Manny the sage of sands, and Frank the agile trickster led them to the Crystal Cathedral— a marvel crafted from pure crystalline light that gleamed with an otherworldly radiance. As they stood in awe before its majestic splendor, they marveled at the cosmic energies that imbued every facet of its structure.

Lili: (her wings shimmering with reflected light) Friends, behold the Crystal Cathedral! It's as if the stars themselves were woven into its very essence.

Silvia: (her presence commanding yet reverent) Lili, Manny, Frank— this place resonates with a purity and harmony that transcends mortal understanding. We stand on sacred ground, bathed in the light of cosmic wisdom.

Manny: (his eyes reflecting the cathedral's ethereal glow) Indeed, Silvia. The Crystal Cathedral— it's a testament to the craftsmanship of celestial artisans, whose artistry rivals the beauty of the heavens.

Frank: (his demeanor playful yet awestruck) Now this is a palace fit for cosmic adventurers like us! I wonder what mysteries await us within its crystalline embrace.

As they approached the entrance of the Crystal Cathedral, the air hummed with a harmonious resonance, welcoming them into its sanctum with a gentle warmth that spoke of ancient knowledge and timeless truths. Inside, they found themselves surrounded by walls that shimmered with iridescent hues, casting prisms of light that danced like ethereal fireflies around them.

Lili: (her voice soft with wonder) This place— it's alive with the whispers of stars and the echoes of distant galaxies. I can feel the cosmic energies swirling around us.

Silvia: (her gaze fixed on the cathedral's intricate architecture) Lili, Manny, Frank— within these walls lie secrets that span the breadth of creation. Let us tread carefully, for every step may uncover truths that shape our understanding of the cosmos.

Manny: (tracing patterns in the air with a finger of sand) Silvia speaks true, my friends. The Crystal Cathedral— it holds the knowledge of ages, waiting to be discovered by those who seek its enlightenment.

Frank: (his eyes scanning the cathedral's corridors with curiosity) Knowledge and mysteries, huh? I wonder what celestial puzzles we'll unravel in this shimmering palace of light.

Within the depths of the Crystal Cathedral, they embarked on a journey of exploration and discovery. Each corridor revealed ancient tapestries that depicted cosmic events, crystalline sculptures that captured the essence of celestial beings, and illuminated manuscripts that whispered secrets of stars and galaxies.

Lili: (as she traced her fingers along a glowing mural) This mural— it tells a story of creation and transformation. The cosmos unfolds before us in colors that defy imagination.

Silvia: (studying a crystalline sculpture with reverence) Each sculpture— it's as if the essence of celestial beings has been crystallized in time. They watch over us with eyes that have witnessed the birth of stars.

Manny: (immersing himself in an illuminated manuscript) These manuscripts— they hold the wisdom of ages, written in languages that transcend mortal comprehension. Here, the answers to our questions may lie.

Frank: (examining a celestial puzzle with a mischievous grin) Puzzles and riddles— they're the spice that keeps our cosmic journey exciting. Let's see if we can unlock the secrets hidden within these shimmering walls.

As they delved deeper into the Crystal Cathedral, the boundaries between space and time seemed to blur. They encountered celestial guardians who tested their intellect and resolve, challenging them to prove their worthiness to unravel the mysteries held within the palace of light.

Lili: (her melodies echoing through the corridors) Music— it's a language that transcends words. Let these melodies resonate with the guardians and open the way to deeper understanding.

Silvia: (her strength resonating with the cathedral's energies) Strength and resilience— they are our allies in this journey. Let us face these trials with courage, knowing that each challenge brings us closer to enlightenment.

Manny: (his runes glowing with ancient power) Knowledge— it's the key that unlocks the mysteries of the cosmos. With each symbol, let us decipher the celestial puzzles that guard the secrets of the Crystal Cathedral.

Frank: (his illusions dancing like stardust) Trickery and laughter— they're the unexpected allies in any cosmic adventure. Let these illusions confound our foes and lead us to the truths hidden within these shimmering walls.

Through trials and tests of their abilities, Lili the melodic butterfly, Silvia the majestic hippo, Manny the sage of sands, and Frank the agile trickster pressed onward. They knew that within

the Crystal Cathedral lay the answers they sought— knowledge that could shape their understanding of the universe and their place within it.

Lili: (as they approached a vault of ancient tomes) Friends, these tomes— they hold the stories of civilizations that have risen and fallen, each page a testament to the tapestry of cosmic existence.

Silvia: (her presence commanding yet serene) Lili, Manny, Frank— let us delve deeper into the heart of the

Crystal Cathedral. Here, amidst the light that illuminates the darkest corners of the cosmos, we may find the wisdom we seek.

Manny: (his eyes alight with anticipation) Indeed, Silvia. Within these hallowed halls, the knowledge of ages awaits us. Let us embrace the journey, for every revelation brings us closer to enlightenment.

Frank: (his laughter echoing through the cathedral's corridors) Knowledge and adventure— they're the treasures we seek in this palace of light. Let's make every discovery count, my friends!

As they continued their exploration of the Crystal Cathedral, Lili, Silvia, Manny , and Frank stood united in their quest for knowledge and understanding. Together, they navigated the shimmering corridors and whispered chambers, ready to uncover the secrets that would shape their destinies as cosmic adventurers in the grand tapestry of creation.

Lili: (raising her voice to the cosmos) To discovery— to the journey that expands our minds and enriches our spirits amidst the splendor of the Crystal Cathedral!

Silvia: (joining her voice with Lili's) To enlightenment— to the wisdom that guides our path through the stars and illuminates the mysteries of the universe!

Manny: (his words a quiet prayer amidst the cathedral's ethereal glow) To knowledge— to the insights that deepen our understanding and connect us to the cosmic dance of creation!

Frank: (his laughter echoing like celestial fireworks) To adventure— to the trials that remind us of the joy and wonder in shaping our own destinies amidst the grandeur of the Crystal Cathedral!

Together, they stood as friends bound not only by their quest for knowledge and understanding but by the bonds of friendship forged in the cosmic splendor of the Crystal Cathedral. In its shimmering light and whispered echoes, they found the promise of discovery and the allure of mysteries yet to be unraveled in the celestial realms where stars whispered secrets and galaxies spun tales of cosmic wonder.

Within the sacred confines of the Crystal Cathedral, they wandered amidst corridors that shimmered with ethereal light. Each step echoed softly against crystalline walls that seemed to breathe with the wisdom of ages, whispering secrets of enlightenment that illuminated their path forward.

Lili: (her wings fluttering with anticipation) Friends, do you hear it? The whispers— they speak of truths that resonate with the stars themselves.

Silvia: (her presence commanding yet reverent) Lili, Manny, Frank— these whispers, they carry the echoes of cosmic knowledge. Let us listen, for within their words lie revelations that may guide our journey.

Manny: (his eyes alight with curiosity) Indeed, Silvia. The whispers— they weave tales of ancient civilizations and celestial wonders. Let us embrace their guidance as we navigate the mysteries of the Crystal Cathedral.

Frank: (his demeanor playful yet attentive) Whispers of enlightenment, huh? I wonder what cosmic secrets we'll uncover next. Let's keep our ears open and our minds sharp, my friends!

As they ventured deeper into the heart of the Crystal Cathedral, the whispers of illumination grew stronger, weaving a tapestry of cosmic understanding that unfolded with each passing moment. They encountered glowing orbs of knowledge that hovered in mid-air, emanating ancient wisdom in soft, melodic tones that resonated with the rhythms of the universe.

Lili: (as she reached out to touch a glowing orb) These orbs— they're like celestial storytellers, weaving tales of creation and transformation. Each whisper adds another thread to the tapestry of cosmic enlightenment.

Silvia: (her gaze fixed on the orbs with reverence) Lili, Manny, Frank— let us listen closely. The whispers— they reveal the interconnectedness of all things, from the smallest quark to the grandest galaxy. In their words, we find the threads that bind us to the cosmic dance.

Manny: (as he absorbed the orbs' radiant energy) Knowledge— it flows through these whispers like a river of light. With each revelation, we gain a deeper understanding of the cosmos and our place within it.

Frank: (his eyes dancing with reflected light) Whispers and secrets— they're the treasures we seek in this celestial sanctuary. Let's embrace the whispers of illumination and follow their guidance through the corridors of enlightenment.

Amidst the whispers of illumination, they encountered holographic projections that depicted cosmic phenomena— stellar nurseries where stars were born, nebulae that shimmered with iridescent hues, and galaxies that spun in graceful arcs across the celestial canvas. Each projection unfolded like a cosmic symphony, revealing the beauty and complexity of the universe in breathtaking detail.

Lili: (her voice filled with wonder) Friends, look at these projections— they're like windows into the heart of creation itself. In their light, we witness the beauty of galaxies unfolding across the vast expanse of space.

Silvia: (her presence commanding yet serene) Lili, Manny, Frank— these projections, they offer glimpses into the cosmic tapestry that connects us all. Let us immerse ourselves in their stories and learn from the wisdom they impart.

Manny: (tracing constellations in the air) Each projection— it's a chapter in the saga of cosmic evolution. From the birth of stars to the dance of galaxies, we witness the wonders that shape the universe.

Frank: (his illusions weaving through the projections like stardust) Cosmic tales and celestial wonders— they're the stories that inspire us to explore, to discover, and to embrace the unknown.

As they continued to wander through the Crystal Cathedral, the whispers of illumination guided them through corridors that shimmered with the light of a thousand stars. They encountered celestial beings whose presence transcended time and space, offering cryptic insights and riddles that challenged their intellect and expanded their understanding of the cosmos.

Lili: (her melodies echoing through the cathedral's chambers) Music— it's a language that bridges the gap between mortal understanding and cosmic wisdom. Let these melodies harmonize with the whispers and lead us deeper into enlightenment.

Silvia: (her strength resonating with celestial energies) Strength and resilience— they are our allies in this journey of cosmic discovery. Let us face these challenges with courage, knowing that each trial brings us closer to the truths we seek.

Manny: (his runes glowing with ancient symbols) Knowledge— it's the key that unlocks the mysteries of the Crystal Cathedral. With each symbol, let us decipher the cosmic puzzles that guard the secrets of enlightenment.

Frank: (his illusions dancing through the cathedral's corridors) Trickery and laughter— they're the unexpected allies in any cosmic adventure. Let these illusions confound our foes and lead us to the revelations hidden within these shimmering walls.

Through trials of intellect and tests of resolve, they embraced the whispers of illumination. They knew that within the Crystal Cathedral lay the answers they sought— knowledge that could shape their understanding of the universe and their place within it.

Lili: (as they approached a radiant altar of cosmic wisdom) Friends, look— this altar, it pulses with the light of a thousand suns. Here, amidst the whispers of illumination, we may find the answers we seek.

Silvia: (her presence commanding yet serene) Lili, Manny, Frank— let us approach with reverence. The altar— it holds the essence of cosmic enlightenment. Let us open our minds and hearts to its guidance.

Manny: (his eyes alight with anticipation) Indeed, Silvia. Within this sacred space, the knowledge of ages awaits us. Let us embrace the journey, for every revelation brings us closer to cosmic understanding.

Frank: (his laughter echoing through the cathedral's chambers) Knowledge and adventure— they're the treasures we seek in this palace of light. Let's make every discovery count, my friends!

As they stood before the radiant altar of cosmic wisdom, Lili the melodic butterfly, Silvia the majestic hippo, Manny the sage of sands, and Frank the agile trickster felt a profound sense of unity and purpose. In the celestial light that bathed them, they knew that their journey through the Crystal Cathedral was not just a quest for knowledge, but a testament to the transformative power of courage, unity, and the relentless pursuit of cosmic enlightenment.

Lili: (raising her voice to the cosmos) To discovery— to the journey that expands our minds and enriches our spirits amidst the whispers of illumination!

Silvia: (joining her voice with Lili's) To enlightenment— to the wisdom that guides our path through the stars and illuminates the mysteries of the universe!

Manny: (his words a quiet prayer amidst the cathedral's ethereal glow) To knowledge— to the insights that deepen our understanding and connect us to the cosmic dance of creation!

Frank: (his laughter echoing like celestial fireworks) To adventure— to the trials that remind us of the joy and wonder in shaping our own destinies amidst the grandeur of the Crystal Cathedral!

Within the luminous expanse of the Crystal Cathedral, Lili the melodic butterfly, Silvia the majestic hippo, Manny the sage of sands, and Frank the agile trickster found themselves drawn deeper into its crystalline embrace. As they wandered through corridors that shimmered with ethereal light, they encountered reflections of their true selves within the cathedral's crystalline walls— mirrors that revealed their innermost desires and fears.

Lili: (her wings fluttering with a gentle glow) Friends, do you see it? These reflections— they reveal truths that lie hidden within our hearts.

Silvia: (her presence commanding yet introspective) Lili, Manny, Frank— these mirrors, they reflect the depths of our souls. Let us gaze upon them with courage, for within their reflections, we may find the keys to understanding ourselves.

Manny: (his eyes reflecting the cathedral's radiant energy) Indeed, Silvia. The mirrors— they offer glimpses into our true selves, mirroring our hopes and fears with crystalline clarity. Let us confront these reflections with open hearts and minds.

Frank: (his demeanor thoughtful yet lighthearted) Mirrors and reflections, huh? I wonder what cosmic truths we'll uncover next. Let's embrace these reflections and see where they lead us, my friends!

As they approached the first mirror, each of them saw their reflection shimmer and transform. Lili saw herself surrounded by a symphony of melodies that resonated with cosmic harmony, embodying the essence of creativity and expression. Silvia beheld an image of strength and resilience, her reflection towering like a beacon of steadfastness amidst cosmic challenges. Manny witnessed runes and symbols dancing across his reflection, embodying the wisdom and knowledge that had shaped him into the sage of sands. Frank saw illusions and pranks playing out in his reflection, revealing the playful spirit that added joy to their cosmic adventures.

Lili: (her voice filled with wonder) This reflection— it's like a portrait of my journey through melodies and dreams. The cosmic symphony within me resonates with the harmony of the universe.

Silvia: (her gaze fixed on her reflection with introspection) Strength and resilience— they define me in ways I never fully realized. In this mirror, I see the guardian and protector that I strive to embody for our cosmic journey.

Manny: (tracing the runes in his reflection with reverence) These symbols— they are the language of cosmic understanding. Through them, I have learned to navigate the mysteries of the universe and guide us on our path.

Frank: (his illusions dancing around his reflection with mischief) Tricks and laughter— they're not just tools of mischief. They remind me of the joy and camaraderie we share in our cosmic escapades.

As they climbed higher through the crystalline corridors, they encountered celestial staircases that seemed to spiral upwards towards infinity. Each step brought them closer to the summit, where the cathedral's highest spires gleamed with a radiance that surpassed even the brightest stars.

Lili: (as she admired the celestial architecture) These spires— they're like beacons of cosmic understanding, reaching towards the heavens with a grace that defies mortal comprehension.

Silvia: (her gaze fixed on the summit with determination) Lili, Manny, Frank— let us climb together. Each step is a testament to our journey and the insights we have gained along the way. Together, we ascend towards enlightenment.

Manny: (tracing ancient symbols along the staircase) Symbols— they're the threads that weave together the tapestry of cosmic knowledge. With each step, let us reflect on the wisdom we carry in our hearts.

Frank: (his eyes scanning the horizon from the staircase) Vistas and horizons— they're the rewards of our cosmic climb. Let's keep pushing onward, my friends. The summit awaits!

As they reached the higher reaches of the Crystal Cathedral, the air seemed to hum with a harmonious resonance, as if welcoming them to the realm of cosmic enlightenment. They passed through corridors adorned with glowing constellations and ancient runes that whispered tales of cosmic creation and the interconnectedness of all things.

Lili: (her voice echoing through the cathedral's heights) Music— it's a language that transcends words. Let these melodies guide us as we ascend to the highest spires of cosmic understanding.

Silvia: (her strength resonating with celestial energies) Strength and perseverance— they are our allies on this ascent. Let us climb with determination, knowing that each step brings us closer to the clarity we seek.

Manny: (his runes glowing with ancient wisdom) Knowledge— it's the compass that guides us through the stars. With each symbol, let us navigate the heights of enlightenment and embrace the cosmic truths that await us.

Frank: (his illusions shimmering with celestial light) Illusions and revelations— they're the steps that lead us to the summit. Let's climb together, my friends. The pinnacle of enlightenment beckons!

At last, they stood before the summit of the Crystal Cathedral, where the highest spires bathed in a luminous glow that seemed to merge with the stars themselves. Here, amidst the celestial heights, they felt a profound sense of accomplishment and unity— a testament to their journey through the depths of cosmic knowledge and self-discovery.

Lili: (raising her voice to the cosmos) To ascension— to the journey that elevates our minds and spirits amidst the celestial spires of the Crystal Cathedral!

Silvia: (joining her voice with Lili's) To clarity— to the understanding that illuminates our path through the stars and reveals the mysteries of the universe!

Manny: (his words a quiet prayer amidst the cathedral's ethereal glow) To enlightenment— to embracing the cosmic truths that shape our understanding and connect us to the cosmic dance of creation!

Frank: (his laughter echoing like celestial fireworks) To unity— to the bonds that unite us as friends and friends on our cosmic ascent through the Crystal Cathedral!

Together, they stood at the summit of the Cathedral, united in their quest for cosmic enlightenment and the boundless wonders of the universe. In the radiant glow that bathed them, they knew that their journey was not just a climb towards knowledge, but a testament to the transformative power of courage, unity, and the relentless pursuit of cosmic understanding.

Lili: (gazing out at the cosmic expanse) Friends, look— this vista, it stretches beyond the horizon of our understanding. Here, amidst the spires of enlightenment, we find the clarity we seek.

Silvia: (her presence commanding yet serene) Lili, Manny, Frank— let us embrace this moment with gratitude. The summit— it offers us a glimpse into the vastness of the cosmos and the mysteries that await us.

Manny: (his eyes alight with cosmic insight) Indeed, Silvia. Within this celestial sanctuary, the knowledge of ages unfolds before us. Let us savor this ascent, for every step has led us closer to cosmic enlightenment.

Frank: (his laughter echoing through the cathedral's heights) Ascension and discovery— they're the treasures we seek in this cosmic sanctuary. Let's cherish this moment, my friends. The summit of enlightenment is just the beginning!

With hearts enlightened by the cosmic truths they had unlocked, Manny and his friends emerged from the Astral Archives, their spirits lifted by the revelations that had reshaped their understanding of the universe. In the echoes of their footsteps and the whispers of celestial wisdom, they knew that their journey was far from over, but that with each step forward, they would continue to uncover the mysteries that bound them to the cosmic dance of creation and eternity.

Silvia the majestic hippo and Frank the agile trickster, alongside their friends, arrived at the Elemental Forge— a place where the primal forces of creation converged, shaping the essence of existence itself. As they stepped into the pulsating heart of the Forge, surrounded by swirling energies and ethereal mists, they felt the weight of cosmic potential and the promise of untold mysteries.

Silvia: (her voice resonant with awe) Frank, do you feel it? This Forge— it hums with the essence of creation, where energies intertwine to shape the fabric of reality.

Frank: (his eyes wide with wonder) Silvia, this place— it's alive with the raw power of creation. I can almost taste the magic in the air.

Around them, streams of elemental energy danced and coalesced into vivid displays of light and color, reflecting the harmonious chaos of creation itself.

Silvia: (surveying the Forge with reverence) Look at these elements— they are the building blocks of worlds, each imbued with the potential to shape destinies and forge new realities. Frank: (as he reached out to touch a swirling vortex of fire and water) Elements in harmony— it's like witnessing the birth of a universe. Silvia, imagine the possibilities that lie within these primal forces.

In the timeless expanse of the Elemental Forge, Silvia and Frank sensed a profound connection to the cosmic forces that governed creation— an understanding that transcended mortal comprehension.

Silvia: (her presence commanding amidst the elemental chaos) Frank, amidst these elemental symphonies, we witness the dance of creation itself. Let us explore with respect and curiosity, for within this Forge lie the secrets that shape our very existence.

As they ventured deeper into the heart of the Elemental Forge, Silvia and Frank knew that their journey was not just a quest for knowledge, but a pilgrimage into the depths of cosmic creation— a journey where each step brought them closer to understanding the primal forces that shaped the universe and defined their place within it.

Silvia the majestic hippo and Frank the agile trickster stood before the Elemental Forge, surrounded by swirling energies of fire, water, earth, and air. With determination in their hearts, they began to harness the raw power of these elements, weaving them together to craft their desires into reality.

Silvia: (her voice steady amidst the elemental chaos) Frank, together we stand at the nexus of creation. Let us channel these elemental energies with respect and purpose.

Frank: (his eyes gleaming with excitement) Silvia, watch closely. Fire and water, earth and air— they are our tools. With their dance, we shape the very essence of existence.

With practiced movements, Silvia and Frank wove their intentions into the fabric of reality, drawing upon the primal forces that surged through the Elemental Forge. Flames leapt and twisted into intricate patterns, water flowed and ebbed with controlled grace, earth shifted and molded beneath their touch, and air whispered secrets of unseen currents and gentle breezes.

Silvia: (her presence commanding as she shapes a sculpture from elemental earth) See, Frank? The earth yields to our will, forming shapes that echo the landscapes of distant worlds.

Frank: (weaving intricate patterns of fire and water) And here, Silvia, fire and water entwine— powerful yet harmonious, like the dance of celestial bodies in the night sky.

As they worked, each element responded to their intentions, creating manifestations of their thoughts and desires. The Forge resonated with their efforts, a symphony of elemental energies that harmonized in the act of creation.

Silvia: (as they completed their creations, the Forge glowing with their efforts) Frank, look around us. In this Forge, we have harnessed the essence of creation itself, shaping realities with the power of elemental energies.

Frank: (breathing deeply, a smile of satisfaction on his face) Silvia, together we have forged wonders from fire, water, earth, and air. The potential within this Forge— it knows no bounds.

With their creations completed and the Forge still humming with elemental vitality, Silvia and Frank felt a deep sense of accomplishment and connection to the cosmic forces that governed creation. In the heart of the Elemental Forge, they had not only harnessed elemental energies but also discovered a deeper understanding of their own potential to shape the universe and forge their destinies amidst the endless expanse of existence.

Silvia the majestic hippo and Frank the agile trickster stood before the Elemental Forge, their creations shimmering with elemental energies. Yet, before them loomed guardians— ethereal beings of fire, water, earth, and air, tasked with protecting the Forge and testing the mastery of those who sought to wield its powers for noble purposes.

Silvia: (her voice resolute, addressing the guardians) Guardians of the elements, we come in peace and with reverence for the power you protect. Allow us to prove our mastery over these forces, that we may harness them for the greater good.

Guardian of Fire: (flames flickering with intensity) Mortals, show us your control over the flame— the spark that ignites and purifies, yet can also destroy.

Frank: (stepping forward, his movements fluid and confident) Guardian of Fire, watch as I tame your flames with respect and understanding.

With a focused mind and precise gestures, Frank manipulated the fire, shaping it into intricate patterns that danced and flickered in harmony with his will. The Guardian of Fire observed, its fiery gaze acknowledging Frank's command over the element.

Guardian of Water: (a serene presence amidst flowing streams) Mortals, demonstrate your mastery over the currents— the flow that sustains and cleanses, yet can also overwhelm.

Silvia: (approaching the Guardian of Water with calm assurance) Guardian of Water, witness how I guide your currents with gentle strength and purpose.

Silvia's movements were graceful yet firm, as she directed the water to form intricate sculptures and gentle waves that shimmered with reflections of distant stars. The Guardian of Water nodded, acknowledging Silvia's control over the element's ebb and flow.

Guardian of Earth: (solid and steadfast) Mortals, prove your mastery over the earth— the foundation that supports and nurtures life, yet can also quake and reshape.

Together, Silvia and Frank approached the Guardian of Earth, their steps steady upon the shifting ground. With coordinated efforts, they molded the earth into sculptures that echoed the majesty of mountains and valleys, demonstrating their unity and mastery over the element.

Guardian of Air: (elusive and ever-changing) Mortals, exhibit your mastery over the winds— the breath that carries life and whispers secrets, yet can also rage and devastate.

In unison, Silvia and Frank turned their attention to the Guardian of Air, their movements synchronized as they shaped the winds into gentle breezes and swirling vortexes that danced with leaves and petals. The Guardian of Air observed, the currents of wind responding to their harmonious control.

As they completed their trials, the elemental guardians conferred silently amongst themselves, their forms shimmering with approval. The Forge resonated with a sense of harmony, the elemental energies acknowledging Silvia and Frank's mastery and noble intentions.

Silvia: (addressing the guardians with gratitude) Guardians of the elements, we thank you for testing our resolve and mastery. With your guidance, we have affirmed our commitment to wield these powers for noble purposes and the greater good of all existence.

Frank: (smiling with satisfaction) Together, with the blessings of the elemental forces, we shall continue to shape realities that reflect the harmony and balance of the cosmos.

In the presence of the elemental guardians and within the Elemental Forge, Silvia the majestic hippo and Frank the agile trickster had proven their mastery over the primal forces of nature. Their journey through the Forge had not only deepened their bond with the elements but also strengthened their resolve to wield these powers responsibly in their quest for cosmic enlightenment and the fulfillment of their noble aspirations.

Silvia the majestic hippo and Frank the agile trickster stood within the Elemental Forge, surrounded by the pulsating energies of fire, water, earth, and air. With every hammer blow and every flicker of flame, they embarked on a journey to forge their destiny anew, shaping the world around them with the power of creation.

Silvia: (her voice resonant with determination) Frank, together we stand at the precipice of creation. With each act, we mold our destinies and the destinies of worlds yet unseen.

Frank: (his movements precise and deliberate) Silvia, watch closely. With each flicker of flame and each stroke of earth, we craft realities that reflect our hopes and dreams.

With focused minds and unwavering resolve, Silvia and Frank channeled the elemental energies into their creations. Flames danced and twisted into sculptures that radiated warmth and light, water flowed and shimmered with the clarity of untouched streams, earth yielded to their touch, forming landscapes of towering mountains and sweeping valleys, and air whispered secrets of unseen currents and gentle breezes.

Silvia: (as she shapes a sculpture from elemental earth) Look, Frank— the earth yields to our will, forming shapes that echo the landscapes of distant worlds. With each stroke, we shape the foundation upon which futures will be built.

Frank: (weaving intricate patterns of fire and water) And here, Silvia— fire and water entwine, powerful yet harmonious, like the dance of celestial bodies in the night sky. With each flicker, we ignite possibilities that stretch beyond the horizon.

In the heart of the Elemental Forge, amidst the symphony of elemental energies, Silvia and Frank forged their destiny with each creation. The Forge resonated with their efforts, a testament to the power of their dreams and the potential within each act of creation.

Silvia: (her gaze steady as they complete their creations) Frank, look around us. In this Forge, we have harnessed the essence of creation itself, shaping realities with the power of

elemental energies. Let us continue to wield this power responsibly, guided by our aspirations for a better world.

Frank: (nodding in agreement, a smile of satisfaction on his face) Silvia, together we have forged our destiny anew. With every hammer blow and every flicker of flame, we shape realities that reflect the harmony and balance of the cosmos.

With hearts full of purpose and minds enlightened by the journey through the Elemental Forge, Silvia the majestic hippo and Frank the agile trickster emerged, their spirits lifted by the realization that they held the power to shape their destinies and the destiny of the world around them. In the echoes of their creations and the whispers of elemental wisdom, they knew that their journey through the Forge was not just a quest for power, but a sacred commitment to use their abilities for the greater good and the fulfillment of their noble aspirations.

XXXXXXX Silvia the majestic hippo, Frank the agile trickster, Manny the sage of sands, and Lili the melodic butterfly stood at the precipice of the Echoing darkness, shrouded in darkness, where the echoes of past trials reverberated ominously. The air was thick with the weight of forgotten memories and the whispers of those who had faced the darkenss before them.

Silvia: (her voice steady, despite the looming darkness) Friends, we have faced Manny challenges together, but this darkness will test our resolve like never before. We must be prepared for the echoes of our past trials.

Frank: (grinning, trying to lighten the mood) Sounds like a blast from the past! Let's hope these echoes have some useful tips for us.

Manny: (his gaze serious, peering into the darkness) This darkness holds more than just memories, Frank. It is a place where shadows of our deepest fears may come to life. We must confront them with courage and unity.

Lili: (fluttering her wings, a soft light emanating from them) We are stronger together. My melodies will guide us through the darkness, providing us with the light of hope and clarity. Together, they began their entry into the Echoing darkness, the path narrow and treacherous. The deeper they went, the more the darkness closed in around them, and the whispers of the past grew louder.

Echo of the Past: (a disembodied voice, haunting and familiar) Remember the trials you have faced— the doubts, the fears, the moments of despair. They await you here, in the depths of the darkness.

Silvia: (her voice firm, addressing the echoes) We remember, but we have also grown stronger. Each trial has forged us into who we are today. We will not be swayed by shadows.

As they ventured further, the darkess seemed to come alive with the echoes of their past experiences. The ground beneath their feet felt unstable, shifting with each step as if testing their determination.

Frank: (his voice echoing with resolve) Shadows and whispers won't stop us. We've faced worse and come out stronger. Together, we'll conquer whatever this darkness throws at us.

Manny: (nodding, his staff glowing faintly) Frank is right. We must hold onto our strengths and the bonds we've forged. The darkness can only consume us if we let it.

Lili: (her melody filling the air with soothing light) Let my song guide us through. Follow the light, my friends, and remember the hope that has always carried us forward.

The group pressed on, guided by Lili's melody and the unwavering determination that had seen them through countless trials. The darkness seemed less oppressive with each step, the echoes of past fears diminishing as they confronted them head-on.

Silvia: (leading the way, her spirit unwavering) We are more than the sum of our fears and doubts. Together, we forge our path through the darkness, emerging stronger and more united.

As they reached the heart of the Echoing darkness, the darkness began to lift, and the echoes faded into silence. They stood together, having faced the shadows of their past and emerged victorious, their spirits strengthened by the trials they had endured.

Frank: (looking around, a smile of triumph on his face) We did it, team. The echoes are behind us, and we've proven once again that nothing can break our spirit.

Manny: (his voice filled with wisdom and pride) Indeed. The journey through the darkness has reminded us of our strength and the power of unity. Let us carry this lesson forward as we continue our quest.

Lili: (her melody now bright and uplifting) Onward, friends. The light of our journey shines ever brighter, guiding us to the next chapter of our adventure.

With renewed resolve and the echoes of the past now silent, Silvia, Frank, Manny, and Lili emerged from the Echoing darkness, ready to face whatever challenges awaited them next in their quest for cosmic enlightenment.

Silvia the majestic hippo, Frank the agile trickster, Manny the sage of sands, and Lili the melodic butterfly had emerged from the heart of the Echoing darkness, their spirits fortified by the trials they had overcome. However, as they ventured on, they encountered a new and unsettling phenomenon— the whispers of the void. These whispers seemed to emanate from the very walls of the darkness, filling the air with an eerie sense of foreboding.

Silvia: (her ears twitching at the faint whispers) Do you hear that? The darkness is speaking to us, but its voice is filled with something dark and unsettling.

Frank: (his usual bravado tempered by caution) Yeah, I hear it too. It's like the walls themselves are alive with voices— voices that don't sound too friendly.

Manny: (his eyes narrowing in concentration) These whispers are more than just echoes. They are the remnants of despair and sorrow from those who have come before us. We must tread carefully and remain vigilant.

Lili: (her wings shimmering as she emits a calming melody) Let my song guide us, friends. The light of hope will dispel the shadows and give us strength to face whatever lies ahead.

As they continued their descent, the whispers grew louder, weaving a tapestry of despair that seemed to tug at their very souls. Each step they took resonated with the voices of the void, filling their minds with unsettling thoughts and fears.

Whisper of the Void: (a disembodied voice, cold and haunting) You will never escape the darkness. The void consumes all who enter, leaving nothing but despair and regret.

Silvia: (her voice steady but firm) We are not afraid of the void. We have faced darkness before and emerged stronger. These whispers cannot deter us from our path.

Frank: (clenching his fists, his resolve unwavering) Nice try, void. But we've got each other's backs, and there's nothing you can throw at us that we can't handle together.

Manny: (his staff glowing with a protective light) The void may whisper lies and fears, but we know the truth of our strength and unity. We will not be swayed by shadows and echoes.

Lili: (her melody rising in defiance of the void's whispers) Let my song banish the darkness and fill our hearts with light. We are stronger than the fears that seek to consume us.

With Lili's melody guiding them, the group pressed on, each step defying the whispers of the void. The darkness' oppressive darkness seemed to lift slightly, as if retreating in the face of their unwavering determination.

Whisper of the Void: (growing fainter, as if conceding defeat) You may resist, but the void is eternal. You will face it again and again.

Silvia: (her voice filled with conviction) Perhaps, but each time we face the void, we will emerge stronger and more united. Your whispers hold no power over us.

Frank: (grinning) That's right. We're not just surviving— we're thriving. And nothing can stop us from reaching our goals.

Manny: (nodding) Together, we will continue to forge our path, no matter how Manny whispers of the void seek to deter us.

Lili: (her song triumphant) Onward, friends. The light of our journey shines ever brighter, guiding us through the darkness and into the dawn of new possibilities.

With the whispers of the void fading into the background, Silvia, Frank, Manny, and Lili continued their descent into the Echoing darkness. Their spirits were unyielding, fortified by the bond they shared and the knowledge that no darkness could ever extinguish the light of their collective resolve.

The descent into the echoing darkness grew more challenging for Silvia the majestic hippo, Frank the agile trickster, Manny the sage of sands, and Lili the melodic butterfly. The whispers of the void, though quieter now, had left an indelible mark on their minds, and the path ahead seemed to twist and turn with a malevolent intent. It was as if the darkness itself was leading them deeper into their own psyches, forcing them to confront the shadows within.

Silvia: (her voice steady but with a hint of unease) We've faced external threats before, but this journey feels different. The darkness is making us confront something deeper— something within ourselves.

Frank: (his usual bravado tempered by a rare seriousness) Yeah, I've been feeling it too. It's like the darkness is digging into our minds, bringing out fears and doubts we thought we'd buried.

Manny: (his eyes reflective, staff glowing softly) This is a place of deep introspection. To emerge stronger, we must face these inner demons and understand their hold on us.

Lili: (her wings shimmering as she emits a soothing melody) We've always found strength in each other. Let's face these fears together, and remember that we are never truly alone.

As they ventured on, the environment around them began to shift and distort, reflecting their innermost fears and insecurities. The darkness seemed to pulse with life, conjuring visions that confronted them with their deepest anxieties.

Silvia: (confronted by a vision of herself weighed down by darness) I've always feared failing those who depend on me. The weight of responsibility feels overwhelming, but I must break these chains and believe in my strength.

With a mighty effort, Silvia shattered the chains, her determination breaking through the illusion. The darkness around her receded slightly, her inner demon vanquished by her resolve.

Frank: (facing a doppelgänger that mocks his confidence) You think you're so clever, Frank, but deep down, you fear you're just a jester— someone who hides behind jokes to mask your insecurities.

Frank took a deep breath, his usual grin replaced by a look of steely determination. "I am more than my fears. I am more than my jokes. I am a protector, a friend, and I will not be defined by my doubts." With that, he dispelled the illusion, the mocking figure dissipating into the shadows.

Manny: (standing before a vision of a crumbling sandcastle) The sands of time never stop, and I fear I haven't done enough— that my wisdom will fail those I care about.

Manny raised his staff, its light growing brighter. "Wisdom is not about knowing everything, but about learning and growing with every experience. I will not be paralyzed by fear." The sandcastle reformed into a sturdy structure, symbolizing Manny's unyielding resolve.

Lili: (seeing herself trapped in a dark cocoon) I fear that my light isn't strong enough to guide others— that I will be lost in the darkness.

Lili's wings glowed brighter, her song rising in defiance. "My light is not just for others— it is also for me. I will shine through the darkness, for myself and for my friends."

As they confronted and overcame their inner demons, the path ahead began to clear. The oppressive darkness lifted, and the echoes of their fears faded into silence. They stood together, their bond stronger than ever.

Silvia: (her voice filled with newfound strength) We've faced our fears and emerged victorious. The darkness tried to break us, but it only made us stronger.

Frank: (his grin returning, but with a deeper understanding behind it) Yeah, those inner demons didn't stand a chance against us. We've got each other's backs, and that's all we need.

Manny: (his eyes shining with wisdom and pride) Our journey through the darkness has revealed our true strength. Together, we can overcome any challenge.

Lili: (her melody bright and uplifting) Let's continue forward, friends. The light of our journey shines ever brighter, guiding us through the darkness and into the dawn of new possibilities.

With their inner demons vanquished and their spirits fortified, Silvia, Frank, Manny, and Lili pressed on, ready to face whatever challenges lay ahead in their quest for cosmic enlightenment.

They continued their journey, following the path illuminated by the radiant light they had embraced. Their next destination lay ahead— a place known as the Temple of Tranquility, a serene sanctuary where peace and harmony reigned supreme.

As they approached the temple, they were struck by the tranquil beauty of their surroundings. The temple was nestled within a lush, verdant valley, surrounded by gently swaying trees and vibrant flowers. A calm river flowed nearby, its waters shimmering with an ethereal glow. The air was filled with the soothing sounds of nature, creating a sense of profound peace.

Silvia: (her voice soft and reverent) This place— it's like a dream. I can feel the tranquility in every breath I take.

Frank: (looking around in awe) Yeah, it's pretty amazing. After everything we've been through, this is exactly what we needed— a place to rest and find peace.

Manny: (his eyes reflecting the serene surroundings) The Temple of Tranquility is a sanctuary for the soul. Here, we can reflect on our journey and find harmony within ourselves.

Lili: (her wings gently fluttering as she takes in the beauty) Let's take this time to rejuvenate our spirits. The serenity here will strengthen us for the challenges ahead.

They entered the temple grounds, their steps light and unburdened. The temple itself was a marvel of architecture, constructed from pristine white marble that gleamed in the sunlight.

Intricate carvings adorned the walls, depicting scenes of nature and cosmic harmony. The atmosphere inside the temple was filled with a profound sense of stillness and peace.

Silvia: (sighing contentedly as she settled on a soft patch of grass) This place feels like a balm for the soul. I could stay here forever.

Frank: (sitting down beside her, his usual energy replaced by a calm contentment) It's nice to just... be. No pressures, no fears. Just peace.

Manny: (sitting in a meditative pose, his staff resting beside him) This sanctuary offers us a chance to center ourselves and find balance. Let's embrace this moment of tranquility.

Lili: (hovering nearby, her wings casting a gentle light) I'll play a melody to enhance the serenity. Let's immerse ourselves in the harmony of this place.

Lili's wings began to shimmer with a soft, soothing light as she played a gentle melody. The music blended seamlessly with the sounds of nature, creating a symphony of peace that enveloped the group. They closed their eyes, letting the tranquility wash over them, and for a time, they were lost in the serene embrace of the Temple of Tranquility.

As they rested, each member of the group reflected on their journey and the trials they had overcome. The peace of the temple allowed them to see their experiences in a new light, recognizing the growth and strength they had gained along the way.

Silvia: (her voice a quiet murmur) I feel like I've shed a heavy burden. The tranquility here has helped me see our journey with fresh eyes.

Frank: (nodding in agreement) Yeah, me too. We've faced a lot, but we've come out stronger. This place is a reminder of that strength.

Manny: (opening his eyes, his expression serene) The Temple of Tranquility has shown us the importance of inner peace. It is this harmony that will guide us through future challenges.

Lili: (her melody softening to a close) Let's carry this peace with us as we continue our journey. The harmony we've found here will be our beacon in times of darkness.

With their spirits rejuvenated and their hearts filled with tranquility, Silvia, Frank, Manny, and Lili rose from their peaceful rest. The Temple of Tranquility had given them the strength and clarity they needed to face whatever lay ahead. As they left the sanctuary, they carried with them the serenity and harmony of the temple, ready to continue their quest for cosmic enlightenment.

Having found respite in the serene embrace of the Temple of Tranquility, they felt their spirits renewed. As they wandered through the temple, they began to hear gentle whispers, almost like a soft breeze, carrying messages of serenity and enlightenment.

The whispers seemed to emanate from the very walls of the temple, resonating with the harmony and peace that permeated the sacred space. Each whisper was a gentle reminder of the tranquility that surrounded them, filling their hearts with calm and clarity.

Silvia: (her ears twitching as she listens to the whispers) Do you hear that? The temple is speaking to us, sharing its wisdom through these whispers.

Frank: (his usual energy subdued by the calm) Yeah, it's like the walls are alive with a kind of peaceful energy. It's comforting.

Manny: (nodding thoughtfully) These whispers are echoes of the temple's ancient wisdom. They remind us of the peace we carry within and the enlightenment we seek.

Lili: (her wings glowing softly as she listens) Let's follow these whispers and see where they lead us. They might reveal deeper truths about our journey and ourselves.

As they moved deeper into the temple, the whispers grew clearer, each one carrying a distinct message of serenity and insight. The temple seemed to guide them along a path, each step bringing them closer to a deeper understanding of tranquility.

Whisper of Serenity: (a gentle voice, filled with calm) Peace is found within, not without. Let go of your fears and embrace the harmony that resides in your heart.

Silvia: (her voice a quiet murmur) I feel the truth of these words. Peace is not something we find outside ourselves— it's something we nurture within.

Whisper of Enlightenment: (a soothing tone) True wisdom comes from understanding oneself. In the stillness of the mind, clarity is found.

Frank: (nodding) It's like the temple is telling us that we've had the answers all along. We just needed to quiet our minds to hear them.

Whisper of Harmony: (a harmonious voice) The universe is a tapestry of interconnected energies. Embrace the flow of life and find your place within it.

Manny: (his eyes reflecting a deep understanding) We are all part of a greater whole. By embracing this connection, we find balance and purpose.

Whisper of Tranquility: (a calm, serene voice) In every moment of stillness, there is a chance to reconnect with the essence of your being. Let tranquility be your guide.

Lili: (her melody blending with the whispers) These whispers are like a song of the soul, guiding us toward a deeper understanding of our journey.

As they listened to the whispers, the group felt a profound sense of peace and enlightenment wash over them. Each message resonated deeply within their hearts, reaffirming the lessons they had learned and the strength they had gained.

Silvia: (her voice filled with gratitude) The temple has given us more than just a place to rest. It has shared its wisdom with us, guiding us toward a deeper understanding of ourselves and our journey.

Frank: (smiling softly) These whispers have reminded us of the importance of inner peace and self-awareness. It's something we can carry with us, no matter where we go.

Manny: (his expression serene) The Temple of Tranquility has shown us the path to true enlightenment. By embracing these whispers, we can navigate any challenge with calm and clarity.

Lili: (her wings shimmering with light) Let's honor the wisdom we've received here and let it guide us forward. The whispers of serenity will be our beacon in times of doubt.

With the whispers of serenity echoing in their hearts, they felt a renewed sense of purpose and tranquility. The Temple of Tranquility had not only provided them with a sanctuary of peace but also with the wisdom and enlightenment to continue their journey with calm and clarity. As they left the temple, the whispers of serenity accompanied them, a gentle reminder of the tranquility that now guided their path.

Having absorbed the whispers of serenity and enlightenment from the Temple of Tranquility, they felt a profound sense of calm and purpose. As they explored further, they discovered a quiet garden within the temple grounds, a perfect place for meditative practices. Here, they would find balance and harmony within themselves, transcending the distractions of the outside world.

The garden was a haven of tranquility, filled with blooming flowers, gently swaying trees, and a central pond whose surface mirrored the sky above. The air was filled with the soft hum of nature, creating an ideal environment for deep meditation.

Silvia: (settling down on a grassy patch) This garden feels like the heart of the temple. Let's take this time to find our inner balance.

Frank: (choosing a spot by the pond) Sounds good to me. It's been a while since we've had a moment to just breathe and center ourselves.

Manny: (sitting cross-legged under a tree) Meditation is a powerful tool. By calming our minds, we can find the clarity and harmony needed to face any challenge.

Lili: (hovering above a bed of flowers, her wings gently fluttering) I'll accompany us with a soothing melody to enhance our meditation. Let's focus on finding balance within.

As Lili played a gentle, calming tune, they each closed their eyes and began their meditative practices. The garden's serene ambiance enveloped them, allowing them to focus inwardly and transcend the distractions of the outside world.

Silvia: (her thoughts serene) In this stillness, I can feel the harmony within me. It's like the tranquility of the garden is a mirror of my own inner peace.

Frank: (his mind clearing of distractions) Meditation helps me see beyond the chaos. It's a reminder that balance is always within reach, no matter the circumstances.

Manny: (his breathing steady and deep) Through meditation, we connect with the essence of our being. This balance is our anchor in the ever-changing currents of life.

Lili: (her melody weaving through their thoughts) Let the music guide us to a place of perfect harmony. In this state, we are aligned with the universe itself.

As they continued to meditate, each of them experienced a profound sense of unity and balance. The distractions of their journey melted away, replaced by a deep sense of harmony and connection with the world around them.

Silvia: (her voice a calm whisper) I feel a deep connection to the earth and the life within it. This balance grounds me and gives me strength.

Frank: (his voice reflecting inner peace) Meditation has shown me that balance isn't something we find— it's something we create within ourselves.

Manny: (his tone serene) By embracing this inner harmony, we can face any challenge with a clear mind and a steady heart.

Lili: (her melody softening to a close) Let's carry this balance with us, a reminder of the tranquility we've found here. It will guide us through whatever lies ahead.

With their spirits balanced and their minds clear, they— Silvia, Frank, Manny, and Lili— rose from their meditative states. The Temple of Tranquility had given them not only serenity but also the tools to find harmony within themselves. As they prepared to continue their journey, they felt a renewed sense of purpose and inner peace, ready to face the challenges of the cosmos with a balanced and harmonious spirit.

With hearts full of peace and spirits uplifted by the wisdom they had gained, they— Silvia, Frank, Manny, and Lili— rose from the alcove. The Temple of Tranquility had not only provided them with a sanctuary of calm but also helped them embrace the inner peace that would guide them through the cosmos. As they left the temple, they carried with them the tranquility and wisdom they had found, ready to face whatever challenges awaited them with clarity and confidence.

Their journey through the cosmos brought them to a place unlike any they had encountered before: the Portals. Here, the boundaries between dimensions blurred, and the very fabric of reality seemed to bend and twist. The air was charged with a surreal energy, and the landscape shifted and shimmered with every step they took.

Silvia: (looking around in awe) This place... it's like nothing I've ever seen. The dimensions here are blending together.

Frank: (his eyes wide with amazement) Yeah, it feels like reality itself is warping. Every step we take changes everything around us.

Manny: (studying the surroundings with a thoughtful expression) The Potal is a convergence point where different realms intersect. It's a place of immense power and potential.

Lili: (her wings shimmering with excitement) We must be careful, but also open to the possibilities this place offers. It's an opportunity to learn and grow.

As they ventured further into the Portals, the air around them seemed to hum with a strange, otherworldly energy. Colors and shapes shifted constantly, creating an ever-changing landscape that defied description. The group felt both exhilarated and cautious, aware that they were treading on the very edge of reality.

Silvia: (her voice filled with wonder) The energy here is so intense. I can feel it resonating within me, like it's trying to tell me something.

Frank: (grinning) It's like a playground of possibilities! But we need to stay focused. This place could be as dangerous as it is amazing.

Manny: (nodding) Indeed. The portal is a place where the rules of reality are flexible. We must stay grounded and maintain our sense of purpose.

Lili: (hovering close to Manny) Let's use this opportunity to explore the portal and see what it has to offer. There's so much we can learn here.

They continued to explore the portal, moving cautiously but with a sense of excitement and curiosity. The boundaries between dimensions were thin, and occasionally, they glimpsed

other worlds and realities through shimmering portals. Each vision was a tantalizing glimpse into the mysteries of the cosmos.

Silvia: (pointing to a portal) Look at that! It's like another world just beyond our reach. The possibilities here are endless.

The Celestial Odyssey: Journey Through Portals

Frank: (peering into a swirling vortex) I wonder if we can step through these portals. Imagine where we could go!

Manny: (placing a calming hand on Frank's shoulder) We must be careful. The portal is unpredictable. We should observe and learn before we act.

Lili: (her wings glowing softly) The portal is showing us the interconnectedness of all things. Each portal is a thread in the vast tapestry of the universe.

As they navigated through the shifting landscape, they encountered beings of pure energy and consciousness. These entities seemed to move effortlessly between dimensions, embodying the fluid nature of the portals.

Silvia: (watching the entities with fascination) These beings... they're like manifestations of the potals itself.

Frank: (waving to an energy being) Hey there! Can you tell us more about this place?

Manny: (observing the beings) They communicate in ways we might not fully understand. We need to be open to new forms of interaction.

Lili: (her melody blending with the energy around them) Let's listen and learn from them. They hold the key to understanding the potal.

Through their encounters and observations, they began to piece together the nature of the portal. It was a place where dimensions converged, and the fabric of reality was malleable.

They realized that their journey through the portal was not just about exploration, but also about understanding the fundamental interconnectedness of the universe.

Silvia: (reflecting on their experiences) This place has shown us that all realms are connected. We are part of a much larger whole.

Frank: (nodding) Yeah, it's like we're seeing the universe from a completely new perspective. It's incredible!

Manny: (his eyes filled with wisdom) The portal has taught us that reality is not fixed. By embracing this fluidity, we can navigate our journey with greater insight.

Lili: (her wings shimmering with light) Let's carry this understanding with us. The interconnectedness of all things will guide us on our path.

With a deeper understanding of the portals and the interconnectedness of all realms, Silvia, Frank, Manny, and Lili continued their journey. The wisdom they had gained in this place of convergence would serve them well as they ventured further into the mysteries of the cosmos.

As they continued their exploration of the portals, the air around them filled with faint whispers and echoes. These sounds seemed to emanate from the very fabric of the multiverse, offering tantalizing glimpses into realms beyond their current understanding. The whispers carried with them the mysteries of the cosmos, drawing the group deeper into the astral pathways.

Silvia: (her ears perked) Do you hear that? It's like the universe is speaking to us in whispers.

Frank: (looking around curiously) Yeah, it's almost like the walls of reality are sharing their secrets. We should listen carefully.

Manny: (nodding) These whispers are echoes from other realms, fragments of knowledge and insight. They could guide us in our journey.

Lili: (her wings fluttering excitedly) Let's open our hearts and minds to these whispers. They might reveal the mysteries of the multiverse.

As they walked through the shifting landscape, the whispers grew more distinct. They seemed to come from all directions, filling the air with a symphony of distant voices. Some whispers spoke of ancient civilizations and forgotten knowledge, while others hinted at future possibilities and untapped potential.

Silvia: (listening intently) I can hear stories of distant worlds and ancient beings. It's like a history lesson from the cosmos itself.

Frank: (his eyes wide with wonder) I hear whispers of technologies and wonders beyond our wildest dreams. The multiverse is so vast!

Manny: (thoughtfully) Each whisper is a piece of the greater puzzle. If we can understand them, we might uncover the true nature of the universe.

Lili: (her melody harmonizing with the whispers) Let's follow the whispers and see where they lead us. They could guide us to new realms of knowledge.

The group followed the ethereal pathways, guided by the whispers that surrounded them. As they moved deeper into the portal, the echoes grew louder and more coherent, forming a chorus of cosmic wisdom. Each step they took brought them closer to understanding the vast interconnectedness of all things.

Silvia: (her voice filled with awe) The whispers are becoming clearer. I can feel the knowledge they carry resonating within me.

Frank: (grinning) It's like we're tuning into the universe's own radio station. This is incredible!

Manny: (his eyes reflecting deep thought) By listening to these whispers, we're tapping into the collective consciousness of the multiverse. This knowledge can guide us.

Lili: (her wings glowing softly) The whispers are a gift, a way for us to connect with the infinite wisdom of the cosmos. Let's embrace them.

As they continued to listen, the whispers began to form coherent messages, offering insights and revelations. They learned of ancient prophecies and cosmic events, of worlds yet to be discovered and realms that defied imagination. Each whisper was a thread in the intricate tapestry of the multiverse, weaving together the stories of countless beings and civilizations.

Silvia: (reflecting on what she's heard) The whispers have shown us that we are part of something much greater than ourselves. Our journey is just one thread in the vast tapestry of existence.

Frank: (nodding) It's humbling to think about how interconnected everything is. Every action we take can ripple through the multiverse.

Manny: (his voice filled with determination) The knowledge we've gained here will help us navigate our path. By understanding the multiverse, we can find our place within it.

Lili: (her melody a soothing counterpoint to the whispers) Let's carry these insights with us. The wisdom of the cosmos will be our guide.

With their minds opened to the whispers of the multiverse, Silvia, Frank, Manny, and Lili felt a renewed sense of purpose. The knowledge they had gained would serve them well as they continued their journey through the portals and beyond. Each whisper had revealed a piece of the cosmic puzzle, bringing them closer to understanding the mysteries of the universe.

In their journey through the portals, the group found themselves navigating through a labyrinthine network of pathways that seemed to stretch endlessly through the cosmos. Here, the boundaries between dimensions were blurred, and the very fabric of reality shimmered with the presence of beings of pure energy and consciousness.

Silvia: (gazing around in wonder) These pathways... they're like threads in a cosmic web. It's overwhelming yet fascinating.

Frank: (eyes wide with amazement) Look at those beings! They're not like anything I've ever seen before. Pure energy and consciousness, huh?

Manny: (studying the beings thoughtfully) These entities exist beyond mortal comprehension. Their presence here signifies the immense power of the portals.

Lili: (her wings fluttering with excitement) Let's approach them with respect and curiosity. They might have knowledge that could illuminate our path.

As they ventured deeper into the portals, they encountered beings of various forms and energies. Some shimmered with radiant light, while others pulsed with a quiet intensity. These entities seemed to move effortlessly through the astral pathways, their movements fluid and purposeful.

Silvia: (approaching a radiant being) What are you? Where do you come from?

Radiant Being: (communicating through pulses of light) We are beings of the astral realms, manifestations of cosmic energies that traverse the portals.

Frank: (amazed) So, you're like guardians of this place? What is your role here?

Pulsing Entity: (its presence felt rather than heard) We exist to maintain the balance of energies within the portals, ensuring harmony across dimensions.

Manny: (nodding in understanding) Your presence here speaks volumes about the interconnectedness of all things. How can we learn from you?

Flowing Essence: (its voice echoing through their thoughts) To navigate the cosmic web, one must understand the ebb and flow of energies. It requires attunement and respect for the interconnected nature of existence.

Lili: (her melody blending with the energy beings) Let us learn from your wisdom. Show us how to traverse these pathways with clarity and purpose.

The beings of pure energy and consciousness guided them through the cosmic web, teaching them how to navigate the intricate pathways of the portals. They learned to sense the subtle shifts in energy, to read the patterns of light and shadow that marked the boundaries between realms.

Silvia: (absorbing the teachings) Each pathway holds a different energy signature. It's like reading a map of the cosmos.

Frank: (adjusting his perception) Navigating here requires a different kind of awareness. It's not just about physical senses— it's about attuning to the vibrations of the portals.

Manny: (his mind expanding with new knowledge) By understanding these energies, we can move through the portals with greater clarity and purpose. It's a journey of spiritual growth as much as exploration.

Lili: (her wings glowing with newfound understanding) The cosmic web connects all realms and dimensions. Let's embrace this interconnectedness as we continue our journey.

As they continued to navigate through the cosmic web, guided by the beings of pure energy and consciousness, they felt a profound sense of connection to the universe. Each encounter, each lesson learned, brought them closer to understanding the intricate tapestry of existence.

Silvia: (reflecting on their journey) Navigating the cosmic web has taught us that everything is connected. We are part of a vast, interwoven fabric of energies.

Frank: (nodding in agreement) Yeah, it's like we're seeing the universe from a whole new perspective. There's so much more to explore and understand.

Manny: (his voice filled with reverence) The beings of the portals have shown us the beauty of harmony and balance. We must carry these lessons with us as we continue our journey.

Lili: (her melody resonating with cosmic energy) Let's honor this interconnectedness in all that we do. The cosmic web will guide us if we listen closely.

With their minds expanded and their spirits uplifted by the wisdom of the portals beings, they continued their journey through the portals. The lessons they had learned would serve them well as they navigated through the complexities of the cosmos, always guided by the interconnected energies that bound all realms together.

As they journeyed deeper into the portals, they felt a profound shift in their understanding of the cosmos. Here, amidst the swirling energies and cosmic pathways, they began to grasp the interconnectedness of all things and the pivotal role they played in shaping the destiny of the multiverse.

Silvia: (gazing into the cosmic expanse) The more we explore, the more I sense how everything is intertwined. Our actions ripple through the fabric of reality.

Frank: (nodding thoughtfully) It's like we're threads in a grand tapestry. Each decision we make, each path we take, influences the greater whole.

Manny: (his eyes reflecting cosmic wisdom) The portal has shown us that we are not separate from the universe. We are integral parts of its unfolding story.

Lili: (her wings shimmering with cosmic energy) Let's embrace our role as custodians of destiny. We have the power to shape the multiverse with every thought and action.

As they ventured deeper into the portals, they encountered echoes of past events and glimpses of future possibilities. They saw how their choices reverberated through time and space, creating patterns of cause and effect that spanned across dimensions.

Silvia: (observing a vision unfold) This vision... it's showing us the consequences of our actions. Every decision matters.

Frank: (pointing to another vision) And look there! Our presence here, in this moment, affects the outcomes of countless realities.

Manny: (contemplating the revelations) The portal of fates binds us all. Our journey is intertwined with the destinies of countless beings across the multiverse.

Lili: (her melody carrying through the visions) Let's tread carefully yet boldly. Our choices can shape a future filled with harmony and balance.

They continued to journey through the portals, guided by their growing understanding of the interconnectedness of all things. Each encounter, each revelation, deepened their sense of purpose and responsibility as stewards of cosmic balance.

Silvia: (reflecting on their discoveries) The nexus has shown us that our journey is not just about exploration—it's about understanding our place in the grand scheme of things.

Frank: (nodding solemnly) Yeah, we're not just travelers. We're architects of destiny, weaving our stories into the fabric of the multiverse.

Manny: (his voice resonating with conviction) By embracing our interconnectedness, we can forge a future where harmony and balance prevail. It's our duty and privilege.

Lili: (her wings glowing with determination) Let's continue to navigate the portal with wisdom and compassion. Together, we can shape a universe where all beings thrive.

With newfound clarity and resolve, they embarked on the next phase of their journey with the Sage. Armed with the knowledge of their interconnectedness and the impact of their choices, they moved forward with purpose, ready to shape their destiny with the Sage one step at a time.

Manny, the wise red Mule, breaks the silence first, his voice carrying a solemn weight. "The Sage's words hold truth," he begins, his gaze sweeping over his friends. "We must remain vigilant, for the path ahead is fraught with challenges that will test not only our abilities but also our unity."

Lili, the singing butterfly, nods thoughtfully, her wings fluttering softly as she speaks. "She spoke of darkness lurking beneath beauty," Lili muses, her voice a gentle melody. "We must be wary of illusions and trust in the bonds we share."

Frank, the mischievous white monkey, grins mischievously as he adds, "Allies in unexpected forms, eh? Sounds like my kind of adventure!" His eyes sparkle with excitement, though a hint of seriousness underlies his playful demeanor.

Silvia, the serene hippopotamus, listens to each of them with quiet contemplation. "Hope lies in our choices and our unity," she reflects, her voice steady and reassuring. "We must remember that we are stronger together."

Manny nods in agreement. "Indeed," he says, his tone filled with determination. "Let us proceed with caution, but also with open hearts and minds. The Zoo of Wonders holds Manny mysteries yet to be unraveled."

As they prepare to continue their journey through the enchanted realm, they share a moment of silent solidarity, each drawing strength from the shared purpose that binds them.

With the Sage's guidance echoing in their hearts, they set forth once more, ready to face whatever challenges and revelations await them on their quest.

In the aftermath of their encounter with the Sage, the group found themselves in a secluded clearing deep within the Zoo of Wonders. Here, surrounded by ancient trees whose leaves whispered secrets of the ages, they gathered to study the signs and omens revealed by the Sage.

Manny, the wise red Mule, sat cross-legged on a moss-covered rock, a parchment spread out before him. His keen eyes scanned the notes he had taken during their audience with the Sage, searching for patterns and connections amidst the cryptic words.

"Lili, do you recall the Sage's mention of darkness beneath beauty?" Manny asked, his voice a low murmur that echoed through the tranquil glade.

Lili, the singing butterfly, hovered nearby, her delicate antennae twitching with concentration. "Yes," she replied softly, her wings fluttering as she recalled the Sage's words. "It could mean illusions or hidden dangers lurking within the enchantments of the zoo."

Frank, the mischievous white monkey, swung down from a nearby branch, landing with a playful grin. "And what about the part where she mentioned allies in unexpected forms?" Frank interjected, his eyes sparkling with curiosity. "Could there be creatures or beings here that appear one way but are something else entirely?"

Silvia, the serene hippopotamus, approached silently, her presence calming the air around them. "Perhaps the Sage speaks of trust," Silvia suggested, her voice resonating with wisdom. "We must trust not only in each other but also in our instincts to discern truth from deception."

Manny nodded thoughtfully, jotting down notes on the parchment. "Indeed," he agreed. "Our journey through the Zoo of Wonders is not just about unraveling its physical mysteries but also about understanding the deeper truths that bind us to this realm."

As the group continued to study the signs and omens revealed by the Sage, they pieced together fragments of prophecy, slowly unraveling the mysteries of their destiny. Each clue, each whispered echo from the depths of time, brought them closer to the heart of existence itself— a journey of discovery that would shape their understanding of the cosmos and their place within it.

With renewed determination, they set forth once more, their minds sharpened by the Sage's guidance and their hearts attuned to the echoes of destiny that resonated through the enchanted forests and celestial observatories that awaited them.

In the heart of the Zoo of Wonders, beneath a canopy of ancient trees that whispered tales of ages past, our band of travelers stood united. They had journeyed through mystical landscapes, deciphered cryptic prophecies, and now, with newfound clarity, they stood ready to embrace their fate.

Manny, stood at the forefront, his scarlet coat shimmering in the dappled sunlight filtering through the leaves. "We have unraveled the signs and omens," Manny proclaimed, his voice carrying a solemn weight. "The path laid out before us is one of challenges and revelations, but also of profound discovery."

Lili, fluttered gracefully beside him, her wings reflecting hues of gold and azure. "The Oracle spoke of darkness and illusions," Lili reminded them, her voice a gentle melody that resonated in the stillness of the glade. "We must trust in our instincts and in each other as we navigate through the unknown."

Frank, swung down from a branch overhead, his gaze intense yet filled with determination. "And allies in unexpected forms," Frank added eagerly, his adventurous spirit undeterred. "Who knows what allies— or adversaries— we may encounter along this journey?"

Silvia, approached quietly, her presence grounding them all with a sense of calm assurance. "Whatever lies ahead," Silvia began, her voice steady and reassuring, "we face it together. Our unity is our strength, and our bonds will guide us through even the darkest of trials."

Manny nodded in agreement, his eyes scanning the horizon with a mix of anticipation and resolve. "Let us embrace our fate," Manny declared, his voice ringing with conviction. "For it is through our journey that we will uncover the secrets of the cosmos and forge our destinies anew."

With their hearts united and their minds sharpened by the Sage's guidance, the group set forth once more. They traversed enchanted forests and celestial observatories, their steps echoing with purpose and their spirits buoyed by the promise of enlightenment.

The Celestial Odyssey: Journey Through Portals

As they embarked on the next leg of their odyssey through the Zoo of Wonders, they knew that each challenge they faced, each revelation they unearthed, brought them closer to the heart of existence itself. With newfound clarity and unwavering determination, they embraced their fate and the path laid out before them, ready to face whatever challenges the future may hold.

Deep within the heart of the Zoo of Wonders, where ancient trees whispered secrets and the air crackled with mystical energy, our band of travelers encountered a powerful guardian. It stood tall and imposing, a creature of elemental might whose very presence seemed to challenge their resolve.

Manny, took a cautious step forward, his gaze fixed on the guardian before them. "Who dares trespass in this sacred realm?" the guardian's voice boomed, echoing through the glade like thunder.

Lili, fluttered nervously beside Manny, her wings quivering with trepidation. "We seek passage through this land," Lili spoke softly, her voice barely audible amidst the guardian's

formidable presence. "We are travelers on a quest to uncover the mysteries that bind this realm."

The guardian regarded them with eyes that gleamed with an ancient wisdom. "To continue your journey, you must prove your worthiness," the guardian declared, its voice resonating with authority. "Only those who possess courage, compassion, and understanding may pass beyond this threshold."

Frank, grinned confidently, his eyes gleaming with excitement. "Courage, compassion, and understanding? Sounds like a challenge fit for heroes!" Frank exclaimed, his adventurous spirit undeterred by the guardian's imposing stature.

Silvia, stepped forward gracefully, her presence radiating calm assurance. "We accept your challenge," Silvia stated firmly, her voice steady and unwavering. "We are bound by a shared purpose and united in our quest for enlightenment."

The guardian nodded solemnly, acknowledging their resolve. "Very well," it intoned, its voice softening slightly. "Know that the path ahead is fraught with trials that will test your unity and strengthen your bonds."

With a resolute nod from Manny, the group steeled themselves for the challenges ahead. They faced the guardian with hearts united and minds sharpened by their journey through the Zoo of Wonders. Each member of the group drew strength from the others, their unity a beacon of hope amidst the trials that lay ahead.

As they prepared to prove their worthiness and continue their odyssey through the mystical landscapes and ancient mysteries of the zoo, they knew that confronting destiny was not just about overcoming obstacles, but about discovering the true essence of their purpose and the interconnectedness of all things.

With courage in their hearts, compassion in their actions, and understanding in their minds, they stood ready to face the guardian and whatever challenges fate had in store for them next.

The group ventured deeper into the heart of the Zoo of Wonders, where they encountered a series of intricate puzzles and riddles that tested their intellect and wit.

Manny studied the first puzzle with furrowed brow, analyzing the intricate symbols carved into the ancient stone. "This puzzle requires careful observation and logical deduction," he remarked, his voice steady as he began to decipher its meaning.

Lili hovered delicately around the second challenge, her keen eyes scanning the patterns that adorned the walls. "Patience and intuition will guide us through," she murmured, her wings fluttering softly as she contemplated the riddle before them.

Frank leaped eagerly onto the third puzzle, his agile mind racing to unravel its complexities. "A challenge of strategy and cunning," he declared with a grin, his enthusiasm undimmed by the puzzle's daunting appearance.

Silvia approached the fourth trial with serene determination, her wisdom shining through as she offered insights that illuminated the group's path forward. "Each puzzle reveals a piece of the greater puzzle," she mused, her voice a beacon of clarity amidst the labyrinth of challenges.

Together, they pooled their strengths and forged ahead, their minds sharp and their spirits buoyed by the thrill of discovery. Each puzzle they solved brought them closer to unlocking the secrets that lay hidden within the Zoo of Wonders, a testament to their unity and resilience in the face of adversity.

As they navigated through the trials of mind, they realized that the true test was not just in solving the puzzles themselves, but in the bonds they forged and the lessons they learned

along the way. With each challenge they overcame, they grew stronger and more attuned to the cosmic mysteries that awaited them.

With unwavering determination and a shared purpose that transcended individual abilities, they embraced the trials of mind as an opportunity to prove their worthiness and uncover the deeper truths that awaited them on their celestial odyssey.

They stood before the final trial set by the guardian, their hearts united and their spirits fortified by the challenges they had overcome. The air crackled with anticipation as they prepared to demonstrate their courage, compassion, and understanding.

The guardian's voice echoed through the clearing, reverberating with ancient power. "You have journeyed far, seekers of truth," it intoned, its eyes gleaming with a mixture of skepticism and respect. "But before you may continue, you must prove your worthiness one final time."

Manny stepped forward, his gaze unwavering as he met the guardian's imposing stare. "We have faced trials that tested our unity and strengthened our resolve," Manny declared, his voice ringing with conviction. "Together, we have learned the true meaning of courage, compassion, and understanding."

Lili fluttered gracefully beside Manny, her wings shimmering with determination. "We have navigated through mysteries and challenges," Lili added, her voice a gentle melody that resonated with unwavering faith. "Our journey has forged bonds that transcend the trials we face."

Frank bounded forward with boundless energy, his eyes alight with determination. "And we've done it together!" Frank exclaimed eagerly, his spirit undimmed by the guardian's formidable presence. "As allies in unexpected forms, we've proven our strength and unity!"

Silvia approached with serene grace, her presence a calming influence amidst the tension that hung in the air. "We embrace our fate," Silvia affirmed, her voice steady and resolute. "With courage in our hearts and understanding in our minds, we are ready to face whatever challenges await us."

The guardian regarded them with a mixture of solemnity and approval. "Very well," it conceded, its voice softer now, tinged with a hint of respect. "You have shown yourselves worthy to continue on your celestial odyssey."

With a resounding sense of triumph, they emerged victorious from the guardian's trial. Their unity had been tested and proven, their bonds strengthened by the challenges they had faced together.

As they prepared to venture deeper into the Zoo of Wonders, they carried with them the lessons learned and the victories earned through unity and determination. The guardian's trial had not just marked a passage; it had affirmed their purpose and solidified their resolve to uncover the secrets of the cosmos.

With hearts ablaze with courage and minds sharpened by understanding, they embraced their triumph over adversity as a testament to the power of unity and the strength of their shared journey through "The Celestial Odyssey."

Manny walked with a renewed sense of purpose, his scarlet coat now a symbol of resilience rather than burden. He embraced the complexities of leadership, acknowledging that true strength lay not in perfection but in the willingness to learn and grow from mistakes.

Lili fluttered gracefully beside Manny, her wings shimmering with newfound confidence. She had confronted her insecurities head-on, recognizing that her voice and presence mattered, even in moments of doubt. She embraced her uniqueness, knowing that true beauty lay in authenticity and self-acceptance.

Frank swung through the trees with renewed vigor, his mischievous grin now tempered with introspection. He had faced the shadows of his past, understanding that vulnerability was not weakness but a testament to his humanity. Frank accepted his flaws as integral parts of his adventurous spirit, shaping him into a friend and ally worthy of trust.

Silvia moved with serene grace, her ivory tusks gleaming with inner peace. She had confronted her fears of failure and loss, realizing that strength came from compassion and empathy. Silvia embraced her role as a pillar of support, knowing that her kindness and understanding were gifts to be shared with those around her.

Together, they embraced the process of self-discovery, understanding that growth was a journey, not a destination. They accepted their flaws and imperfections as essential parts of their identities, recognizing that true strength lay in embracing their vulnerabilities and learning from them.

As they continued their odyssey through "The Celestial Odyssey,", they carried with them the lessons learned from their journey of self-discovery. They faced the challenges ahead with renewed courage and unity, knowing that their collective strength lay in their acceptance of each other and themselves.

With hearts open to growth and minds enriched by introspection, they ventured forth into the unknown realms of mystical landscapes and ancient mysteries. The journey continues, and they ere ready to embrace the limitless possibilities that awaite them on their quest for enlightenment.

In the tranquil aftermath of their trials within their journey they embarked on a journey of profound self-discovery and inner peace. Each reflection they had encountered had brought them closer to acceptance and love for themselves, embracing both their strengths and their imperfections.

Manny stood at the edge of a serene pond, the waters reflecting the starlit sky above. As he gazed into the peaceful surface, he found a sense of inner peace, accepting himself as a leader who could learn and grow from every experience. He knew that true strength lay in humility and compassion, qualities he now cherished.

Lili perched delicately on a blossoming branch nearby, her wings catching the gentle breeze. In the quietude of the moment, she felt a deep sense of acceptance for her own voice and presence. She embraced her uniqueness, understanding that her song carried beauty and meaning, resonating with those who listened.

Frank swung playfully from tree to tree, the rustling leaves whispering tales of adventure. Amidst the lush greenery, he found a sense of peace in acknowledging his vulnerabilities and past mistakes. He realized that his journey was not about perfection but about the courage to explore, learn, and grow.

Silvia rested beside a tranquil waterfall, its cascading waters a soothing melody. As she observed the natural rhythm of life around her, she felt a profound acceptance of her role as a pillar of support and kindness. She embraced her ability to bring comfort and solace to others, finding strength in her empathy.

Together, they embraced the journey towards inner peace, knowing that self-love was a journey of acceptance and growth. They celebrated their strengths and learned from their challenges, understanding that every aspect of themselves contributed to the unity and resilience of their group.

As they continued their odyssey through "The Celestial Odyssey," they carried with them the tranquility of inner peace. They faced the mysteries and challenges ahead with renewed clarity and harmony, knowing that their journey was guided by self-acceptance and love.

With hearts open to the beauty of their own souls and minds enriched by introspection, they ventured forth into the boundless realms of mystical landscapes and ancient mysteries. The path ahead shimmered with possibility, illuminated by the inner peace they had discovered within themselves.

As they ventured deeper into the cosmic web, Manny led the group with unwavering determination. His scarlet coat glowed softly amidst the swirling energies that surrounded them, a beacon of resilience in the face of the unknown. He sensed the presence of beings whose forms shimmered with ethereal light, their consciousness reaching out across the cosmic expanse.

Lili fluttered beside Manny, her wings shimmering with curiosity and awe. She marveled at the beings of pure energy that they encountered, their forms fluid and ever-changing. Each encounter offered new insights into the nature of existence, expanding her understanding of the interconnectedness that bound all realms together.

Frank swung through the cosmic branches with a mix of excitement and caution. His mischievous grin widened as they encountered beings whose thoughts resonated like celestial melodies. He engaged in playful exchanges with these entities, learning that communication transcended language in the cosmic web.

Silvia moved with serene grace, her ivory tusks gleaming with inner peace amidst the swirling energies. She approached the beings of pure consciousness with a sense of reverence, recognizing the profound wisdom they possessed. Through silent communion, she understood that existence was not bound by physical form but by the essence of being itself.

Lili fluttered beside Manny, her wings aglow with the realization that every song she sang echoed through the multiverse. She understood that her voice carried not just beauty but also the power to inspire and connect disparate realms. Through her melodies, she bridged gaps between dimensions, weaving unity and harmony into the fabric of existence.

Frank swung through the nexus with a newfound appreciation for the chaos and order that intertwined across realities. He reveled in the diversity of experiences and perspectives they encountered, realizing that their journey was a testament to the infinite possibilities that existed within the multiverse. He embraced his role in disrupting and reshaping boundaries that defined existence.

Together, they navigated the convergence of realities within the Celestial Junction, each revelation deepening their understanding of their place in the grand tapestry of existence. They witnessed the ripple effects of their choices and actions, realizing that they were not just travelers but custodians of the multiverse's destiny.

As they journeyed deeper into the nexus, they felt a profound sense of unity and purpose. They embraced the interconnectedness of all things, knowing that their quest for enlightenment was intertwined with the fate of countless beings across dimensions.

With hearts open to the vastness of existence and minds enriched by their experiences, they ventured forth into the ever-expanding mysteries of the Clestial Junction. The journey ahead promised further revelations and challenges, each step bringing them closer to the heart of existence itself in "The Celestial Odyssey."

Arriving at the Ethereal Observatory, they stood in awe before a structure that seemed to reach towards the heavens themselves. Perched atop a celestial plateau, the observatory shimmered with an otherworldly light, its domes and spires adorned with ancient symbols that spoke of timeless wisdom and cosmic knowledge.

Manny led the group towards the entrance, his scarlet coat vibrant against the backdrop of the observatory's ethereal glow. He felt a sense of reverence for the mysteries that awaited them within, knowing that the stars held secrets that could illuminate their path through the multiverse.

Lili fluttered beside Manny, her wings catching the faint starlight that filtered through the observatory's intricate windows. She felt a deep connection to the celestial energies that permeated the air, sensing that each twinkling star held a story waiting to be told, a song waiting to be sung.

Frank swung through the observatory gates with his usual enthusiasm, his eyes sparkling with curiosity and wonder. He marveled at the celestial instruments that adorned the observatory's chambers, each one a testament to the ingenuity of those who sought to understand the cosmos.

Silvia moved with serene grace, her presence a calming influence amidst the vastness of the celestial observatory. She embraced the stillness of the cosmic currents that flowed around them, understanding that the stars whispered secrets of creation and destiny.

Together, they ascended the spiraling staircases and traversed the labyrinthine corridors of the Ethereal Observatory. They encountered celestial charts that mapped the movements of stars and galaxies, telescopes that peered into distant realms, and manuscripts that chronicled the histories of cosmic beings.

As they delved deeper into the mysteries of the cosmos within the Ethereal Observatory, they felt a profound sense of awe and wonder. They understood that the stars were not just distant lights in the night sky but portals to realms of knowledge and enlightenment.

With minds open to the mysteries of the cosmos and hearts attuned to the celestial harmonies, they ventured forth into the boundless expanse of the Ethereal Observatory. The journey ahead promised revelations that would illuminate their understanding of existence itself in "The Celestial Odyssey."

Under the vaulted dome of the Ethereal Observatory, they stood before a towering telescope that promised glimpses into the farthest reaches of the cosmos. As they peered through its lens, marveling at the celestial wonders that unfolded before them, they couldn't help but share their thoughts and observations.

Silvia: (gazing at a distant galaxy) "Look at the spiral arms of that galaxy. It's as if each star is a brushstroke in a cosmic painting."

Lili: (with awe in her voice) "Oh, the colors! I've never seen such hues. It's like the stars are painting the canvas of space with their light."

Manny: (nodding thoughtfully) "Every twinkle we see represents a story untold, a history written in stardust and time. It's humbling to witness the vastness of the universe."

Frank: (grinning widely) "Imagine the adventures waiting out there! Who knows what kind of creatures and worlds we might find beyond our own?"

Silvia: "And yet, despite the vastness, there's a sense of interconnectedness in everything we observe. We're all part of this grand cosmic dance."

Lili: "I wonder if there are beings out there looking back at us, wondering the same things we are."

Manny: "Perhaps they are, Lili. The stars connect us all, across space and time. They remind us of our place in the universe."

Frank: (leaning closer to the telescope) "Hey, look! There's a nebula shaped like a giant dragon. It's like the myths come alive in the heavens."

Silvia: "It's moments like these that remind us why we embarked on this journey. To understand, to explore, and to marvel at the beauty of creation."

As they continued to gaze at the celestial wonders through the observatory's telescopes, Manny, they felt a profound sense of unity and purpose. They knew that their journey through the cosmos was not just about discovery but also about embracing the mysteries that bound them together as travelers in "The Celestial Odyssey."

"Reflecting on the passages we've traversed, they mirror the confusion in life and the repetitive daily routines we endure. Yet, amidst this, what truly matters is the experience gained from exploring new paths. Our souls crave nourishment to thrive. With that said, here's the continuation of the story in 'The Celestial Odyssey.'"

As the journey in "The Celestial Odyssey" unfolds, Manny finds himself in a moment of profound introspection. Amidst the swirling energies of the cosmic nexus, he pauses to contemplate the path he has walked.

Manny gazes into the infinite expanse of stars above, each one a reminder of the vastness of the universe and the complexity of existence. Thoughts of his past trials and triumphs swirl through his mind like constellations in the night sky.

"I've faced fears and conquered challenges," Manny whispers to himself, his voice carried away by the gentle cosmic breeze. "But have I truly embraced who I am?"

Manny's thoughts turn inward. He recalls moments of doubt and insecurity, times when he questioned his worth and purpose. Yet, with each trial overcome, he discovered a strength within himself that he never knew existed.

"And now," Manny muses, "here I am, amidst the wonders of the cosmos, realizing that happiness isn't found in changing who I am, but in accepting and embracing the person I've become."

A sense of peace washes over Manny as he acknowledges the journey of self-discovery he has embarked upon. He understands now that true happiness lies not in seeking external validation or conforming to others' expectations, but in honoring his own truth and essence.

"I am content," Manny declares softly, a smile spreading across his face. "Content with the challenges I've faced, the lessons I've learned, and the person I've grown to be."

With newfound clarity, Manny continues his journey through the cosmic nexus, his heart lightened by the realization that happiness blooms from within. As he ventures onward, he carries with him a profound understanding: that embracing oneself is the key to unlocking the boundless potential of the soul.

Lili, the Melodic Singing Butterfly, finds a serene clearing bathed in the soft glow of twilight. The air is filled with the gentle hum of nature's symphony, and Lili perches delicately on a blooming flower, her wings shimmering in the fading light.

As she gazes at the tranquil surroundings, Lili's thoughts drift to the journey she has embarked upon. The melodies she has sung, the challenges she has faced—each note and every obstacle has shaped her into the butterfly she is today.

"I've always sought harmony in every melody," Lili murmurs softly, her voice carrying a melody of its own. "But have I found harmony within myself?"

With the grace of a dancer, Lili reflects on moments of uncertainty and the times when she felt her song falter. Yet, with each trial overcome, she discovered a resilience within herself that resonated deeper than any melody she could sing.

"Now, amidst the beauty of this forest," Lili muses, "I realize that happiness isn't about the perfection of every note, but in embracing the unique melody that is mine alone."

A sense of peace envelops Lili as she embraces the truth of her journey. She understands now that true happiness lies not in seeking approval of others, but in honoring the purity of her own song.

"I am joyful," Lili whispers, her wings fluttering with contentment. "Joyful in the melodies I've sung, the challenges I've overcome, and the soulful essence of who I am."

With a renewed sense of purpose, Lili continues to flutter gracefully through the enchanted forest, her heart lifted by the realization that happiness blooms from within. As she explores further, she carries with her a profound revelation: that embracing her true melody is the key to unlocking the boundless beauty of her soul.

Frank stands amidst swirling galaxies and pulsating stars. The vastness of the universe stretches out before him, a canvas of endless possibilities and unseen forces. As he contemplates the journey he has undertaken, Frank feels a sense of introspection wash over him.

"I've traversed countless realms and faced formidable challenges," Frank reflects, his voice steady amid the cosmic symphony. "But have I truly embraced the essence of who I am?"

Memories flicker through Frank's mind like constellations in the night sky— moments of doubt, triumphs of courage, and the profound lessons learned along the way. Each experience has shaped him, molding his character into one tempered by resilience and wisdom.

"Now, amidst the celestial expanse," Frank muses, "I realize that happiness isn't found in conquering every obstacle, but in embracing the journey and finding peace within myself."

A profound stillness settles over Frank as he acknowledges the path of self-discovery he has walked. He understands now that true contentment lies not in external achievements or accolades, but in honoring the integrity of his own spirit.

"I am at peace," Frank declares softly, a smile touching his lips. "At peace with the challenges I've faced, the growth I've experienced, and the person I've become."

With renewed clarity, Frank continues to navigate the cosmic nexus, his heart lifted by the realization that happiness springs from within. As he explores further, he carries with him a

deep-seated understanding: that embracing his true essence is the key to unlocking the boundless potential of his soul.

Amidst the tranquil shores of the Luminous Lagoon, Silvia the Hippo finds a moment of quiet contemplation. The waters shimmer with ethereal light, casting a gentle glow upon her massive form. Silvia gazes out across the lagoon, the reflection of the stars above dancing upon its surface.

Silvia's thoughts drift to the journey she has embarked upon alongside her companions. She recalls the challenges faced, the friendships forged, and the wisdom gained from each encounter. Yet, amidst the beauty of the lagoon, she feels a stirring within her soul—a yearning for deeper understanding.

"I've navigated turbulent waters and stood against formidable adversaries," Silvia reflects, her voice resonating with a soothing cadence. "But have I truly embraced the fullness of my being?"

Silvia recalls moments of self-doubt and the times when she felt her strength tested. Through perseverance and resilience, she discovered an inner fortitude that surpassed her physical prowess.

"Now, here in the serenity of this lagoon," Silvia muses, "I realize that happiness isn't about the battles won or the challenges overcome, but in embracing the harmony of mind, body, and spirit."

A sense of tranquility envelops Silvia as she acknowledges the journey of self-discovery she has undertaken. She understands now that true happiness lies not in seeking external validation or power, but in honoring the peace that comes from within.

"I am fulfilled," Silvia declares softly, a smile gracing her lips. "Fulfilled by the bonds forged, the lessons learned, and the acceptance of who I am."

With a profound sense of peace, Silvia continues to bask in the luminous glow of the lagoon, her heart uplifted by the realization that happiness springs from embracing one's true essence. As she moves forward, she carries with her a profound insight: that embracing inner harmony is the key to unlocking the boundless potential of the soul.

Frank sits by a crackling campfire, the flames casting dancing shadows on his weathered face. The air is crisp with the scent of pine and the distant echoes of nocturnal creatures. As he gazes into the flickering embers, Frank allows his thoughts to drift back to the countless journeys he has undertaken.

Memories surge forth like waves crashing upon the shore— moments of triumph and moments of doubt, each etched into the fabric of his being. He recalls the first time he stepped through a portal, heart racing with anticipation and fear. The unfamiliar landscapes, the challenges faced, and the friendships forged in the crucible of adversity.

Yet, amidst the thrill of exploration, there lingers a shadow— a deep-seated fear that has haunted him for as long as he can remember. It is the fear of failure, of letting down those who have placed their trust in him, and of confronting the darkest corners of his own soul.

Tonight, beneath the canopy of stars that have witnessed countless tales of heroism and heartache, Frank confronts his deepest fears. He replays pivotal moments in his mind, dissecting his actions and choices with a clarity born of introspection. Each memory is a stepping stone, leading him deeper into the labyrinth of his emotions.

As the fire crackles and fades into embers, Frank realizes that true courage lies not in the absence of fear, but in the willingness to confront it. He acknowledges the lessons learned from his past journeys— the resilience gained from overcoming obstacles, the wisdom gleaned from unforeseen challenges, and the strength found in moments of vulnerability.

With a newfound resolve burning within him, Frank embraces the dawn of a new day. He knows that the path ahead will not be without its trials, but he faces the future with a clarity of purpose and a steadfast determination to conquer his fears.

As the first light of morning paints the horizon in hues of gold and amber, Frank rises from his reverie. The echoes of his reflections linger in the crisp morning air, a testament to his journey of self-discovery and the unwavering spirit that guides him through the celestial odyssey.

Nestled within the embrace of an ancient grove, Silvia the Hippo finds herself drawn to the tranquil beauty of the Enchanted Forest. Shafts of golden sunlight filter through the dense canopy above, dappling the forest floor with a mosaic of light and shadow. The air is alive with the gentle rustling of leaves and the sweet melody of birdsong.

Amidst this symphony of nature, Silvia wanders along a winding path that meanders through towering trees and lush ferns. Her footsteps are slow and deliberate, each one grounding her deeper into the natural rhythm of the forest. With each breath, she inhales the crisp scent of pine and earth, feeling a sense of peace settle within her.

Silvia's thoughts turn inward as she seeks solace amidst the chaos that often surrounds their celestial odyssey. She reflects on the challenges they have faced as a group— the trials of courage, the bonds of friendship tested, and the uncertainty of their quest. Yet, amidst it all, she finds a sanctuary in the quiet solitude of the forest.

She pauses beside a tranquil pond, its surface reflecting the azure sky like a mirror. Silvia gazes into the crystal-clear waters, seeing her own reflection amidst the ripples that dance upon the surface. In this moment of stillness, she discovers a profound sense of inner peace

— a serenity that transcends the tumultuous journey they have undertaken.

The forest whispers its ancient secrets to Silvia, a gentle reminder of the interconnectedness of all living things. She observes the delicate balance of nature— the harmony of predator and prey, the cycles of life and death— and finds solace in the simplicity of existence.

As the sun begins its descent towards the horizon, casting a warm glow over the forest, Silvia feels a deep sense of gratitude welling up within her heart. She is grateful for the beauty that surrounds her, for the strength she has discovered within herself, and for the companions who have stood by her side through every trial and triumph.

With renewed clarity and a tranquil heart, Silvia continues her journey through the Enchanted Forest. Each step is a testament to her resilience and her unwavering commitment to finding peace amidst the chaos of their celestial odyssey.

High atop a sun-kissed hill in the realm of Melodia, Lili the Melodic Singing Butterfly finds herself enveloped in a symphony of sound. The air resonates with the melodic strains of unseen choruses, each note weaving together in a tapestry of harmony and rhythm. Lili flutters gracefully amidst a field of blossoming wildflowers, her wings shimmering in the gentle breeze.

As she hovers above the vibrant blooms, Lili closes her eyes and listens intently to the melodies that fill the air. Each song tells a story— a tale of love and loss, of joy and sorrow, of dreams pursued and challenges overcome. Yet amidst the beauty of the melodies that surround her, Lili senses a yearning deep within her soul.

With a flutter of wings, Lili descends to rest upon a petal-soft petunia, its delicate hues mirroring the colors of the sunset. She takes a moment to gather her thoughts, reflecting on the journey they have embarked upon and the melodies she has sung along the way. Memories flicker through her mind like flickering candlelight— moments of triumph on stage, the camaraderie shared with her companions, and the lessons learned from each performance.

Yet amidst the crescendo of songs and applause, Lili realizes that there is more to her melody than meets the ear. She longs to explore the depths of her own voice— to uncover new harmonies that resonate from the core of her being. With each breath, she inhales the essence of creativity and exhales a melody that is uniquely her own.

Lili begins to sing— a lilting, ethereal tune that rises and falls like the ebb and flow of the tide. Her voice intertwines with the natural symphony of the realm, blending seamlessly with the rustling leaves and the gentle hum of bees.

As she sings, Lili discovers new harmonies within herself— notes that resonate with clarity and purpose. She embraces the freedom of expression, letting her song soar into the boundless sky, carrying with it the emotions and experiences of her celestial odyssey.

With each verse, Lili feels a sense of liberation— a release of pent-up emotions and untapped potential. She realizes that her melody is not just a means of communication, but a journey of self-discovery and personal growth.

As the last echoes of her song fade into the twilight, Lili opens her eyes to the fading light of the setting sun. She feels a deep sense of fulfillment and contentment, knowing that she has found new harmonies within her soul and embraced the beauty of her own voice.

With a heart full of joy and renewed inspiration, Lili takes flight once more, her wings carrying her towards the next chapter of their celestial odyssey. Each note she sings is a testament to her resilience and her unwavering commitment to explore the depths of her melody, wherever the journey may lead.

Beneath the sprawling branches of an ancient baobab tree, Manny the Lion finds a quiet sanctuary amidst the bustling landscapes of the celestial realms. The air is thick with the earthy scent of the savannah, and the distant calls of wildlife echo through the serene surroundings. Manny settles himself upon a bed of soft grass, his mane catching the golden rays of the sun that filter through the leaves above.

As he gazes out across the expansive vista, Manny's thoughts turn inward, retracing the path he has walked throughout their odyssey. He recalls the challenges faced— the fierce battles with adversaries, the moments of uncertainty, and the bonds forged with his companions. Yet amidst the tumultuous journey, Manny finds himself drawn to a simpler truth— a truth that whispers of contentment and acceptance.

"I have roamed far and wide, seeking answers and confronting fears," Manny murmurs softly, his deep voice resonating with introspection. "But perhaps the greatest treasure lies not in conquest, but in the serenity of acceptance."

Manny reflects on the lessons learned from his fellow travelers— the wisdom imparted by their diverse perspectives and the humility gained from shared experiences. He realizes that happiness is not found in the accumulation of victories or accolades, but in embracing the present moment with gratitude and grace.

With each breath, Manny inhales the essence of the savannah— the whispers of the wind, the rustle of leaves, and the heartbeat of the earth beneath his paws. He finds solace in the rhythms of nature, a reminder of the interconnectedness of all living things and the fleeting beauty of each passing moment.

As the sun arcs overhead, casting a warm glow upon the landscape, Manny feels a profound sense of peace wash over him. He understands now that true happiness lies in simplicity— in savoring the quiet moments, in cherishing the bonds of kinship, and in accepting life's inevitable ebbs and flows.

"I am grateful for the journey," Manny declares, his amber eyes alight with newfound clarity. "Grateful for the lessons learned, the challenges overcome, and the wisdom gained along the way."

With a heart full of humility and a spirit uplifted by acceptance, Manny rises from his meditation beneath the baobab tree. Each step forward is a testament to his inner strength

and his commitment to embracing the essence of their celestial odyssey— one grounded in simplicity, gratitude, and the profound joy found in life's simplest pleasures.

Frank stands against the howling wind that whips through the jagged peaks. The air is thin and crisp, carrying with it the scent of frost and the distant echoes of avalanches. Frank surveys the daunting landscape spread out before him— a labyrinth of sheer cliffs and treacherous ravines that stretch as far as the eye can see.

As he prepares to embark on their next quest, Frank feels a flicker of uncertainty gnawing at the edges of his resolve. The challenge ahead looms large, testing the limits of his endurance and courage. Yet amidst the swirling mists and formidable terrain, Frank senses an opportunity for growth— a chance to prove his mettle and strengthen his bond with his companions.

"I have faced many trials on this odyssey," Frank murmurs to himself, his voice firm despite the lingering doubts. "Each challenge has tested my resolve, but I have emerged stronger and wiser because of them."

With a deep breath, Frank steps forward onto the narrow path that winds its way along the cliff's edge. Every footfall is deliberate, every movement calculated to navigate the perilous terrain ahead. The wind buffets against him, threatening to knock him off balance, but Frank remains steadfast in his determination.

As he progresses deeper into Vertigo Peaks, Frank encounters obstacles that demand both physical prowess and mental acuity. He scales sheer rock faces, navigates treacherous crevasses, and confronts adversaries who seek to thwart their quest. With each obstacle overcome, Frank draws upon the lessons learned from past journeys— the resilience gained from adversity, the courage forged in the heat of battle, and the unwavering belief in his own capabilities.

Through sheer grit and determination, Frank pushes forward, driven by a relentless pursuit of their goal and a steadfast commitment to his companions. His resolve strengthens with each passing moment, fueled by the knowledge that every challenge surmounted brings them closer to their ultimate destination.

As the sun sets behind the peaks, casting a fiery glow upon the rugged landscape, Frank reaches the summit of Vertigo Peaks. Exhausted but triumphant, he gazes out across the expanse of the celestial realms spread out below— a testament to his resilience and unwavering determination.

"I am stronger than I was yesterday," Frank declares, his voice echoing against the granite cliffs. "And with each challenge overcome, I grow closer to unlocking the mysteries of our celestial odyssey."

Silvia the Hippo finds herself confronted by a formidable challenge that tests her resolve like never before. The forest is alive with a symphony of murmurs— a chorus of whispers that seem to echo her doubts and fears. Shafts of dappled sunlight filter through the dense canopy above, casting intricate patterns of light and shadow upon the forest floor.

As Silvia navigates the winding paths of the Whispering Woods, her footsteps are steady despite the uncertainty that gnaws at her spirit. She recalls the lessons learned from past adventures— the courage found in moments of adversity, the wisdom gained from unexpected allies, and the unyielding strength of her companions.

Yet amidst the tranquility of the forest, Silvia encounters an obstacle that challenges her in ways she never imagined. A towering thicket of thorns blocks her path, its branches twisted and entangled like a labyrinth of uncertainty. Silvia's heart quickens with apprehension, but she knows that retreat is not an option. She draws upon the reservoir of courage within her, bolstered by the unwavering support of her friends.

With a deep breath, Silvia takes the first tentative step forward, her movements deliberate and measured. Each thorn she navigates is a testament to her resilience and determination— a reminder that strength is not merely physical, but a reflection of inner fortitude and unwavering resolve.

As she presses onward through the tangled thicket, Silvia's thoughts turn inward. She recalls the words of wisdom imparted by her companions— the importance of perseverance in the face of adversity, the power of solidarity forged through shared trials, and the transformative journey of self-discovery.

With each branch she pushes aside and every obstacle she surmounts, Silvia draws closer to the heart of the Whispering Woods. Her determination grows with each passing moment, fueled by the knowledge that every challenge overcome strengthens the bonds of their celestial odyssey.

At last, Silvia emerges into a clearing bathed in golden sunlight. She stands amidst a grove of ancient oak trees, their gnarled branches reaching skyward like sentinels of resilience. Silvia breathes a sigh of relief, her spirit uplifted by the triumph of overcoming adversity and the strength found within herself.

"I am stronger than I knew," Silvia whispers to the whispering leaves that rustle in the gentle breeze. "And with each challenge faced, I grow closer to embracing the fullness of our celestial odyssey."

In the realm of Harmonia, where melodies float on the breeze and every creature has a song, Lili the Melodic Singing Butterfly flutters through a garden of blossoms that hum with vibrant energy. The air is alive with the harmonious symphony of nature, each note blending seamlessly into a chorus of life and beauty.

As Lili hovers above a field of radiant sunflowers, she feels a stirring within her— a sense that there is more to her song than she has yet discovered. She has always been known for her enchanting voice, but now she senses that deeper, hidden talents lie within her, waiting to be uncovered.

Driven by curiosity and a desire for self-discovery, Lili decides to explore the depths of her abilities aside from singing. She finds a quiet glade, where the sounds of the outside world a fade into Driven by curiosity and a desire for self-discovery, Lili decides to explore the depths of her flying abilities. She finds a quiet glade, where the sounds of the outside world fade into a gentle hum. Here, amidst the tranquility of nature, Lili begins to experiment with her flight, pushing the boundaries of her maneuvers and exploring new aerial techniques.

At first, her attempts are tentative, her movements wavering with uncertainty. But as she delves deeper into her creative expression, Lili begins to uncover new facets of her talent. She discovers that her flight can mimic the motions of the forest— the swooping of birds, the fluttering of butterflies, the gentle drift of falling leaves. With each new motion, she feels a surge of confidence, a realization that her abilities extend far beyond what she had ever imagined.

Encouraged by her discoveries, Lili continues to experiment, blending her maneuvers with the natural rhythms of Harmonia. She learns to harmonize with the wind, to create patterns that echo the heartbeat of the earth, and to weave intricate aerial dances that captivate all who see them.

As she embraces her unique abilities, Lili feels a profound sense of empowerment. She realizes that her flight is not just a means of movement, but a powerful force for connection and transformation. With each new aerial performance she creates, she shares a piece of her soul, touching the hearts of those around her and inspiring them to discover their own hidden talents.

In the heart of the garden, surrounded by the vibrant energy of Harmonia, Lili performs a new aerial composition— a symphony of motion that captures the essence of her journey. Her movements rise and fall like the ebb and flow of the tides, carrying with them the wisdom of her experiences and the joy of her discoveries.

As the final moments of her performance fade into the evening air, Lili feels a deep sense of fulfillment. She has uncovered hidden talents within herself and embraced her unique abilities with confidence and grace. She knows that her journey of self-discovery is far from al.

In the heart of the Serengeti Plain, under the vast expanse of a starlit sky, Manny the Lion finds a quiet spot by a shimmering oasis. The water reflects the twinkling stars above, creating a mirror of the universe that stretches infinitely in every direction. The night is serene, yet Manny's mind is a whirlwind of thoughts and reflections.

Manny has always been the epitome of strength and courage, the leader who faces challenges head-on with unwavering resolve. But tonight, as he gazes into the tranquil waters, he contemplates the true essence of courage. He realizes that bravery is not solely defined by physical strength or fearlessness in the face of danger; it is also about embracing one's vulnerabilities and showing strength through honesty and openness.

As the gentle breeze rustles the tall grasses, Manny recalls moments from their celestial journey— times when he felt uncertain, times when he doubted himself. He remembers the battles fought and the victories won, but also the moments of quiet introspection, the nights when fears and insecurities crept into his heart.

"I've faced many foes," Manny murmurs to the still night air, "but the greatest challenge is facing oneself."

Manny's musings lead him to an epiphany: true courage lies in acknowledging one's fears and insecurities, and allowing oneself to be vulnerable. It takes immense bravery to admit when you're scared, to seek help when you're struggling, and to share your true self with others.

With a deep breath, Manny closes his eyes and listens to the sounds of the night— the distant roar of a lion, the chirping of crickets, and the gentle lapping of the water against the shore. He feels a profound connection to the world around him, a reminder that he is not alone in his struggles.

Manny decides to embrace this newfound understanding of courage. He resolves to be more open with his companions, to share his thoughts and fears with them. By doing so, he hopes to strengthen their bond and inspire them to do the same.

The next morning, as the first rays of dawn break over the horizon, Manny gathers his friends— Frank, Silvia, and Lili— by the oasis. With a calm yet resolute voice, he begins to share his thoughts, his musings from the night before. He speaks of his fears and doubts, of the moments when he felt vulnerable, and the strength he has found in acknowledging these feelings.

His friends listen intently, their eyes reflecting understanding and empathy. In sharing his vulnerabilities, Manny not only finds courage within himself but also fosters a deeper sense of trust and connection among his companions.

As the sun rises, casting a warm golden glow over the Serengeti, Manny feels a sense of liberation. He has discovered a new dimension of bravery— one that embraces vulnerability and finds strength in honesty.

With renewed resolve and a heart full of courage, Manny leads his friends onward, ready to face whatever challenges their celestial odyssey may bring. He knows that true bravery lies not just in the battles fought, but in the willingness to be open and vulnerable, to share one's true self with those who matter most.

In the mystical realm of Echoing Canyons, where every sound reverberates through the cliffs and valleys, Frank finds himself standing at the edge of a precipice. The canyon below is a vast expanse of shadow and light, with echoes bouncing off the walls, creating a symphony of natural sounds. Here, amidst the grandeur and isolation, Frank feels the weight of their journey and the questions that have long lingered in his mind.

Silvia the Hippo finds herself drawn to the gentle allure of solitude. The meadow, bathed in the soft glow of the moon, is a haven of peace and tranquility. Fireflies dance in the night air, their light blending with the silvery luminescence of the moon, creating an ethereal landscape that feels like a dream.

Silvia has always been a cornerstone of strength and support for her friends, but she knows that in order to continue their journey, she must also nurture her own soul. She decides to spend some time alone, away from the demands of their quest, to reconnect with her inner voice and desires.

As she wanders through the meadow, Silvia takes in the beauty of her surroundings— the gentle rustle of the leaves, the soft chirping of crickets, and the soothing whisper of the night breeze. She finds a quiet spot by a tranquil pond, where the water reflects the moonlight like a mirror of the heavens. Here, she sits down and closes her eyes, allowing herself to be fully present in the moment.

Silvia's thoughts begin to drift inward, exploring the depths of her heart and mind. She reflects on her journey thus far, the challenges faced, and the triumphs celebrated. She acknowledges the strength she has gained and the lessons learned, but she also recognizes the need to understand her own desires and aspirations.

In the stillness of the night, Silvia's inner voice begins to speak. It is a voice of wisdom and clarity, guiding her to rediscover her true self. She realizes that her desires are not just about the physical journey, but also about personal growth and fulfillment. She yearns for a deeper connection with herself and the world around her.

Silvia's solitude allows her to explore her passions and dreams. She remembers the joy she finds in creating art, the peace she feels when surrounded by nature, and the fulfillment she experiences when helping others. These desires are an integral part of who she is, and she resolves to honor them as she continues her celestial odyssey.

As the night progresses, Silvia feels a sense of renewal and clarity. She understands that her strength comes not just from physical resilience, but from embracing her inner desires and staying true to herself. She knows that by nurturing her own soul, she will be better equipped to support her friends and face the challenges ahead.

With a heart full of gratitude and a renewed sense of purpose, Silvia rises from her spot by the pond. She takes one last look at the moonlit meadow, feeling a deep connection to the beauty and tranquility of the night. She knows that she will carry this sense of peace and clarity with her, no matter where their journey takes them.

Driven by curiosity and a desire for self-discovery, Lili decides to explore the depths of her flying abilities. She finds a quiet glade, where the sounds of the outside world fade into a gentle hum. Here, amidst the tranquility of nature, Lili begins to experiment with her flight, pushing the boundaries of her maneuvers and exploring new aerial techniques.

At first, her attempts are tentative, her movements wavering with uncertainty. But as she delves deeper into her creative expression, Lili begins to uncover new facets of her talent. She discovers that her flight can mimic the motions of the forest— the swooping of birds, the fluttering of butterflies, the gentle drift of falling leaves. With each new motion, she feels a surge of confidence, a realization that her abilities extend far beyond what she had ever imagined.

Encouraged by her discoveries, Lili continues to experiment, blending her maneuvers with the natural rhythms of Harmonia. She learns to harmonize with the wind, to create patterns that echo the heartbeat of the earth, and to weave intricate aerial dances that captivate all who see them.

As she embraces her unique abilities, Lili feels a profound sense of empowerment. She realizes that her flight is not just a means of movement, but a powerful force for connection and transformation. With each new aerial performance she creates, she shares a piece of her soul, touching the hearts of those around her and inspiring them to discover their own hidden talents.

In the heart of the garden, surrounded by the vibrant energy of Harmonia, Lili performs a new aerial composition— a symphony of motion that captures the essence of her journey. Her movements rise and fall like the ebb and flow of the tides, carrying with them the wisdom of her experiences and the joy of her discoveries.

As the final moments of her performance fade into the evening air, Lili feels a deep sense of fulfillment. She has uncovered hidden talents within herself and embraced her unique abilities with confidence and grace. She knows that her journey of self-discovery is far from over, but she faces the future with a renewed sense of purpose and an unshakable belief in her own potential.

The memories are vivid, and for a moment, Manny feels the sting of nostalgia and longing. But as the whispers of the woods surround him, he begins to see these memories in a different light. He understands that his time spent at the zoo was a cherished part of his past, a place where he felt connected to nature and its wonders. He realizes that holding onto regret only binds him to the past, preventing him from embracing the present.

Manny's reflections lead him to the concept of appreciation. He sees that missing the zoo is not just about longing for what was, but about recognizing the joy and fulfillment it brought him. It is about honoring those moments and allowing himself the grace to cherish them without letting the absence weigh him down. Appreciation is a path to healing, a way to free the heart from the chains of longing and regret. With this newfound understanding, Manny decides to embrace his memories. He starts by acknowledging the happiness the zoo brought into his life. He recalls the vibrant sights and sounds, the sense of wonder and discovery, and he feels a warmth in his heart.

Next, Manny thinks of the animals and the experiences that made his visits so special. He realizes that missing them is a testament to the impact they had on him. With a deep breath, he sends thoughts of gratitude and love to those memories. He understands that while he cannot relive those moments, he can carry their essence within him.

As the sun begins to set, casting a golden glow over the Whispering Woods, Manny feels a profound sense of peace. His reflections have led him to a place of wisdom and understanding. He sees that appreciation is a powerful tool for healing and growth, a way to transform longing into gratitude and regret into fond remembrance. With a renewed spirit, Manny rises from his spot. He is ready to rejoin his friends, carrying with him the lessons learned in the Whispering Woods. He knows that the journey ahead will still have challenges, but he is now equipped with the wisdom of appreciation and the strength to face whatever comes their way.

Frank has been feeling the weight of their journey, the physical and emotional toll of countless adventures and battles. Though he is strong and resilient, he often finds himself wishing for a stronger tail, one that could provide more balance and power during their celestial odyssey.

As Frank approaches the Radiant Springs, he is greeted by the gentle sound of flowing water and the invigorating scent of blooming flowers. The springs sparkle with a glow, their crystal- clear waters inviting him to immerse himself. He senses that this place holds the key to his renewal, a transformative experience that will reignite his spirit.

With a deep breath, Frank steps into the water. Immediately, he feels a soothing warmth envelop him, as if the springs are embracing him with their healing energy. He wades further in, letting the water wash over him, cleansing away the fatigue and stress that have accumulated over time.

As he stands in the middle of the spring, Frank closes his eyes and allows himself to be fully present in the moment. The gentle current massages his tired muscles, and he feels a deep sense of relaxation spreading through his body. He takes another deep breath, inhaling the fresh, fragrant air, and begins to meditate.

In his meditation, Frank visualizes the journey they have been on, the challenges they have faced, and the victories they have achieved. He acknowledges the strength and wisdom he has gained, but also the burdens he has carried. He sees the faces of his friends, the moments of camaraderie and support that have sustained him. These reflections fill him with gratitude, but he knows that he needs to let go of the past to fully embrace the present and future.

Suddenly, Frank feels a surge of energy coursing through him, as if the springs are infusing him with their magical properties. His mind becomes clear, and he experiences a profound sense of peace and clarity. He sees visions of the cosmos, the interconnectedness of all things, and the boundless potential that lies within him.

This transformative experience awakens a new sense of purpose in Frank. He realizes that renewal is not just about physical rest, but about reconnecting with the core of his being, reigniting his passion, and embracing the journey ahead with a rejuvenated spirit.

He understands that his strength comes from within, from his ability to adapt, grow, and remain steadfast in the face of adversity.

As the sun begins to set, casting a golden glow over the Whispering Woods, Frank feels a profound sense of peace. His reflections have led him to a place of wisdom and understanding.

He sees that his longing for a stronger tail is a metaphor for the deeper inner strength he seeks. With a renewed spirit, Frank rises from his spot. He is ready to rejoin his friends, carrying with him the lessons learned in the Whispering Woods. He knows that the journey ahead will still have challenges, but he is now equipped with the wisdom of inner strength and the resilience to face whatever comes their way.

In the serene realm of Verdant Vale, Silvia the Hippo discovers a hidden sanctuary, a place where nature's beauty is in perfect harmony. The vale, nestled between rolling hills and dense forests, is a lush paradise filled with vibrant flowers, tranquil streams, and an abundance of wildlife. It is a place where time seems to stand still, offering a respite from the demands of their celestial odyssey.

Silvia has been feeling the pressures of their journey, the constant need to be strong and resilient for her friends. She knows that to continue supporting them, she must first take care of her own well-being. The Verdant Vale, with its promise of tranquility and rejuvenation, beckons her to find sanctuary within its embrace.

As Silvia enters the vale, she is greeted by a chorus of birds singing in the treetops and the gentle rustling of leaves in the breeze. The air is filled with the sweet scent of blooming flowers, and the warm sunlight filters through the canopy, casting dappled shadows on the forest floor. Silvia feels an immediate sense of peace wash over her, as if the vale itself is welcoming her with open arms.

She wanders through the vale, taking in the breathtaking beauty that surrounds her. Each step brings her deeper into a world of natural wonder. She follows a winding path that leads to a secluded meadow, where a crystal-clear stream flows gently through the grass. The sound of the water is soothing, a gentle melody that calms her mind and soul.

Silvia finds a comfortable spot by the stream and sits down, allowing herself to fully relax. She closes her eyes and takes a deep breath, inhaling the fresh, fragrant air.

She feels the warmth of the sun on her skin and the cool touch of the grass beneath her. In this moment, she feels completely connected to the earth, grounded in the beauty and tranquility of the vale.

As she sits in quiet contemplation, Silvia's thoughts begin to drift. She reflects on the challenges they have faced, the moments of doubt and fear, and the times when she felt overwhelmed by the weight of their journey. But she also remembers the moments of joy and triumph, the times when they overcame obstacles and grew stronger together.

Amid these reflections, a specific memory comes to her mind: the day she lost her beloved red high heel. It was a symbol of her unique style and confidence, something that always made her feel special. The thought of it brings a pang of nostalgia and a wish that she had it with her now, a reminder of her individuality and strength.

Silvia realizes that just as the vale is a sanctuary for her body, it is also a sanctuary for her mind and soul. She understands that finding balance and inner peace is essential for her well- being. She takes this time to reconnect with herself, to listen to her inner voice and desires, and to find clarity amidst the chaos.

The natural beauty of the vale inspires Silvia to embrace a new perspective. She sees that nature thrives through cycles of growth and renewal, and she too must allow herself to rest and rejuvenate. She acknowledges the importance of self-care and the need to nurture her own spirit.

With each passing moment, Silvia feels a sense of renewal. The tranquility of the vale rejuvenates her, filling her with a profound sense of peace and strength. She knows that she can draw upon this inner sanctuary whenever she needs to, finding solace and clarity in the beauty of nature.

As the sun begins to set, casting a golden glow over the vale, Silvia rises from her spot by the stream. She feels refreshed and invigorated, ready to continue their journey with a renewed spirit. She takes one last look at the meadow, grateful for the sanctuary it has provided, and, with a smile, she holds onto the memory of her red high heel, a symbol of her inner strength and unique charm.

"As our celestial odyssey continues, our courageous companions— Frank, Silvia, Lili, and Manny— have traversed realms brimming with both enchantment and adversity.

Each portal they pass through unveils new trials that challenge their resolve and deepen their understanding of the cosmic tapestry they navigate.

They have come to realize that the most profound journeys are not just about external conquests, but about the internal conquest of their own fears and shadows.

Through these experiences, they discover that true liberation lies not in escaping adversity, but in confronting and mastering their inner demons.

Each lesson learned becomes a beacon of light, guiding them towards a life unbound by limitations— a life where wisdom and resilience pave the way to freedom."

Frank, the steadfast monkey, steps into the swirling vortex of the Mental Portal, unsure of what awaits him on the other side.

As he emerges into the new realm, he finds himself surrounded by a labyrinthine landscape shrouded in mist.

Within this mysterious place, Frank encounters various manifestations of knowledge and wisdom. Each step forward leads him to new insights and profound understandings about life and its complexities.

He encounters ancient texts that reveal the secrets of resilience, scrolls that illustrate the power of compassion, and symbols that represent the interconnectedness of all beings. These lessons resonate deeply with Frank, expanding his perspective and enriching his spirit.

Throughout his journey in the labyrinth, Frank absorbs the wisdom from these encounters. He learns about the importance of balance, the strength found in vulnerability, and the beauty of continuous growth. These teachings shape his understanding of the world and his place within it.

At the heart of the labyrinth, Frank encounters a mirror that reflects his truest self— not just a reflection of his physical form, but a representation of his newfound wisdom and enlightenment.

He realizes that he is now equipped with a deeper understanding of life, a knowledge that he is eager to share with others.

With renewed determination, Frank steps out of the Mental Portal, carrying with him the wisdom gained from his journey.

He knows that the road ahead will still have challenges, but he is now prepared to guide others, using the lessons he has learned.

Frank is ready to teach others the meaning of life. He understands that true wisdom lies in growth, resilience, and the courage to embrace one's journey with an open heart.

With a newfound sense of purpose, he is eager to share these lessons, helping others to discover their own paths to enlightenment and fulfillment.

Silvia, with a heart as vast as the cosmos, steps into the swirling vortex of the Mental Portal. As she emerges into the mirrored realm, she is surrounded by reflections of herself— each mirror casting back her doubts, fears, and insecurities with stark clarity.

The first mirror she encounters shows her a vision of doubt, whispering echoes of inadequacy and questioning her strength.

Silvia sees herself hesitating, moments where she doubted her ability to carry the weight of their celestial odyssey. The doubts grow louder, threatening to overshadow her resolve. But Silvia does not turn away. With each mirror she faces, she confronts a different facet of her inner conflicts.

In one reflection, she sees her fear of vulnerability— of showing her true self and being seen as weak. In another, she confronts her doubts about her worthiness to lead, to guide her friends through the challenges they face. As she navigates through the mirrored realm, Silvia realizes that strength does not come from denying vulnerability, but from embracing it.

Each reflection teaches her that vulnerability is a wellspring of courage— a source of inner strength that allows her to connect deeply with others and herself. In the heart of the mirrored realm, Silvia encounters a mirror that shows her a different perspective— a reflection bathed in resilience and acceptance. Here, she sees herself as she truly is: compassionate, determined, and capable of leading her friends with unwavering strength.

With newfound clarity, Silvia touches the mirror's surface, feeling a surge of empowerment within her. She understands that redemption lies not in erasing her doubts, but in acknowledging them and growing stronger because of them. She embraces her vulnerabilities as part of her journey, knowing that they are integral to her growth and understanding.

As she steps out of the Mental Portal, Silvia carries with her the lessons learned from confronting her inner conflicts. She knows that true redemption comes from within, from trusting in her abilities and embracing the journey ahead with courage and resilience.

Lili, the Melodic Singing Butterfly whose wings carry the wisdom of ancient melodies, steps into the swirling vortex of the Mental Portal. As she emerges into the surreal dreamscape, she finds herself surrounded by a landscape cloaked in shadows, where fierce dragons and formidable demons lurk, ready to challenge her at every turn.

The first dragon that materializes is a massive beast, its scales shimmering with an eerie glow. It roars with a ferocity that shakes the ground, its eyes burning with malice. Without hesitation, Lili spreads her wings, and the air fills with the sound of her powerful melody. The dragon lunges at her, but she dodges with grace, using her song to create barriers of sound that deflect its fiery breath.

As Lili moves forward, she encounters a swarm of demons, each one representing a different threat to her journey. They snarl and snap at her, trying to bring her down. But Lili's voice rises in a harmonious crescendo, and her melodies weave through the air like a powerful force, pushing back the demons and dissolving their dark forms.

One particularly menacing demon, towering over the rest, charges at her with relentless aggression. Lili focuses her energy and lets out a piercing, high-pitched note that shatters the demon's form into a thousand pieces. She doesn't waver, her determination growing with each victory.

In the heart of the dreamscape, Lili encounters the fiercest dragon of all, a colossal creature that embodies her deepest fears and doubts. Its scales are like obsidian, and its roar echoes with a sinister resonance. But Lili stands her ground, drawing upon the wisdom and strength she has cultivated throughout her journey.

With a powerful and melodic battle cry, Lili launches herself at the dragon. Her wings emit a brilliant light, and her voice reaches an ethereal pitch. She weaves through the dragon's attacks with agility and precision, each note of her song striking the beast with the force of a thunderbolt.

As the battle rages on, Lili's melody grows stronger, overpowering the dragon's roars. With a final, triumphant note, she sends a wave of sound that envelops the dragon, disintegrating it into a cascade of shimmering light.

Victorious, Lili emerges from the dreamscape, carrying with her the strength and confidence gained from defeating these formidable foes. She understands now that her unique abilities are powerful weapons, and she is ready to face any challenge that comes her way.

As she steps out of the Mental Portal, Lili knows that she is prepared to teach others the meaning of resilience and courage. Her battles with the dragons and demons have shown her that true strength lies in embracing one's gifts and facing adversity head-on. With unwavering determination, she is ready to guide others on their journeys, helping them to discover their own inner power and wisdom.

"As our celestial adventurers— Frank, Silvia, Lili, and Manny— emerge from the depths of self-discovery, they realize that the journey of understanding oneself is but a single step in the vast expanse of the universe's knowledge. There are still countless portals yet to be explored,

each offering new challenges and revelations. Armed with newfound insights into their inner selves, they embark once more, ready to uncover the mysteries that await them."

Manny, shape-shifting , steps into the swirling vortex of the Mental Portal.

As he emerges into the surreal dreamscape, he finds himself surrounded by a landscape cloaked in shadows. The air is thick with tension, and Manny senses a malevolent presence hunting him down.

Suddenly, Manny's form begins to shift and change, contorting into a dark, maleficent thought that embodies his deepest fears and insecurities. This dark manifestation, born from his own mind, has come to torment him and make him suffer.

The thought, now a towering figure of pure malice, charges at Manny with relentless aggression. Its eyes glow with a sinister light, and its voice echoes through the dreamscape, taunting him with whispers of doubt and despair.

But Manny does not falter. Drawing upon his inner strength, he prepares to face this twisted version of himself. He understands that this battle is not just physical but a test of his resolve and self-belief.

With each confrontation, Manny uses his shape-shifting abilities to outmaneuver the dark thought. He transforms into agile, swift forms to dodge its attacks, then into powerful, resilient forms to strike back with force. The battle is fierce, but Manny's determination grows with each passing moment.

As Manny fights, he realizes that defeating this malevolent thought requires more than just physical prowess. He must confront the very essence of his fears and insecurities, accepting them as part of his journey. With a deep breath, Manny taps into the wisdom he has gained from his experiences, using it to fuel his resolve.

In a moment of clarity, Manny transforms into a radiant, enlightened version of himself. His form glows with a brilliant light, and his presence exudes calm and confidence. The malevolent thought recoils, its power waning in the face of Manny's newfound strength.

With a final, powerful move, Manny dispels the dark thought, sending it scattering into a million harmless fragments. The dreamscape shifts, the shadows receding as Manny's inner light banishes the darkness.

Victorious, Manny emerges from the dreamscape, carrying with him the wisdom gained from confronting his inner demons. He understands now that true strength comes from embracing his fears and turning them into sources of power.

As he steps out of the Mental Portal, Manny knows that he is prepared to teach others the meaning of resilience and self-acceptance. His battle with the malevolent thought has shown him that true enlightenment lies in facing one's inner darkness and transforming it into light. With unwavering determination, he is ready to guide others on their journeys, helping them to discover their own inner strength and wisdom.

Frank, the adventurous Monkey, stands before the Celestial Guru in a chamber filled with the soft glow of celestial light. The Guru, an embodiment of serene wisdom and ancient knowledge, gazes at Frank with eyes that seem to peer into his very soul.

"What is the true meaning of resilience, and how have you exemplified it in your journey?" the Guru's voice resonates through the chamber, carrying the weight of centuries of wisdom.

Frank pauses, reflecting on his journey through portals and realms that tested his resolve. Memories flood his mind— moments of uncertainty when fear threatened to paralyze him, yet he found the strength to move forward.

"Resilience," Frank begins, his voice steady yet reflective, "is the ability to endure and adapt in the face of adversity. It is not merely surviving challenges but emerging stronger from them."

He recalls a time when he encountered overwhelming obstacles that seemed insurmountable. In those moments, resilience was about finding new ways to navigate the difficulties, refusing to be defeated by setbacks.

"In my journey," Frank continues, "I have embodied resilience by embracing change and learning from every experience. Each portal, each challenge, has been an opportunity to grow resilient— to face setbacks with determination and to discover the depth of my own perseverance."

He remembers the unwavering support of his friends— Silvia's calming presence, Lili's inspiring melodies, Manny's steadfast encouragement— all of whom stood by him during trials and reinforced his resilience.

The Celestial Guru listens intently, nodding in understanding as Frank speaks. "Resilience," the Guru replies, "is indeed a cornerstone of spiritual growth. Through your journey, you have demonstrated the strength to overcome adversity and the wisdom to inspire others to do the same. Continue to embody resilience, Frank, and you will illuminate the path for others seeking inner strength."

With a renewed sense of purpose, Frank bows respectfully to the Celestial Guru, knowing that his commitment to resilience will guide him and others on their celestial odyssey. Silvia, the gentle Hippo with a heart as vast as the cosmos, approaches the Celestial Guru in a tranquil chamber adorned with celestial symbols. The Guru, emanating an aura of profound wisdom and serenity, meets her gaze with understanding eyes that seem to penetrate her very essence.

"How do you balance strength and vulnerability, and what have you learned from embracing both?" the Guru's voice resonates gently, carrying the weight of countless lifetimes of insight.

Silvia takes a moment to gather her thoughts, her mind drifting back to the many challenges and triumphs she has faced alongside her friends. She recalls moments when her strength guided them through adversity, her determination unwavering in the face of uncertainty.

"Strength," Silvia begins, her voice soft yet resolute, "is not merely about physical prowess or unyielding resolve. It is about inner resilience— the ability to persevere even when the path ahead seems daunting."

She reflects on how her gentle demeanor belies a profound strength rooted in compassion and empathy. "In embracing vulnerability," Silvia continues, "I have discovered that it is not a weakness, but a source of deep connection with others. It allows me to empathize, to understand, and to offer support in ways that transcend mere strength."

The Guru nods in quiet acknowledgement, sensing the depth of Silvia's understanding. "Vulnerability," the Guru replies, "is indeed a gateway to profound growth and connection. It requires courage to embrace, yet it opens doors to empathy and authenticity."

Silvia reflects on moments when her vulnerability led to profound connections with her friends— moments of shared laughter, tears, and understanding. "By balancing strength with vulnerability," Silvia concludes, "I have learned that true resilience lies in accepting all facets of myself and others, and in forging bonds that transcend adversity."

The Celestial Guru smiles warmly, a silent affirmation of Silvia's journey of enlightenment. "Continue to walk your path with compassion and empathy, Silvia," the Guru says, "and you will illuminate the way for others seeking balance and understanding."

With a heart filled with newfound clarity, Silvia bows respectfully to the Celestial Guru, grateful for the wisdom imparted. As she leaves the chamber, she carries with her a deeper appreciation for the delicate balance between strength and vulnerability— a balance that will guide her through the celestial realms yet to be explored in "The Celestial Odyssey."

Lili, the Melodic Singing Butterfly whose wings carry the wisdom of ancient melodies, steps forward with a gentle flutter of anticipation. She stands before the Celestial Guru in a chamber bathed in celestial light, feeling a sense of serenity wash over her in the presence of such wisdom. The Guru, a beacon of tranquility and profound insight, meets her gaze with eyes that seem to hold the secrets of the cosmos.

"What is the melody that guides your soul, and how has it shaped your understanding of the universe?" the Guru's voice resonates softly, carrying the essence of countless harmonies and celestial rhythms.

Lili closes her eyes briefly, letting the echoes of her melodic journey reverberate through her being. She recalls the melodies that have echoed through the celestial realms— the soothing lullabies that brought comfort, the triumphant anthems that inspired courage, and the melancholic ballads that spoke of loss and longing.

"The melody that guides my soul," Lili begins, her voice as delicate as the flutter of butterfly wings, "is a symphony of emotions and experiences woven together in harmony. It is the essence of joy, sorrow, and everything in between— a melody that transcends words and speaks directly to the heart."

She reflects on how each melody has shaped her understanding of the universe— how the rhythms of nature intertwine with the celestial symphonies, creating a tapestry of interconnectedness. "Through music," Lili continues, "I have learned to listen deeply— to the whispers of the wind, the song of the stars, and the heartbeat of the universe itself."

The Guru nods thoughtfully, acknowledging the depth of Lili's connection to the cosmic melodies. "Music," the Guru replies, "has the power to transcend boundaries and connect us to the essence of existence. Your journey of discovery through melody illuminates the interconnectedness of all things."

Lili smiles softly, a butterfly of understanding unfolding within her. "By embracing the melodies that guide my soul," she concludes, "I have discovered that music is not just a sound, but a language of the universe— a language that speaks of unity, diversity, and the beauty of every note."

The Celestial Guru's eyes shimmer with approval, a silent affirmation of Lili's journey of discovery. "Continue to listen to the melodies of the cosmos, Lili," the Guru says, "and you will find wisdom in the harmonies that resonate within and around you."

With a heart brimming with newfound insight, Lili bows respectfully to the Celestial Guru, grateful for the wisdom imparted. As she leaves the chamber, she carries with her a deeper appreciation for the melodies that guide her soul— a guiding light that will illuminate the celestial realms yet to be explored in "The Celestial Odyssey."

Manny, the Lion whose mane shimmers with the wisdom of the cosmos, stands with quiet strength before the Celestial Guru. The chamber is bathed in cosmic light, lending an air of reverence to the encounter. The Guru, radiating tranquility and ancient wisdom, gazes at Manny with eyes that seem to see beyond the physical realm.

"How have forgiveness and acceptance transformed your journey, and what wisdom do you offer to those who seek inner peace?" the Guru's voice resonates gently, carrying the weight of countless lifetimes of introspection.

Manny takes a moment to gather his thoughts, recalling the turbulent currents of his journey— the challenges, the triumphs, and the moments of profound self-discovery. He reflects on how forgiveness and acceptance have been pivotal in shaping his path.

"Forgiveness," Manny begins, his voice deep yet resonant, "is a journey of liberation— an act of releasing the burdens of resentment and judgment that weigh upon the spirit. In forgiving others, I have learned to release the grip of anger and find peace within myself."

He remembers a time when forgiveness was the bridge that healed rifts and restored harmony among his companions. "Acceptance," Manny continues, "is the companion to forgiveness. It is the willingness to embrace life as it unfolds, with all its imperfections and uncertainties."

Through acceptance, Manny has found a profound sense of serenity amidst the chaos of existence. "I offer this wisdom to those who seek inner peace," Manny says thoughtfully, "that forgiveness is not an act of weakness, but of strength. And acceptance is not resignation, but a path to understanding and growth."

The Guru nods in quiet acknowledgment, sensing the depth of Manny's insights. "Forgiveness and acceptance," the Guru replies, "are indeed pillars of inner peace. Your journey exemplifies the courage to confront the shadows of the past and embrace the light of compassion."

Manny, stood before the Celestial Guru in a chamber suffused with the gentle glow of celestial light. The Guru, embodiment of timeless wisdom and knowledge, regarded Manny with eyes that seemed to peer into the depths of his soul.

"What has wisdom taught you, Manny, and how has it shaped your journey?" The Guru's voice echoed through the chamber, carrying the weight of centuries of insight.

Manny paused, his thoughts retracing the winding path through portals and realms that had tested his resolve. Memories flooded his consciousness— moments of doubt and discovery, where wisdom had illuminated his path and guided him through uncertainty.

"Wisdom," Manny began, his voice resonant with reflection, "is the culmination of experience and understanding. It's not merely knowledge, but the discernment to apply that knowledge with clarity and compassion."

He recounted a time when he faced perplexing challenges that defied conventional solutions. In those pivotal moments, wisdom meant navigating complexities with patience and insight, seeking resolutions that honored the interconnectedness of all beings.

"In my journey," Manny continued, "wisdom has been my guiding light. It has taught me to listen deeply— to the whispers of the wind, the murmurs of the earth, and the echoes of my own heart. Each portal, each encounter, has revealed new facets of wisdom, deepening my appreciation for the interconnectedness of life."

Manny reflected gratefully on the invaluable lessons imparted by his companions— Silvia's serene wisdom that grounded him in times of turmoil, Lili's intuitive understanding that resonated with his own quest for enlightenment, and Frank's irrepressible spirit that embodied the joy of learning.

The Celestial Guru nodded in quiet acknowledgement, a serene smile touching their lips. "Wisdom," the Guru affirmed gently, "is indeed a journey of profound discovery and growth. Your path exemplifies the depth of insight gained through experience and reflection. Embrace this wisdom, Manny, and continue to illuminate the way for those seeking enlightenment."

With a sense of reverence, Manny bowed deeply to the Celestial Guru, acknowledging the wisdom that had guided him thus far and would continue to shape his journey through the celestial realms, where each challenge was an opportunity to deepen his understanding and share his newfound wisdom with others.

Frank's Challenge: Deciphering the Riddle

Frank steps forward in the chamber, his gaze fixed on the riddle inscribed on an ancient scroll before him. The celestial symbols around the scroll shimmer softly, hinting at the complexity of the puzzle he must unravel.

The riddle poses a question that transcends mere words, probing deep into the essence of courage and resilience.

As Frank reads the riddle aloud, its meaning begins to unfold like a tapestry woven with threads of his past challenges. Each line of verse echoes the trials he has faced— the moments of doubt, the battles fought, and the victories won through sheer determination and steadfastness. The riddle challenges him to synthesize these experiences into a coherent answer that captures the essence of courage in its myriad forms.

Drawing upon his encounters with diverse adversaries and challenges throughout the Celestial Odyssey, Frank reflects on the wisdom gained. He recalls the times when courage meant standing firm in the face of uncertainty, leading others with conviction, and making decisions guided by integrity rather than fear. Each memory serves as a beacon, illuminating the path to understanding the riddle's cryptic message.

With each passing moment, Frank's resolve strengthens. He pieces together fragments of insight gleaned from his journey, weaving them into a tapestry of wisdom that speaks to the heart of the riddle. Finally, with a clarity born of introspection and experience, Frank formulates his answer— a testament to the transformative power of courage in the face of adversity.

As he presents his solution to the celestial guardian, there is a brief moment of silence, filled with anticipation. The guardian's eyes, ancient and wise, gleam with approval. Frank's journey through the Test of Wisdom has not only affirmed his understanding of courage but also deepened his connection to the cosmic tapestry that binds all beings together.

Silvia's Challenge: Unraveling Symbolic Clues

Meanwhile, Silvia stands before a series of celestial symbols etched onto a luminous mosaic. Each symbol resonates with the interconnectedness of life and the cosmos, reflecting the harmony and balance she has sought throughout her odyssey. The task before her is to decipher the symbolic clues that illuminate the profound truths hidden within.

As Silvia studies the mosaic, she recognizes familiar patterns that mirror the rhythms of nature and the celestial spheres. The symbols whisper tales of cosmic dances and universal harmony, inviting her to contemplate the interplay between strength and vulnerability, resilience and surrender. Each clue she unravels unveils a deeper layer of understanding, revealing how every action resonates across the cosmic tapestry.

Drawing upon her experiences with the companions she has met along her journey— each bringing their own melody to the symphony of life— Silvia begins to decipher the symbolic language before her. She reflects on the moments when strength emerged from vulnerability, when courage blossomed amidst doubt, and when unity transcended differences.

With each symbolic clue decoded, Silvia's perception of interconnectedness deepens. She realizes that every being, every experience, and every challenge is a thread woven into the fabric of existence. Her journey through the Test of Wisdom becomes a pilgrimage of enlightenment, guided by the celestial symbols that illuminate her path.

As she completes the final puzzle, the mosaic glows with a soft radiance, harmonizing with the celestial guardian's approving gaze. Silvia's journey through the Test of Wisdom has not only enriched her understanding of life's interconnected nature but has also fortified her spirit for the challenges that lie ahead in the quest to return to the Zoo of Wonders.

Lili's Challenge: Philosophical Discussions with Celestial Scholars

In the chamber of wisdom, Lili is surrounded by celestial scholars adorned in robes that shimmer with cosmic hues. They beckon her to engage in philosophical discussions, their eyes twinkling with curiosity and wisdom accumulated over eons. Lili, with her wings fluttering in anticipation, steps forward to join them.

The discussions delve into the melodies and harmonies that have guided Lili's journey through the Celestial Odyssey. She recounts the moments when music became her solace, weaving through challenges and illuminating paths forward. The scholars listen intently as Lili shares her insights— how melodies echoed the rhythms of life, resonating with emotions and transcending barriers of language and form.

As the discussions unfold, Lili finds herself immersed in a symphony of ideas and perspectives. The scholars pose questions that probe the essence of harmony and balance in the universe. They challenge her to articulate how music has shaped her understanding of existence and interconnectedness, drawing parallels between celestial melodies and the cosmic order.

With each exchange, Lili gains clarity and depth of insight. She reflects on the melodies that mirrored moments of growth and transformation, harmonizing with the cosmic symphony that binds all beings together. Through these philosophical dialogues, Lili not only embraces her role as a seeker of truth but also discovers the profound wisdom hidden within the harmonies of the universe.

As the celestial scholars nod in acknowledgment of her revelations, Lili feels a sense of fulfillment. Her journey through the Test of Wisdom has affirmed her connection to the cosmic tapestry, where melodies intertwine with the fabric of existence, guiding souls on their celestial odyssey.

Manny's Challenge: Confronting Ethical Dilemmas and Moral Quandaries

Meanwhile, Manny stands before a series of ethical dilemmas and moral quandaries presented by the celestial guardian. These challenges test his principles of forgiveness, acceptance, and inner peace— cornerstones he has embraced throughout his odyssey.

The dilemmas Manny faces are not mere hypothetical scenarios but reflections of his past and present interactions with others. Each dilemma poses a choice that demands introspection and a deep understanding of the consequences of his actions. Manny must navigate through the complexities of moral decision-making, guided by the principles he holds dear.

Drawing upon his experiences of reconciliation and redemption, Manny confronts the dilemmas with courage and humility. He reflects on moments when forgiveness bridged divides, when acceptance healed wounds, and when inner peace became a sanctuary amidst turmoil. These principles, once abstract concepts, now serve as compass points guiding him through the labyrinth of ethical challenges.

As Manny deliberates each dilemma, he weighs the impact of his choices on others and himself. He seeks not just answers but a deeper understanding of the interconnectedness of actions and consequences in the cosmic order. Through introspection and empathy, Manny navigates the moral landscapes laid bare before him, guided by the lessons learned from his journey.

With each ethical dilemma resolved, Manny feels a sense of clarity and purpose. The celestial guardian, observing his journey with keen interest, nods in acknowledgment of his growth and wisdom. Manny's passage through the Test of Wisdom has not only fortified his principles but also prepared him for the challenges that lie ahead on the path back to the Zoo of Wonders.

After proving their courage, the characters stand ready for the celestial guardian's next challenge: a test designed to measure their wisdom. They are ushered into a chamber adorned with towering shelves of ancient scrolls, where celestial symbols glow softly in the ambient light. Enigmatic puzzles, crafted with precision, await their deciphering.

Within this sanctum of knowledge, each character is called upon to demonstrate their profound understanding of the lessons woven into the fabric of their journey. Frank pores over scrolls depicting heroic tales of courage and sacrifice, seeking insights into the nature of leadership and perseverance.

Silvia deciphers celestial symbols that illuminate the interconnectedness of all life forms, contemplating the balance between strength and vulnerability. Lili's keen eyes trace patterns in the enigmatic puzzles, unraveling the melodies of resilience and self-discovery hidden within. Meanwhile, Manny delves into philosophical treatises that explore the complexities of forgiveness and acceptance, grappling with the universal truths that transcend time and space.

As they delve deeper into the chamber's mysteries, the characters draw upon their experiences and reflections, piecing together the wisdom gained from their odyssey. Each puzzle solved, each symbol interpreted, and each scroll deciphered brings them closer to the realization that wisdom is not merely knowledge, but the application of understanding to illuminate the path forward.

Under the watchful gaze of the celestial guardian, their minds sharpened by the challenges of the chamber, Frank, Silvia, Lili, and Manny emerge with newfound clarity and insight. They stand united, their spirits enriched by the wisdom acquired, ready to face the next phase of their journey back to the Zoo of Wonders.

As each character solves their respective challenges with wisdom and insight, the celestial guardian nods once more, impressed by their growth and understanding. They are deemed worthy of progressing further on their journey back home.

Frank's Compassion:

Frank, known for his courage and steadfastness, approaches a troubled soul in the celestial realm. This soul is engulfed in a haze of self-doubt, their essence dimmed by shadows of insecurity. As Frank draws near, he senses the weight of uncertainty that burdens the soul— a reflection of struggles he himself has faced on his journey.

With a gentle voice that carries the wisdom of experience, Frank begins to share his own tale of overcoming insecurities. He speaks of moments when doubt threatened to overshadow

his path, recounting how each challenge became a stepping stone to greater resilience. His words, infused with empathy, resonate deeply with the troubled soul.

Frank listens attentively, offering reassurance and encouragement rooted in his journey's lessons. He acknowledges the soul's fears without judgment, guiding them to recognize their own strength and worth.

Through patient dialogue and heartfelt sincerity, Frank helps the troubled soul see beyond their doubts, fostering a renewed sense of hope and self-belief.

Silvia's Compassion:

Silvia, with her innate sensitivity and profound understanding of vulnerability, approaches a lost spirit adrift in the celestial realm. The spirit's essence flickers with echoes of past hardships, their light dimmed by a sense of abandonment and despair. Silvia's heart goes out to them, recognizing the familiar ache of loneliness and uncertainty.

With a serene presence that emanates warmth, Silvia gently embraces the spirit's turmoil. She shares stories woven with threads of resilience and the beauty found in embracing vulnerability. Silvia speaks of moments when she herself felt adrift, yet discovered strength in embracing her true self— the strength born from acknowledging both shadows and light within.

As she speaks, Silvia's words weave a tapestry of hope and courage around the lost spirit. She reassures them that vulnerability is not a weakness but a wellspring of inner power and connection. Through compassionate storytelling and heartfelt empathy, Silvia helps the spirit rediscover their own resilience and potential for growth.

Lili's Compassion:

Lili, with her ethereal melodies that resonate with the rhythms of the universe, approaches a realm where emotional wounds linger as discordant energies. Here, troubled souls are ensnared in a web of unresolved emotions and fractured harmonies, yearning for healing and restoration.

With a gentle touch upon her enchanted instrument, Lili begins to play melodies that echo with compassion and empathy. Each note carries a soothing cadence, weaving through the tangled emotions of those who listen. The melodies unravel knots of pain and sorrow, transforming discord into harmonious resonance.

Lili's music becomes a beacon of healing within the celestial realm, radiating empathy and understanding to every troubled soul. As she plays, she listens with her heart attuned to the unspoken cries for solace. Through her melodies, Lili facilitates emotional release and restoration, restoring harmony to hearts weighed down by anguish.

Manny's Compassion:

Manny, known for his wisdom and capacity for forgiveness, approaches beings burdened by guilt and regret in the celestial realm. These souls carry heavy burdens— mistakes of the past that haunt their present, casting shadows upon their spirits. Manny recognizes the weight of remorse, having journeyed through his own moments of moral reckoning.

With a calm presence and compassionate gaze, Manny offers forgiveness and understanding to those who seek redemption. He listens without judgment, allowing each soul to voice their regrets and fears. Manny shares stories of his own journey towards acceptance, recounting how forgiveness became a beacon of light in his darkest moments.

Through patient guidance and gentle counsel, Manny helps these souls confront their inner turmoil. He encourages them to embrace self-forgiveness and release the shackles of guilt that bind them. Manny's words of wisdom resonate deeply, offering a pathway to reconciliation and inner peace.

These compassionate acts by Frank, Silvia, Lili, and Manny resonate throughout the celestial realm, bringing solace and healing to those in need. Their journeys through the Test of Compassion not only deepen their understanding of empathy but also prepare them for the final phase of their celestial odyssey— to return to the Zoo of Wonders, where their compassion will continue to illuminate the path ahead.

In the final trial of the Celestial Odyssey, each character faces a personal challenge that tests their ability to work together as a cohesive team, harmonizing their strengths and supporting each other through collaborative efforts.

Frank's Challenge - Courageous Leadership:

Frank steps into the cosmic maze with determination etched on his face. As the leader of the group, his challenge is to navigate through the maze's shifting realities and lead the team with unwavering courage. He encounters obstacles that require decisive action and fearless resolve. Frank's role is pivotal in motivating the group and setting the tone for their unified effort.

Silvia's Challenge - Resilient Support:

Silvia brings her innate resilience and nurturing spirit to the forefront. Her challenge within the maze is to provide unwavering support to her teammates. She helps navigate the emotional complexities of the trials they face, offering comfort and guidance when doubts arise. Silvia's ability to uplift and reassure the team strengthens their resolve and fosters a sense of unity.

Lili's Challenge - Harmonious Guidance:

Lili's journey through the cosmic maze centers around her unique ability to harmonize energies and guide the team with her melodies. Her challenge is to use her musical talents not only to overcome obstacles but also to bring harmony to discordant energies within the maze. Lili's melodies resonate through the corridors, inspiring her teammates and aligning their efforts with a unified purpose.

Manny's Challenge - Wise Navigation:

Manny's wisdom and insight are crucial as he navigates the intricate passages of the maze. His challenge is to interpret cosmic symbols and decipher the deeper meanings behind the trials they face. Manny provides strategic guidance, helping the team unlock celestial gates and pathways that lead closer to their ultimate goal. His ability to see the bigger picture and offer profound insights strengthens the team's cohesion.

Unity in Action:

Throughout the trials, Frank, Silvia, Lili, and Manny synchronize their efforts seamlessly. They communicate effectively, leveraging each other's strengths to overcome challenges that require teamwork and mutual support. Together, they confront the final challenge— a daunting trial that demands they merge their individual experiences into a unified vision of hope and determination.

Conclusion:

As they pass each test of unity, the celestial guardian observes with approval. Their journey through the Celestial Odyssey has not only transformed them individually but has also forged a bond of friendship and unity that transcends time and space. With their collective strengths and newfound unity, they approach the portal home with renewed purpose and a deep sense of accomplishment.

As the celestial journey of Frank, Silvia, Lili, and Manny nears its conclusion, a shimmering portal suddenly materializes before them. This portal, radiant with cosmic energies, signifies their passage back home to the Zoo of Wonders— a sanctuary they had embarked from on their extraordinary odyssey through celestial realms.

Meanwhile, nestled in a cozy corner of the Zoo of Wonders, Nataly, a young and vibrant zookeeper, awakens from a refreshing nap after her lunch break. Disoriented and still caught in the haze of sleep, she murmurs to herself, "What happened? Oh my god, what a dream that was! I must have slept deeply." Slowly gathering her bearings, she realizes it's time to return to her duties at the zoo.

Confused by the vividness of her dream, Nataly recounts the surreal adventures to a curious coworker. "I dreamt I was on this incredible journey through celestial realms and my name was Lili, I had tree friends with me and we were encountering mystical beings and facing profound trials," she explains, shaking her head in disbelief.

Her coworker offers a thoughtful response, "You know, dreams can be reflections of our subconscious mind, working through our thoughts and emotions. Maybe it's your mind's way of processing things."

Reflecting on the dream, Nataly finds herself intrigued by the symbolism and meaning woven into her subconscious narrative. Despite its fantastical elements, the journey had touched upon themes of courage, resilience, harmony, and wisdom— qualities she aspires to embody in her own life.

As Nataly returns to her tasks at the Zoo of Wonders, she carries with her the lingering impressions of the dream. Though it was just a dream, its impact on her perspective remains profound. She approaches her work with renewed vigor, recognizing that sometimes, the most fantastical journeys can offer insights that resonate deeply within us.

THE END

Dear Readers

As we conclude this journey through the Celestial Odyssey together, I want to extend my deepest gratitude for joining me on this adventure of exploration and discovery. Throughout our odyssey, we've encountered challenges that tested our courage, moments of introspection that deepened our understanding, and glimpses of wonder that expanded our perspectives.

Life, much like our celestial journey, is a series of pathways where we encounter both light and shadow. It teaches us that facing our challenges head-on, without fear, is key to growth and resilience. Each obstacle is an opportunity to learn, to evolve, and to discover the strength within ourselves.

Remember, no matter what twists and turns life presents, it continues forward. It is in embracing these challenges with courage and determination that we find our truest selves and forge paths of meaning and fulfillment.

As we part ways, may the lessons learned from our celestial odyssey inspire you to confront life's challenges with an open heart and unwavering resolve. Let us carry forward the spirit of adventure, the wisdom gained, and the friendships forged along the way.

Thank you for embarking on this journey with me. May your own path be filled with courage, resilience, and the boundless beauty of discovery.

Warm regards,

Angel Viera,

Author of "The Celestial Odyssey"

CR 2009/2024

About The Author

Angel Viera, a multi-talented artist and writer, has always been deeply immersed in the world of artistic expression. With an inherent inclination towards creativity, he effortlessly weaves together various art forms, embracing music, painting, and literature as integral parts of his artistic repertoire.

Angel's passion for classical music finds solace in the melodies he composes on his piano, filling his home with harmonious compositions that reflect the depths of his emotions. The ethereal notes that resonate from his fingertips carry the essence of his soul, a testament to his ability to communicate and evoke emotions through the power of music.

In addition to his musical talents, Angel has also found immense joy and fulfillment in the realm of visual arts. His oil and acrylic paintings, showcased in art galleries across Chicago, unveil yet another dimension of his artistic prowess. With bold brushstrokes, vibrant colors, and a keen eye for detail, Angel captures the essence of his subjects, revealing his unique perspective and unbridled creativity.

While Angel's artistic journey began with a love for music and painting, his literary aspirations have been with him from a young age. Since his early years, he has poured his thoughts, dreams, and vivid imagination onto paper, weaving captivating stories that captivate and transport readers to new worlds. It is now, at this juncture in his life, that Angel embraces the opportunity to share his literary collection with the world, offering a glimpse into the rich tapestry of his storytelling.

While Angel academic background in not included in this introduction is good to know that is very extensive. At the tender age of 21, Angel was granted a scholarship by the prestigious Art Institute of Chicago to pursue a formal education in the arts. However, driven by his own creative instincts and a desire to forge his own path, he made the brave decision to follow his artistic vision independently, charting his course through the vast realm of artistic exploration.

Since 1992, Angel has made Miami his home, finding inspiration in its vibrant culture, diverse community, and picturesque surroundings. The dynamic energy of the city and its fusion of influences have undoubtedly shaped his artistic perspective, infusing his works with a distinct flair and a sense of wonder.

Angel's literary collection is a testament to his versatility as a writer, spanning across genres such as fiction, love stories, and thrilling adventures. With over 60 titles to his name, each book is a testament to his boundless imagination and his ability to craft narratives that resonate deeply with readers.

As you embark on this literary journey with Angel Viera, be prepared to immerse yourself in a world where music, painting, and literature intertwine. His works invite you to explore the depths of human emotion, to dance with the melodies of his compositions, and to experience the transformative power of storytelling.

Angel Viera's artistic endeavors are an invitation to engage with the beauty of his creations, to delve into the depths of his imagination, and to embark on a journey of self-discovery through the medium of art.

www.ingramcontent.com/pod-product-compliance
Lightning Source LLC
Chambersburg PA
CBHW041134110526
44590CB00027B/4008